Prop Trading Secrets

Prop Trading Secrets

How Successful Traders are Living off the Markets

Kathy Lien

Etienne Crete

WILEY

Published by John Wiley & Sons, Inc., Hoboken, New Jersey.
Published simultaneously in Canada.

For general information on our other products and services or for technical support, please contact our Customer Care Department within the United States at (800) 762-2974, outside the United States at (317) 572-3993 or fax (317) 572-4002.

Wiley also publishes its books in a variety of electronic formats. Some content that appears in print may not be available in electronic formats. For more information about Wiley products, visit our web site at www.wiley.com.

Library of Congress Cataloging-in-Publication Data

Names: Lien, Kathy, 1980- author. | Crete, Etienne, author.
Title: Prop trading secrets : how successful traders are living off the markets / Kathy Lien, Etienne Crete.
Description: First edition. | Hoboken, New Jersey : Wiley, [2025] | Includes index.
Identifiers: LCCN 2024046181 (print) | LCCN 2024046182 (ebook) | ISBN 9781394243167 (Cloth) | ISBN 9781394243181 (adobe pdf) | ISBN 9781394243174 (epub)
Subjects: LCSH: Foreign exchange futures. | Foreign exchange market. | Speculation.
Classification: LCC HG3853 .L545 2025 (print) | LCC HG3853 (ebook) | DDC 332.4/5—dc23/eng/20241004
LC record available at https://lccn.loc.gov/2024046181
LC ebook record available at https://lccn.loc.gov/2024046182

Cover Design: Wiley
Cover Image: © mineart1995/Adobe Stock Photos
Author Photos: Courtesy of the author

SKY10091218_111824

Contents

Preface

Whether it's the pursuit of financial freedom, the desire to boost income, or the challenge of finding new opportunities after a job loss, more and more people are turning to trading. The universal appeal of earning extra cash and generating additional income streams is undeniable. Since the 2020 pandemic, the way we work has transformed. With more people working from home, there's a newfound flexibility to explore side hustles like trading, and many are eager to leave the 9-to-5 grind behind.

While investing in retirement accounts, stocks, and real estate has long been seen as the golden path to financial freedom, not everyone has the extra cash or income to invest in the future. That's where trading comes in, offering a chance to build capital and create a steady income stream that can eventually be invested in long-term wealth. The rise of modern prop trading has made this opportunity even more exciting and accessible.

Unlike traditional prop trading, once reserved for Wall Street professionals, the modern prop trading model is designed for the everyday trader. These firms enable traders to access substantial capital – whether real or simulated – and earn a portion of the profits, sometimes as much as 90%.

To seize this opportunity, traders need to qualify by hitting a profit target without exceeding the maximum daily loss limit. Each firm has its own set of rules, but generally, traders are required to generate an 8–10% profit on the capital while keeping losses under 5%. Some firms add extra conditions, like restrictions on trading during news events or using automated trading systems. Others assess traders' competence through scoring methods. With so many firms offering different paths, including free funding from some brokers, you could be trading with $100,000 or more in capital for just a few hundred dollars.

As modern prop trading gains popularity, it's easy for newcomers to make rookie mistakes. Even experienced traders can struggle to navigate the rules, leading to disqualification, often known as "blowing up their evaluations."

This book is here to help both new and experienced traders avoid these early missteps and fast-track their journey to becoming successful funded traders. We had the privilege of speaking with 14 accomplished traders – ranging from those with just a few years of experience to trading legends with decades of expertise. This includes trading champions, prop traders managing significant funds, and seasoned pros who trade independently and make a living from the markets. In this book, we explore the shared traits of these traders, from their personalities to their trading strategies, providing valuable insights for anyone looking to succeed in the market.

You'll hear from Rob Hoffman, a day trader with over 30 domestic and international trading competition wins, who emphasizes the importance of patience and taking the right trade at the right time for the right reasons. Davide Biocchi, who has won 10 real-money trading championships, discusses the value of focusing on the visible range and using volume-based tools for precise trade identification. John Bannan, who ranked third in the Robbins World Cup of Futures Trading, shares his unique cycle-based trading technique.

David Floyd, a seasoned veteran with over 30 years of trading experience, speaks about the art of listening to the market. Sunny Harris, a top commodity trading advisor with over 40 years in the markets, stresses the importance of staying focused and not succumbing to the fear of missing out on trades. Ali Crooks shares his inspiring journey from running a failing business to managing a regulated fund. Aatu Kokkila highlights how teamwork skills from his experience on the world's top World of Warcraft team translated into his trading success.

Andres Granger, who manages a $10 million crypto fund, underscores the importance of learning from both positive and negative trades. Jean-Francois Boucher shares his inspirational story of losing everything trading options, battling leukemia, and eventually becoming a profitable funded trader. Austin Silver, a multi-funded trader, discusses the importance of treating trading like a business.

Alyse Amores, a single mother who grew her trading capital from a few hundred dollars to $8 million, shares her practical approach to determining when one's ready to trade full-time. Matt Miller, who focuses on mastering one instrument and one setup, shares how this focus helped him withdraw $300,000 in profits over 85 trading days. Nick Syiek, who made $3 million by the age of 23 trading forex and indices, reveals his unique market approach. Finally, Vince Koehn outlines his journey of blowing up hundreds of accounts before developing a consistent methodology that enabled him to withdraw over $1 million from prop firms.

We hope you find these traders' stories both encouraging and insightful. Each of them has faced their own set of challenges and found unique ways to overcome them. We believe their experiences offer valuable lessons for anyone looking to succeed in trading. Whether you're just starting out or are an experienced trader seeking to refine your approach, we trust that their insights will inspire you, guide your decisions, and ultimately help you on your journey to becoming a successful trader.

About the Authors

Kathy Lien is the Managing Director of FX Strategy for BKTraders.com and an internationally recognized expert in forex trading. A prodigy in finance, Kathy graduated from New York University's Stern School of Business at just 18 and immediately began her career on Wall Street. With over 25 years of experience in the financial markets, she has honed her expertise in foreign exchange, making her a go-to authority in the field.

Kathy's career began at JPMorgan Chase, where she worked on the interbank FX trading desk, making markets in foreign exchange. She later moved to the cross-markets proprietary trading group, where she traded FX spot, options, interest rate derivatives, bonds, equities, and futures. In 2003, Kathy joined FXCM and founded DailyFX.com, a leading online foreign exchange research portal. As Chief Strategist, she led a team of analysts dedicated to providing in-depth research and commentary on the foreign exchange market. By 2008, she had joined Global Futures & Forex Ltd as Director of Currency Research, where she managed a global team and delivered expert analysis to clients.

Kathy is the internationally published author of the best-selling book *Day Trading and Swing Trading the Currency Market*. She has also authored *The Little Book of Currency Trading* and *Millionaire Traders: How Everyday People Beat Wall Street at Its Own Game*, all published by Wiley. Her extensive experience in developing trading strategies through cross-market analysis and her deep knowledge of predicting economic data surprises are integral to BK's analytical techniques.

As a seasoned expert on G20 currencies, Kathy appears frequently on CNBC and is quoted in major sources such as *The Wall Street Journal*, Reuters, Bloomberg, *MarketWatch*, Associated Press, *UK Telegraph*, and the *Sydney Morning Herald*.

Etienne Crete is a swing trader from Montreal, Canada. He is known for traveling the world while trading full-time since 2017 and is the founder of Desire To Trade, aiming to help aspiring traders develop profitable trading methods and achieve financial independence.

Etienne started his trading journey in 2013 and realized that the only way to succeed was by surrounding himself with traders ahead on the journey.

His platform offers a variety of resources, including educational videos, a podcast, and several programs, all designed to help traders get profitable and scale up their trading.

Through the *Desire To Trade Podcast* he has interviewed over 400 successful traders and experts who share their insights into trading for a living. Through his work, Etienne aims to help traders achieve the freedom to travel and live on their terms while following their passion for trading.

CHAPTER 1

The Shift in Prop Trading

From Big Banks to Everyday Traders

Proprietary trading, or prop trading for short, has been around for decades. It started as a way for big banks to use their own capital to profit from market moves. Fast-forward to the 1990s, and advancing technology made markets more accessible, sparking the rise of algorithmic and high-frequency trading. This shift led to the birth of electronic platforms like E-Trade, which provided individual traders with online market access. They quickly gained popularity, with millions opening accounts to trade online.

During this time, modern contracts for differences were introduced to retail traders, followed by the emergence of retail forex trading firms around 1999. The dot-com boom was a real game changer, revealing the endless opportunities in the financial markets to traders worldwide. The global financial crisis slowed things down a bit, but the cryptocurrency bubble and WallStreetBets brought the excitement back in the early 2020s. It was during this time that the modern version of prop trading began to gain significant traction. Between 2020 and 2024, over 120 new prop trading firms were established, attracting more than a million new traders and generating a staggering $70 trillion in trading volume.

There are many differences between traditional and new prop trading firms. Traditional prop trading firms typically use their own capital. They employ traders who are often salaried employees or partners who receive performance-based compensation. This small group of hand-selected traders usually undergo extensive training before they are allowed to trade with the firm's real capital. Once allocated funds, their performance is closely monitored to ensure they stick to strict risk limits.

New funded prop trading firms are shaking things up. Instead of employing traders outright, they offer aspiring traders the chance to prove their skills through evaluation challenges using simulated accounts. Traders pay a fee to enter these challenges, and those who succeed are given access to a larger amount of capital to trade, with profits shared between the trader and the firm. This setup is appealing because it allows traders to control significant amounts of capital – often $10,000 or more – by investing just a few hundred dollars on an evaluation. A $600 fee, for example, might provide access to $100,000 in trading capital, with the possibility to scale up from there.

To access the funds and reach the stage of a funded trader, individuals must pass an evaluation, which involves meeting specific profit targets without exceeding certain loss limits. Some programs require passing two evaluations before funding, but once traders are funded, they can trade larger positions and share profits based on those amounts. The maximum financial risk for a trader is limited to the evaluation fees, which is a low-risk way to access big capital.

This model opens the door to traders from all walks of life, particularly those just out of college or early in their careers who haven't saved large amounts of capital. Saving $10,000 or more can take years, but with just a few hundred dollars these prop firms offer a chance to trade significant amounts if you pass their evaluation. The evaluation is essentially a test to identify skilled traders. Prop firms want to see if you can consistently hit profit targets, like making 6% without losing more than 3%, over a set number of trading days. Each firm has its own rules, but they all aim to find traders who can profit consistently without taking big risks.

Another appealing aspect is that these firms operate primarily online, offering flexibility and remote work opportunities for traders worldwide. This new approach not only opens doors for many aspiring traders but also ensures that only the most capable traders get funded.

Although new funded prop trading firms offer exciting opportunities, there are some downsides to be aware of. One significant drawback is that most traders, whether they are on evaluation or funded accounts, trade with virtual funds. Additionally, regulators are just beginning to look at this space, which could lead to changes in the future. Another concern is that a significant portion of these firms' revenue comes from evaluation fees. This raises concerns about the firms' primary incentives – whether they genuinely aim to find and fund skilled traders or to profit from the steady influx of evaluation fees. As this industry segment is still fairly new, these firms are adapting and evolving to become fairer and align their interests more closely with those of the traders. With so many different prop firms, each with its own unique rules, it's essential for traders to do their homework and fully understand the terms and conditions of these funded prop programs before diving in. This way, they'll be fully aware of both the potential risks and rewards.

The world of prop trading is diverse and exciting, encompassing traders who trade for themselves, those who work for traditional prop firms, and those involved in funded trader programs. In this book, we've had the pleasure of interviewing 14 standout proprietary traders. Among them are three trading champions, each with over a decade of experience, some of the most popular and widely followed funded traders, full-time traders turned professional money managers, and a select group of seasoned trading veterans.

These traders have shared their specific strategies and techniques, providing you with valuable insights. Whether you're just starting or looking to refine your skills, their stories and advice will inspire and guide you on your trading journey. Get ready to dive into their world and discover the secrets to their success.

CHAPTER 2

Prop Trader Secrets

Discover What the Best Have in Common

Through our journey of interviewing successful prop traders, we've uncovered some fascinating traits and practices that contribute to their success. Our conversations were filled with illuminating moments, revealing a mix of grit, strategy, discipline, and community spirit that fuels these prop traders' achievements. From early hustles to mastering a single instrument, and from leveraging trading communities to refining their techniques, these insights are shared with the hope of helping you become a better trader.

STRONG WORK ETHIC AND PERSEVERANCE

By starting work at a young age, some as early as middle school, many of the traders developed a strong work ethic and a deep appreciation for the value of money. Their early ambitions instilled discipline and the importance of perseverance – key qualities for making and maintaining profits in the trading world. Starting with small accounts, they ambitiously grew and stacked them into larger ones, showcasing their consistent and conservative approaches. Their journey from small beginnings to significant successes is a testament to their drive and ingenuity.

CONSISTENCY WITH INITIAL TECHNIQUES

It's remarkable that many of the traders we interviewed have stuck to the same general trading philosophy they learned at the start of their careers. While their techniques and tactics have evolved, their core focus remains on the original concepts that sparked their interest in the market. For example, traders who began with fundamental analysis and trading news events still rely on these methods. Those who started with technical analysis, focusing on volume and price action, have stayed true to these approaches. Likewise, traders who initially learned to trade cycles and breakouts continue to refine and use these strategies over time. This shows that you can be successful with a variety of trading methods, as long as you remain consistent and dedicated to mastering your chosen approach.

YOUR FIRST FEW TRADES SET THE TONE FOR YOUR TRADING DAY

Trading is an emotional roller coaster, and many of the traders we've interviewed know that the first few trades of the day can set the tone. They carefully pick their initial trades, aiming to build a cushion early on. This smart move gives them the confidence and financial buffer to let part of the trades run or take bigger positions later in the day, knowing they've already pocketed some profits. If those early trades go south, they often spend the rest of the day trying to claw back their losses, which can affect their mindset and emotions. This scramble to recover can lead to impulsive decisions and high stress, ultimately hurting their performance. By prioritizing cautious and strategic early trades, traders can dodge this downward spiral and stay calm throughout the day.

FOCUS ON ONE INSTRUMENT OR STRATEGY

Many of the traders we've interviewed achieved success by zeroing in on a single trading instrument. By focusing exclusively on one asset, they develop an intimate understanding of its movements, reactions to news, optimal trading times, and more. Other traders prefer to focus on a single strategy to trade on a small number of instruments. This laser focus reduces the stress of constantly reevaluating different instruments and hunting for new opportunities. Plus, it gives these traders lightning-fast reaction times because they know what they trade so well. This approach enhances their ability to select trades with greater confidence and manage their positions and profits effectively.

SEEKING CONFLUENCE IN TRADES

Confluence is also important to many of the traders we interviewed. They hunt for multiple factors that support a specific trade direction or level, like technical indicators, volume patterns, and prior highs or lows. Finding confluence boosts their confidence in the setup and helps them decide whether to take a smaller or larger position. When several factors align, these traders can make more informed and confident trading decisions.

PREFERENCE FOR BUYING CHEAP

Everyone loves a good deal, and the traders we interviewed are no exception – they don't like to chase price. Instead, they prefer to buy at a discount, often waiting for a pullback before jumping into a trade. This smart tactic boosts their chances of success, reduces risk, and maximizes value. Many of our traders look for breakouts and then wait for a retest of the breakout point before getting in. By doing so, they enter trades at more favorable prices, enhancing their risk-to-reward ratios. This disciplined approach not only helps them be better positioned but also fosters greater patience and strategic thinking in their trading practices.

THREE STRIKES RULE FOR BAD DAYS

In baseball, a player steps away after they miss any pitch that is in the strike zone. Many of the traders we interviewed use a similar three strikes and you're out rule for their trading. If they strike out with three consecutive losing trades, they step away from the market to avoid further emotional and financial damage. This rule helps them stay disciplined and prevents a bad day from turning into a major loss. By taking a break after a rough patch, they keep their cool and come back stronger the next day, ready to hit the market with fresh energy. This straightforward yet powerful strategy ensures that a streak of bad luck doesn't knock them off their game.

LOWER RISK-REWARD RATIOS IN DAY TRADING

Many of our day traders are successful because they use risk-reward ratios, such as 1 : 1 or even lower. While higher reward, low-risk setups sound great in theory, they're rare in day trading. Consistently successful traders know that the real secret to success is maintaining a high win rate. Most of their strategies focus on high accuracy, getting in and out of trades quickly. Protecting profits is also important, so these traders might use emergency stops with a risk-reward ratio of less than 1 : 1. However, they will move their stops up swiftly as the trade moves in their favor, locking in profits and minimizing losses.

DAY TRADING FOR CONSISTENCY AND CASH FLOW

Day trading, or scalping, is the primary focus for most of our traders. Since trading is their main gig, these traders' top priority is to generate steady cash flow and consistent results. Even those who lean toward longer-term swing trades know the importance of consistency, liquidity, and financial stability. If you dream of becoming a full-time trader, you'll need a strategy that provides regular cash flow to cover expenses like rent, bills, childcare, and tuition. A useful tip from one of our traders is to try living off your trading income for a while to see if it's enough. Or aim to match your weekly or biweekly paycheck with your trading profits.

MANAGING SUCCESS EXPECTATIONS

Traders with high expectations often put unnecessary pressure on themselves. Good trading shouldn't be about expecting a certain profitability since there are factors we cannot control. In the end, one can only take what the market gives. Trying to force positive results beyond that is pointless. Start with the expectation that it's going to be really hard to stay consistent in trading. It will not get anyone rich overnight. It's also been emphasized by one of the traders in this book that success comes from expanding your time horizon. Instead of looking for results in the short term (day, week, or month), traders should let the odds play out in their favor and expect results to come only in the long term (quarter, year).

ABILITY TO LEARN AND ADAPT

Mistakes present a great learning opportunity. Traders who stay successful over many decades are lifelong students. They are finding new ways to learn about the market and themselves. They are also highly adaptable. When the market context or other conditions change, these traders are quickly looking at how to pivot. While some would be afraid of change, successful traders look to the future instead of worrying about the past. Whether through a wide collection of books or by talking to others in the industry, the traders interviewed in this book always stay curious and continue evolving.

SELF-AWARENESS AND REGULATION

Knowing who you are and aren't presents an edge for many of the traders interviewed in this book. Consistently profitable traders know their trading strategies and personalities inside and out. Some of the traders we've interviewed have a very specific trading style they like and don't deviate from. Others know when they're not likely to perform well and add trading rules that match themselves better. It's important to be patient with who you are. One can always get better, but it takes time. Self-awareness is also a great way to be more disciplined, since you're more likely to find your pitfalls early.

CUTTING LOSSES INSTEAD OF TRADING MORE

Being profitable in trading isn't about finding more winning trades. It's about minimizing losses that eat into your profits. The traders in this book have shared trade and risk management techniques to reduce their losses. Small mistakes repeated can often lead to large changes in results over time. Tracking and reviewing trades is also one of the key habits to see where money is lost. Any good trader would tell you that this isn't a one-time exercise. It is a principle to continually strive for as one evolves in a trading career.

TRACKING AND REVIEWING TRADES

Keeping track of and reviewing their trades is a habit that all successful traders swear by. It helps them understand their trading patterns, spot strengths and weaknesses, and make the necessary tweaks. By analyzing their own data, they learn from their mistakes and weed out the problems. This process has been a game changer for many of our traders, helping them correct big mistakes and hit their stride. Plus, with tons of journaling platforms available, they can get detailed insights into their trading performance. Using these tools for self-assessment can significantly enhance your understanding of your trading habits, improve your skills, and increase your overall success.

VALUE IN TRADING COMMUNITIES

Community is key in all walks of life, and it's even more essential in trading. Every trader we interviewed raves about the value of trading communities, even if they don't always adopt the strategies shared within them. These communities are a goldmine for exchanging ideas, learning new techniques, and diving into market discussions, which is a lifesaver in the often solitary world of trading. Plus, being part of a trading community means fantastic networking opportunities, a sense of accountability, and opportunities for self-reflection.

PART I

PROP TRADING CHAMPIONS

CHAPTER 3

Rob Hoffman

Rob Hoffman is a 33-time real-money international trading champion born in Germany and raised in northern Illinois. Since the early 2000s, he has won 16 domestic trading competitions in the United States and 17 international competitions in countries such as France, Italy, and the United Kingdom. Rob's interest in trading began just before the 1987 market crash when he recognized the opportunities for gains on the long and short side of the market. At the time he was limited to paper trading because he was only 16 years old, but he knew he wanted to become a trader. Born to an army and law enforcement family, structure, regimentation, and discipline were always a part of his life. In this chapter, you'll learn how Rob's commitment to structure and patience played a pivotal role in his trading decisions, particularly his unwavering approach to selecting the right moments to trade even when facing public embarrassment during competitions.

Today, Rob maintains a disciplined routine, rising at 5 a.m. to trade and run his many trading businesses. This includes Wealth365, which hosts the world's premier online trading and investing summit, and WealthCharts, an award-winning charting and trading solution tailored for the active trader and investor used by traders all over the world. This relentless commitment not only underscores his dedication to trading but also to the enterprises he has built based on this passion.

Q: Rob, how did you get into trading and into the markets?

Rob: When I was a teenager, my passion was the financial markets. I was 16 years old and I knew that I really wanted to do something with the stock market. I believe it came from my love of chess back then, and understanding the game and thinking several moves ahead. I would look at financial publications and watch TV. I'd see charts of different symbols on financial television or *Investor's Business Daily* and the *Wall Street Journal* – the type of publications that were available at the newsstands. I would look at the different stock charts and the rankings for the day. Then I'd go back and see those same stocks listed a week or two later, and I'd compare them to what I thought they were going to do. It was a very early way of spotting and analyzing patterns on the charts.

In January 1987, the year of the '87 crash, it was a real blessing for me. I had no money to trade at the time, I was just a paper-trading kid. However, I was watching, monitoring, and studying the market and this crash taught me to focus on learning how to make money on the way down with short positions, not just on the way up, because there's so much opportunity in falling markets. This was an important key to my future trading endeavors. It's a skill and advantage I see validated over and over to this day when seeing those who only focus on trading and investing in bullish markets really struggle and often give back too much in bearish market environments.

Q: Did you have a trading mentor?

Rob: No, I didn't have a trading mentor, I was completely self-driven. I made a lot of mistakes. Even to this day, as I'm managing a fast-growing charting and trading analysis company, I'm sitting here looking at a wall of charts right now. I love trading so much that I built an international company focused on technical analysis and trading with much higher probabilities. It has been my passion from the very beginning. So I try to be the mentor to others that I didn't have when I was learning to trade and invest.

Q: So it's really interesting that you talked about how you were exposed to chart reading and to looking at charts in the mid-1980s because information flow and chart availability was pretty much nonexistent at that time, especially for someone who didn't have the resources. Someone who was a teenager, not a professional trader. How did you get that information? What were you looking at? How were you getting updated?

Rob: The newspapers! I'd flip through many charts from the *Wall Street Journal* and *Investor's Business Daily* – creating my own off-screen charting view of the market. I was strictly looking at the paper without much more in the way of indicators. I think some of the charts had like a 200-day moving average but that was it. They were just open, high, low, close bars. It was very rudimentary but it allowed me to really focus on price action, and the ebb and flow of trends.

Q: Given the lack of intraday information at the time, were you focusing on a longer time frame?

Rob: Yes, absolutely. The concept of day trading was completely foreign to me. I didn't have the technology or resources to focus on any sort of day trading when I was younger. I was strictly looking at the long-term charts on paper. I'm a day trader now, but honestly, that training was just as good, if not better, to prepare me for day trading. Ultimately, because a chart is a chart is a chart as it relates to technical analysis. So I generally use the same strategies on a one-minute chart that I use on a daily, weekly, or monthly chart.

Q: So you went into law enforcement after graduation? Did you trade while working? How did you get the capital to trade?

Rob: Yes, I traded and worked at the same time. I basically worked the equivalent of two and a half jobs at one point. I had my regular full-time job at the sheriff's department and I did court overtime duty because they had a major jail overflow problem. I'd work a 12-hour shift sometimes at the sheriff's department from 6 p.m. to 6 a.m. Then I would take a quick nap and come right back for court overtime work about 8 a.m. When I was working overtime duty in the judge's chambers court, I had to transport prisoners from the jail to the judge's chambers and my only task after that was to wait. I'd sit there for hours and I'd look at the charts. I printed out hundreds of charts that I'd take with me to work, flipping through them and looking for the ones I thought were the most interesting pattern-wise. If I was out in a patrol car for one of my side gig law enforcement jobs, I'd sit there sometimes in the squad car while on break and looking at charts of indices and individual equities, and I'd dial out for a current quote because I didn't have a computer with me.

Q: What was your strategy back then when you started trading mid-1990s?

Rob: I was doing the equivalent of what they called SOEs, small order executions. Everything was trading in quarter points or so. You could buy on the bid, try to sell on the offer, do a quarter-point trade here and there, and try to make $250 a trade with 1,000-share lots. I would look at daily charts but I was using that for shorter-term trading, looking to hop on a trade near the open and close it by the end of the day for profit.

Q: If you were watching end-of-day charts and trying to forecast moves the following day, were you trading the continuation?

Rob: Yes, at the time I was looking for continuation trades. I'm definitely a trend-based trader, not a counter-trend trader.

Q: How did you decide to transition to full-time trading, and what made you feel prepared to leave your full-time job?

Rob: That's a great question. At some point, I felt that because of all of the jobs I had, the time I had to trade was very limited and I was very tired. One thing I share with people is that if you're in a bad emotional state or you're physically exhausted, or you've had a fight with your spouse that day (especially if about money) or you have health issues requiring heavy medications, it is not a good place to trade from. I realized that I couldn't mentally make good decisions when I was physically exhausted all of the time. I felt confident in my systems but I was always looking for patches of time to trade. So I decided to take the plunge. I didn't have a guaranteed nest egg of a certain amount but I had the confidence that I was going to figure this out as I had with a lot of other things in my life.

I also knew that if I needed to get a part-time job, I could get a moonlighting gig in law enforcement or something else, which ultimately I did at one point as I was getting serious. I knew that I'd land on my feet because I had a lot of skills and certifications. I always encourage people even to this day to consider getting a part- or full-time job if they have bills to pay, money they can't afford to trade, money they can't lose, or they start making terrible mistakes with their money management. When you have extra income coming in, it's a huge psychological comfort.

Q: Did your trading change once you became a full-time trader because you had more time?

Rob: Yes. I came to realize that the more time I had to make money, the more time I had to sit in front of the computer and the more mistakes I would make. I know that may sound counterintuitive, but more screen time was a problem. I came to realize that not every minute of every day should be traded.

That's just a reality, and I wish I could go back to those days with what I know today. I've learned over the years that when you sit in front of the screens, you want to do something. I was constantly looking for the next trade, the next trade, and the next trade, but what I've come to learn after many years, and a few gray hairs later, is that in reality, less trading is more. My strategies today are effectively the inverse of back then by incorporating all of the things I learned, and all of the mistakes that I've made. When you are sitting in front of the computer and you think "I should be trading right now because that's my job to sit here and be in the market all day long" you are setting yourself up for failure. It's just not true that you have to trade, trade, trade like a crazy person. Being slow, steady, and consistent and focusing on the right trade, at the right time, for the right reasons, wins the day, week, or year. The biggest gains are usually made in very finite times. The other times, it's a great opportunity for you to enjoy life, develop additional strategies, and automate the trade-finding process, things of that nature.

The idea that you should be in the market all the time is not the right course of action for me and for many other people who are actively trading. Now, I'm not referring to traditional investing or even swing trading, when you might have several positions open with various options hedging and so forth. I'm referring to day trading specifically in this case.

One of my strategies, the thrust, pullback, thrust (TPT), was developed in the late 1990s during the dot-com bubble when I had all the time in the world to trade tech stocks.

I would be watching the screens looking for a big green bar. The price would creep up and creep up. I'm thinking at the time that this is a new uptrend and then it explodes to the upside. I would jump into a trade because I don't want to miss it, but I didn't realize at that point that every other person in the world is also jumping into that big green bar. Then the market would pull back, pull back, pull back, and stop me out! I didn't realize it at the time but statistically, that's when you're actually most likely going to get a pullback for the next several bars back into the direction of the original trend. At the beginning, I thought, that isn't good, that's not supposed to happen, so I'm going to take my loss like a good trooper because I want to be conscientious about risk-reward and take the loss. Then after I got out, I would watch it go back up without me and I knew I had the direction right, and the trend right, but the timing was off. So I studied it and studied it and that's where the concept of TPT was born. Most of my work even to this day comes out of the idea "don't chase that trade; look for the high probability trend resumption trade!"

"My whole mentality changed from the hunted to the hunter."

When I started developing signals for the reentry rather than chasing, my whole mentality changed from being the hunted to the hunter. Instead of being the hunted, the person running in on the big green bar or after a large move, only to get stopped out and watch it go right back the other way, I started seeing the green bar, watching it pull back, and then I would wait. I wanted to see it come back out of my indicators before I would get in. That way, I'm in the momentum for the new run back into the direction of the trend.

THE SWITCH TO TRADING DOW FUTURES AND MORE

In the late 1990s, when the Dow Futures were launched, I was so excited because it was much easier for me. I didn't have to print out 100+ charts and follow the earnings calendar for each of these companies, their news releases, and similar companies' news cycles as well, all of which would often destroy my trade opportunities if they countered my intended direction. Since I was already looking at the Dow anyway to see which way it would go and how it could affect my trade, it was a logical transition for me to start looking at Futures as well. This way I could go long or short and not have to worry about an uptick rule. I traded Dow Futures primarily until 2008/2009 and at that point there was a lot going on in the currency market. Since I was already trading with the exchanges, the next logical progression was euro, pound, and yen futures. About that time the Russell became very popular. It was $10 a tick and moved like the Nasdaq does by today's standards, which is hyper-parabolic all over the place. I also traded gold and crude oil futures.

Q: You've broadened the instruments that you're trading. How do you manage to follow all of them?

Rob: I built a technology company, now called WealthCharts. I built it for me first and foremost as a hardcore trader. I programmed the strategy into the charts, and then it triggers alerts and scans the market for me. Then it'll email me, text me, and pop up the alert on the screen. It gives me three different forms of communication to say, *Hey, one of those little ideas that you like is happening now.* So now I don't have to sit all day in front of the screen.

Q: So, by harnessing the technology you developed, you've managed to expand the range of instruments you monitor, rather than just concentrating on a single one?

Rob: That's exactly right. Technology helped me diversify the markets I follow, but of course, I still have my favorite instruments that I love to trade; make no mistake about it. I've really enjoyed day trading Nasdaq Futures because of the volatility, the action, the movement, the range, and how that can add up very quickly. It really opens up a lot of opportunities because I thrive on that ebb and flow. I love the movement, that boom, boom, boom, pullback, then resumption! Boom, boom, boom, pullback, then resumption! Whereas a lot of people may feel like "no, no, that's just too much for me. I'm getting heart palpitations. I need something much slower." Everybody has what's interesting to them and there's something for everyone! I personally thrive on that action, plus I'm busy. I still have two lovely little ones at home now, an 8- and a 10-year-old. They're both very active in school and extra-curricular activities and my wife Sarah and I are very active in charitable events and organizations. I run multiple international companies, so as a CEO, as a dad, as a husband, there's a lot of honey-dos on Rob Hoffman's list. I have to be in a situation where I can systematize and automate the trade identification process because I found that it is just not healthy to sit there all day and stare at the screen waiting for something to happen. If you do, your mind starts to trick you into wanting to do something to keep the market interesting. Sometimes I used to find myself wanting to put a trade on just to pay attention more to what's happening in the market. Now with the automation capability, the trade identification where the scanners will just find it and pop it up to me, I can have my cake and eat it, too. That's really the big benefit of the technology. I'll let the system do all the heavy lifting for me, so I can take care of all the other things in my life that need to be well taken care of. I know people have very busy lives trying to grow their businesses, trying to manage their families, and sometimes really recognizing that and trying to look for technical solutions can actually really enhance their trading. I'm a strong believer in that.

Q: Your system scans for trade ideas. Do you take all of them, or are there criteria for selection? Is there room for discretionary decision-making in this process?

Rob: Personally, I'm still a discretionary trader. I like automation, I like bot trading, but until I have my Garry Kasparov moment where the machine beats me consistently, I'm still taking all of my trades manually. (*Note: IBM computer Deep Blue beat Garry Kasparov, a World Chess Champion in 1997. Rob Hoffman is not being beaten regularly by machines at his competitions as of yet.*)

I'm old school and I still enjoy trading manually. It's kind of like pilots. The computers fly the airplane mostly but the pilot is always there, ready to take over. I have a passion for the markets. My wife Sarah is always joking, taking pictures of me because I'm looking at the mobile version of WealthCharts when we're at events for our children's school, a charity event, or out with friends. I'm still a big financial markets geek. I still have this passion, so I keep a very close feel on the market despite the fact that the automation will help identify the trading opportunities. I'm still that person who likes to execute the trade live. I've traded in competitions against bots. I got some great videos and some great pictures where these bots were just green, green, green, and nearly every trade the bots were doing were winners and I still beat them by nearly two to one. I would sit there and wait, and wait, and wait, for a few select trades, then jump in.

Q: How long do you usually hold your trades for?

Rob: With all of the geopolitical risks, trades could figuratively and sometimes do blow up overnight. I'm much more cautious about naked positions. I want to sleep like a baby so I put more intraday trades on and if I am going to swing trade, it will be with options where I have a defined rather than unlimited risk. I like to know where I'm at any time of the day. My holding period, typically for those types of trades, is anywhere from several minutes to several hours within the day. The goal is to exit all of those stock index futures trades by the end of the day so I'm not carrying extremely high leverage positions overnight. If I were to want to carry an overnight position, I'd want to do it more with an options strategy that has a defined risk, and those types of trades could last for days to several weeks depending on the objective of the trade.

Q: Are there certain times of the day when these pullbacks are more effective?

Rob: Yes, for day trading, within the first few hours of the market opening. To be clear, these opportunities happen throughout the day but I'm more focused in the morning and I find the most vigorous moves frequently happen anywhere between 8:30 a.m. Eastern time when news is released pre-US market open and through the lunch hour at noon Eastern. I feel the market often loses some of its energy in the afternoon as far as the speed at which it moves. The exception is when we have news events or a period of time in the markets where there's a lot of risk of black swans and news that is taking place. Then the markets can get very excited in the afternoon and offer the same strategies. You'll see the same opportunity during the European session after the European market opens. There's an energy that takes place for a few hours until they go into their lunchtime, and then again, after 8:30 a.m. Eastern time when we get those morning announcements until about noon. The swing trades are not so dependent on the time of day as they are defined risk trades with options and are taken when the signals fire off. Although I tend to avoid earnings for swing trades.

Q: What's your favorite time frame chart?

Rob: I'm looking for synchronicity between the daily, hourly, five-minute, and one-minute charts wherever possible. If I see a discrepancy between the hourly chart and the daily chart, for instance, that's a market condition I refer to as mom and dad fighting. You have two big heavy hitter time frames where if one is going up, the other one's going down, the market is all but guaranteed to be very choppy intraday. But I'm typically executing off that one- or two-minute time frame. I don't look for extended moves. I'm not looking to try to put on a trade and let it run for hours because statistically speaking, it's not going to.

Q: How do you enter trades? Single entry, single exit, or do you scale in, scale out?

Rob: This may be controversial but what I have found is that adding to winners sounds great on paper but it can be an execution problem for many traders. They can't handle it. The problem with scaling in is that you're basically pyramiding into trades. The trades are going in your direction, you add 3 more contracts, it is still working, let me throw 10 more contracts on this thing because it's continuing to work and this is really exciting. Then suddenly I've got my heaviest load in the market at a point where statistically it is most likely to have a reversal. What I find in real trading is that you're trying to add and add into the winner, but every minute, every hour, every day, depending on the time frame you are trading, that bend in the end is coming closer and closer. I find that for people making money earlier in the trades, they tend to give quite a bit of it back. They find themselves getting in too big, too far into the trend, and then the markets reverse against them. For me, it doesn't work out so well. So, scaling up my size closer to the end doesn't logically work out from my personal perspective based on what I've seen in general in the active trader community. From an exit perspective, typically I exit the whole position at once or scale out part of the position and let the rest run depending on my confidence level, and how far away we are from meaningful price resistance.

I'm looking for very specific types of entries, such as the pullback and resumptions entries mentioned earlier. I've come to realize that not every minute of every day should be traded. I'm trying to focus on extremely high-probability trades. I'm not happy unless I feel like I've got a 90+% chance of this trade working out. I look for a confluence of circumstances that can dramatically increase my probability of success.

That kind of pattern doesn't happen all day every day, week, or month in the same instrument because of the different time frames that play against each other. There can be a lot of disagreement on different time frames. For instance, the five minute is up, but your hourly is down, and your daily is up, so the risk of a reversal against you is very high, and that is not a 90% trade. Same thing for swing traders when looking at the daily, versus weekly, versus monthly. The higher the confluence, the higher the probability when taking resumption trades.

Q: You've won 33 trading competitions. Can you tell me what those competitions are like?

Rob: Some of these events – the international ones in particular – can be very intense. The first time I was invited to do the big international competition in Paris was back in 2012. I'd won some competitions domestically in the United States so I was invited to France. In the beginning, my starting ranking was considered 15 out of 16, because Americans usually don't win these. Traders represent their countries, your flags are in front of you, the competition is very fierce, and everybody's out to win.

Meanwhile, it's a highly regulated environment. You're trading real money, you have to show your trade in a live account, and they've got to verify the accounts. There are all these judges standing behind you and when you trade. They've got to come over to verify the trade, write it down on a board. Most of them were speaking in French, Italian, or broken English, so trying to communicate with them can be difficult. "No, no, I went short, not long" and "Yeah, that was in the S&P." There's that pressure where I'm trying to explain the trade and show it to them to verify on the screen, but I just want to get back to trading.

Then on top of all that, there's often an audience of hundreds of people and they ask questions. What are you doing? What is your strategy? What are you trading? Why are you trading it? Everybody is speaking in different languages so most of the time I don't really understand what everybody else is doing until they give the official rankings that so and so is number one right now and so and so was number two. It can be very confusing and disorientating so I just focus on the charts. It is a lot of pressure. Most of the time I am the only person from the United States so I try to do a good job, explain to the audience what I am doing, and try to make sure I can get to the next round when applicable.

I was actually publicly shamed and embarrassed a couple of times. In a few of the competitions they would say so and so is doing this, and he's up this much money, so and so is in this trade and down this much money. Rob Hoffman's flat. Then so and so is doing this and so and so is doing this . . . Rob Hoffman is still flat. You could hear the audience chuckle. Imagine the pressure, their robots are making trade after trade and I'm sitting there waiting and waiting. I'm trying to explain to the audience that I'm waiting for my signals to come, for the right setup. Then all of a sudden . . . "Hoffman is in first place" and then they didn't laugh at me anymore.

Waiting for the right trade at the right time, for the right reasons, is everything. I've seen this in competitions year over year over year. I wait and wait. Everybody else is trading a lot, some of the algorithms were very impressive, making a little bit of money with every trade and their equity curve was just straight up.

I would take one trade, and all of a sudden, I'm up. Then I would take another trade and another, and I would win two to one. Other traders would constantly be in and out, but I would win by waiting for the right trade no matter what, and I think that's the secret to my success. I didn't care about who was making fun of me or the distractions happening around me. I was representing my country as an individual and trying my best to make the right trades.

Yes, I trade the same way as I do in real life as much as possible, which is why I am so patient during the competition. I am focusing on that TPT resumption. Waiting for the right trade at the right time for the right reasons and accepting no substitute. As soon as you start accepting substitutes, you're accepting a much lower probability of success, which means your failure rate is going to go up. Then you are going to start doubting yourself. Your stop management is going to be thrown out of whack. Your risk management is going to be thrown out of whack and bad things are going to happen real fast. So stick with the best trades if you want to perform the best.

Q: Does everyone have the same starting capital? Did you trade larger amounts than usual to try to win the competition?

Rob: In the French competitions, for instance, everyone starts out with €50,000 and there's only so much you can do with size because there were very specific rules on intraday and overnight margin requirements for most of the instruments, so it's not like you just go big and go home with the big pot of gold at the end for doing some big trade. Everybody can only trade up to a certain amount.

Q: What's your best trade ever?

Rob: I've had very impressive gains, but to be honest it's not about the single best trade; it's about that series of gains that matters. Trading is about consistency, day after day after day, rather than one big win. Everybody focuses on that one big one that they made for bragging rights but the rest of the time they don't have anything to show, which is why I focus on consistency. That's far more important than one big trade. Sure, I've had some really wonderful big trades but the reality is I've had big losers as well. One of which was a big loss over 13 years ago that really defined who I am as a trader today.

I had a huge run of winners with $1,000, $2,000, $5,000, and $10,000+ winning days back to back again for roughly 18 months straight. I was on fire but I was getting sloppier and sloppier. I didn't realize it at the time, but I was lowering those probabilities and one day I woke up and basically traded against my indicators. I had the Superman complex; I felt invincible, I could do no wrong. I was up, my indicators were down, my one-minute chart was down, my five-minute chart was down, my hourly chart was blood red, and the daily chart had been blood red. Everything was down. And guess what I did? I went long. Then Bernanke came out, I was in a heavy position and the market just dropped hundreds of points and that was my biggest loss ever. I went and told my wife what I did, and kind of had my Victor Niederhoffer moment like it was just another day at the office. She said, "Get back at it. Tomorrow you'll do better." So I went back the next day and showed everybody everything I did wrong and got back on track. (*Note: At the end of his book* The Education of a Speculator, *Victor Niederhoffer discusses the concept of "just another day at the office" as a metaphor for the ups and downs of life and trading. Niederhoffer reflects on the lessons learned from his experiences, emphasizing the importance of resilience, continuous learning, and the acceptance of both successes and failures as part of the journey. He underscores that every day, whether filled with triumphs or setbacks, contributes to one's growth and education as a speculator and as an individual.*)

In my specific situation, I woke up one day and had the Superman complex. I had a viable system and a viable strategy. I just got arrogant, cocky, and I thought I *was* Superman. Nothing could stop me but I had something to go back to. I had some consistency, obviously, a great deal of consistency leading up to it. What I had to do was get back to all the things I was doing right.

Thirteen years later, I've gone on to win 33 real-money trading competitions, had my single best year of trading in modern memory as of last year's close, and focus every day on trying to stick to the rules and avoid the Superman–Wonder Woman trap.

Q: Do you recommend paper trading for new traders?

Rob: Yes, to practice the mechanics. The problem with paper trading is that most people don't treat paper trading like it's real money. It is amazing the ridiculous things that we do when we're paper trading. You take a lot more risk, you take bigger positions that will show these huge gains, you don't treat it as seriously, you don't take the loss, and you are less emotionally affected by the loss because it is on paper only. People tend to let paper losses run further than losses in their real accounts and sometimes it'll come back up to profitability and if that happens, you've trained yourself to hold losses for longer. That can be a big problem if you can't afford to lose that money in the first place, money that you may need to pay bills with. What ends up happening is you learn bad habits: you've trained yourself when you are down to hold the trades for longer because it is going to come up. Also, how does paper trading help your fear of pulling the trigger? Trading real money is different.

If you paper trade, you should think about it like back-testing. You're not getting the real-money fear and greed feelings that can affect your decision-making. That said, it allows you to test your concepts under real market conditions instead of back-testing on the charts afterward and thinking, wow, I could have made this much money in this much time. There are a lot of mechanics that go into trading, and it's a great way to practice them. In addition to back-testing, I've built paper trading, trading simulation, and chart replay into my WealthCharts platform to support active traders and investors and their needs. For myself, I use the trade simulator to help me keep my skills sharp and to practice for the yearly trading competitions to simulate the intensity of those events.

Q: You've given us so much valuable information. If there is one tip that you can provide to anyone who wants to become a full-time trader, what would it be?

Rob: Have some humility. The market is always right, only our opinions of the market are wrong, so be patient. I know I've mentioned this several times earlier, but I can't emphasize it enough, I just can't. There's always the next great trade around the corner. So, have the patience to wait for the next great trade, and have the humility to understand that the market is always right. Think like the hunter, not the hunted. It should be respected and not feared.

Many people may have experienced what I did during my 18-month run and that feeling of being untouchable. Then one day, I woke up and had big losses because I had no humility and no patience and I got humbled.

Find a great strategy; concepts like the TPT resumption are wonderful because they leverage the common psychological pattern where people usually enter the market at the wrong time and are stopped out right before the great move.

If you don't have patience, you're going to be the person who is going to win some, lose some, win some, lose some, a pattern that repeats endlessly. You're taking higher probability trades, but mixing in a series of lower probability trades and you're never going to find that consistency due to your lack of patience. Just remember, wait to take the right trade, at the right time, for the right reasons.

ROB'S TRADING TIPS

1. **Stay with the trend until the bend in the end.**

   One of Rob's most valuable lessons is to stay with the trend until the bend in the end. He learned early on that riding the wave of the market's trend rather than trying to fight against it increases your probability of winning. Stay with the trend until you see signs of reversal, then exit; don't counter-trend trade it. This approach is not just about strategy; it's about developing a deep respect for the market's direction.

2. **Take the right trade at the right time for the right reasons.**

   Rob points out that being patient and waiting for that perfect setup – when everything just clicks – is key. This principle is deeply woven into Rob's narrative, reflecting a discipline forged in the heat of trading competitions and honed through years of market engagement. He's learned that in real-world trading, jumping the gun rarely ends well. He waits for that moment when everything lines up just right, ensuring he's not just trading on a whim, but rather with a solid plan.

3. **Don't buy the breakout; wait for the pullback for better risk to reward.**

   In this chapter, Rob shares with us his TPT strategy that outlines a more selective approach to entering trades. This strategy is based on his observation that entering a trade immediately after a breakout often leads to being caught in a pullback, which can prematurely stop out a trade. By waiting for the initial thrust (a strong price move), a pullback, and then another thrust, traders can enter trades with a better risk to reward from entries made at points that have a higher likelihood of continuation.

CHAPTER 4

Davide Biocchi

Davide Biocchi is a 10-time real-money international trading champion. Known for his strategic use of trading range combined with volume, Davide's strategy focuses on analyzing both big and small player trading volumes. He started with trading US stocks but now primarily trades Italian stocks.

Born in Milan, Davide moved to a seaside town on the Liguria coast in his early 20s to help run his family's hotel and restaurant. During the slow times at the hotel, Davide immersed himself in trading, balancing the demands of the hospitality industry with the fast-paced world of trading. In 2003, after making more money trading than from the hotel business, he decided to sell the hotel and become a full-time trader.

Davide has taught trading at 31 universities, primarily in Italy but also across Europe, earning a reputation as a respected trading expert in Italy. He writes a weekly "Traders Corner" column for major Italian newspapers like *La Repubblica* and *il Fatto Quotidiano*, where he explains financial concepts and answers reader questions.

Q: How did you get into trading?

Davide: I was about 34 years old and working in my family-run hotel every afternoon, even during the winter. It was mandatory as a service to the community to stay open. Imagine this, a seaside hotel with no visitors because it's off-season, but we had to stay open just in case someone needed a room. It was incredibly boring.

On Sundays, it was even worse. I often didn't see a single person for hours, and the boredom was unbearable. Then a friend mentioned something intriguing. I already had a computer and internet access in 1995, so when he told me about simulated trading – paper trading, where you start with $100,000 to buy stocks – I was immediately interested.

That very same day, I logged in and started exploring it. I was passionate about finance and had studied economics in college, so it was an easy transition for me. After a few months of paper trading US stocks I was hooked. I had a savings program that wasn't performing well, so I decided to stop it early and get my money back. It took over 10 working days for the funds to arrive, but once they did, I jumped into real trading. I discovered a fascinating new world, with real-time prices updating every second. It was perfect for me.

Q: Were you day trading?

Davide: Yes, I was day trading while working in my own restaurant, surrounded by family because we also ran a hotel with a kitchen, serving food to guests. In Europe, the Wall Street opening bell rings at 3:30 p.m., which was perfect for me. After serving lunch, I would move to my office, and be ready for the US market to open.

At first, I didn't know terms like *swing trading* or *day trading*. I just started buying some stocks. Back then, it wasn't like today, when you can find news and information on trading everywhere online. But there were a few websites that offered good news about trading.

I often bought stocks that were well-established, with my favorites being Intel, Cisco Systems, and Yahoo!. Besides these, I would also look for initial public offerings or newer stocks. That was my activity back then, balancing my time between the restaurant and the trading desk.

Q: Did you rely primarily on news and fundamentals, or did you also look at charts?

Davide: In the beginning, I didn't look at any charts; I focused on fundamentals. I searched for information on the fundamentals of the stocks I was interested in. Eventually, I started looking at charts as well, initially just to understand the market context, and later as part of my trading activity. It's interesting to think that now I'm a professional member of the Italian branch of the International Federation of Technical Analysis. Back then, I was not good at it at all.

Initially, for the first two years, I wasn't very successful. However, my success grew when I discovered the possibility of opening an online trading account in Italy. This made things much easier for me. Everything was in Italian and transferring money within my own country was straightforward, which boosted my confidence. With my experience trading US stocks, I began trading Italian stocks and found it to be a natural progression.

I started being really successful in 2000 and there came a point when it was evident that I was making more money from trading than from the hotel business. In 2003, I decided to end my career in the hospitality industry and focus solely on trading. This shift was challenging because I hadn't initially considered trading as a full-time career that required formal training. Despite this, I managed to balance trading with my work, making trading an integral part of my professional life.

Q: How did you manage running the hotel and trading during the busy months?

Davide: The administrative office of my hotel was visible to everyone since it was adjacent to the concierge. People could see my setup: one monitor for hotel activities like customer registration and billing, and additional monitors displaying charts and stock prices. They would often ask, "What are you doing there?" I'd explain, "I'm passionate about the markets," and they'd get curious, wanting to come in and watch.

My office quickly became a hub of activity, filled with people. While this was encouraging and sparked many interesting conversations, it also created a lot of difficulties. I found it hard to focus on trading because I was constantly distracted. Guests would come in asking for beers, coffee, or cappuccino, and I had to serve them. Running a family hotel meant I had multiple responsibilities, and it was always busy.

At that time, I was already trading US stocks using the order book, like Level 2, which was incredible because it provided 20 levels per side. You could see exactly what was happening, and I fully grasped the difference between having just Level 1 and having Level 2 data. My entire trading activity was based on the order book.

When I moved to trading Italian stocks, they also had order books, but they were much slower compared to the US ones. This actually made it easier to understand and trade. In the beginning, the order books in Italy felt like a chess game. You would enter an order, then take it out, maybe reenter later, or move your order up or down. It was really a strategic mind game, and my experience with US stocks gave me an edge.

I became quite successful with this approach. For several years, I consistently performed well. At one point, I had about 6 million liras in my account, which was a bit more than €2,700 today. Within a year, I had grown that to nearly €80,000. My performance was stellar, almost unbelievable.

Q: Did you use anything else besides the order book to trade?

Davide: In the very beginning, it was all about book trading. As I mentioned, it was really like a chess game. It was a constant struggle, you against the others. You place orders, take them out, and sometimes the market would come closer to your position, and then you could hit them. It was a strategic battle, and it worked. It was successful.

Q: Was there a specific time of day that this technique would work?

Davide: For me, trading the US market was perfect due to the time difference, but it was different when I started trading the Italian market. The Italian market opened at 9:30 in the morning, which coincided with the time I finished serving breakfast to my hotel guests. Later, the market hours were extended, starting at 9 a.m., making it difficult to manage both jobs. I couldn't serve breakfast and trade at the same time, so I always missed the first half-hour of trading, which I found to be the most volatile and, therefore, the most lucrative part of the day.

In the US, you have premarket and after-hours trading, which extends trading opportunities. However, in Italy, the market starts with an auction that lasts for an hour. You can place orders, but executions happen at the end of the auction, depending on your bid. To fully understand and participate in this auction, you need to be present and attentive.

Initially, I tried to manage by enlisting the help of a nephew to monitor the market and alert me, but that didn't work well. Eventually, I hired someone to handle breakfast and other duties, allowing me to move to a quieter office where I could focus on trading.

For about two years, this setup worked well. I was making more money trading than from the hotel business. However, tourism on the seaside was declining, and the industry was shifting from full-service stays to just bed-and-breakfast. This transition was difficult for a family-run business that had to reallocate resources. Additionally, hiring someone to replace my role wasn't as effective as doing it myself.

Ultimately, I decided to sell the hotel. This decision was tough after dedicating 15 years, 7 days a week, to the business. But once I made the switch, things took a downturn. Ironically, as soon as I sold my business, my trading success plummeted. I had a terrible year; it was the only time I lost significant money in my entire trading career.

I later realized that the problem was the pressure of providing for my family solely through trading. At that time, I had a wife, three children, and a house to maintain. Trading had initially been a supplement to my income, helping me pay off debts and support my family. However, relying entirely on trading for all our needs created immense pressure. Trading requires calm and a clear strategy, but the stress of needing money for basic necessities disrupted my focus and effectiveness.

Q: Do you think you traded differently as a result of the pressure?
Davide: Absolutely, when you have to push to make money, its overwhelming pressure. In the beginning, I was earning money that I didn't necessarily need, which made trading less stressful. But later, I needed that money to live, and the pressure increased tremendously. From my perspective, this pressure affected my success. I experienced my biggest loss ever in the market, about €12,000, due to my decision to buy shares of Parmalat.

Parmalat was involved in a major scandal here in Italy. They provided false information to the market, claiming to have funds deposited in Bank of America New York. They even presented a falsified statement created with Photoshop.

At the time, I was both day trading and swing trading. Parmalat's stock was collapsing daily, and when they released their false statement, no one knew it was fabricated. I decided to buy the stock to capitalize on what I thought would be a quick profit, planning to sell later the same day or perhaps the next day. However, in the middle of the afternoon, the stock was suspended and never came back. Eventually, it was delisted from the market, resulting in a significant loss for me.

Q: Was it more painful because it was the company and not your error?

Davide: This is one aspect of trading that I truly love. On the flipside, it's also what makes trading incredibly challenging. Every mistake you make has a cost. It's straightforward: make a mistake, and the market immediately takes money from your portfolio. You can say goodbye to it instantly.

In a way, yes, I perceived myself as a victim of fraud, but ultimately, it was my portfolio that took the hit. Through my experience, I learned that this can happen. I was the victim of revenge trading mentality. I wanted to get my money back from the market as soon as possible, believing that I was a victim of a terrible fraud that affected me and many others.

This led me to trade more aggressively. Even if I had some successes, I wanted more, and sometimes my gains turned into losses. It was a terrible cycle. When you revenge trade, it's quite normal not to recover your losses. In fact, it would take a miracle not to lose even more money. That's essentially what happened to me. The Parmalat scandal hit me hard in December 2003, and I ended that year with a significant loss. In 2004, I managed to break even, with no profits or losses. It took half a year of trading to recover from that situation.

Q: So essentially, you experienced significant losses and then spent six months revenge trading before something clicked and you realized you needed to change your approach?

Davide: Yes, exactly. What saved me was that, starting in 1999, I had also opened an account with an Italian broker. I was trading heavily, sometimes executing 50–100 trades per day. Drawing on my previous experience with a US broker, I saw an opportunity to improve my Italian broker's platform. I reached out to them, and they invited me to Turin to discuss my ideas. They were impressed and implemented some of my suggestions.

Later, they asked me to provide a testimonial for their platform and present the new features to potential clients. By 2004, my collaboration with them intensified. They started paying me for educational events, where I would travel to cities like Milan, Turin, and Rome to share my trading experience and teach customers how to use the platform.

This role was a real benefit for me. It provided a steady income while allowing me the freedom to trade throughout the day. My job was essentially to provide tips for the platform and teach people how to use it. At least one day a week, I dedicated my time to training others, while the rest of the time I could focus on my own trading.

Eventually, my collaboration with the broker grew even more, prompting me to move to Turin to be closer to their office. This allowed me to meet with them regularly and continue trading actively. Despite these changes, I never stopped trading. My best trading day was in August 2011.

Q: Wow, 50–100 executions in one day is a lot. Did you use a trading robot or trade this manually?

Davide: Mostly manual. The number of trades I executed rapidly increased starting about 2006 when the first algorithms began trading in the market. These early algorithms were attempting to simulate the activity of a speculator, like a day trader or a scalper. However, at that time, they were very fast but also quite rudimentary. They were quite "stupid" in a certain way. Old folks like me who have a lot of experience were really capable of trading against the machines and winning.

Q: How did you physically manage to do so many transactions; even 50 is a lot?

Davide: I was using one of the first trackpads and became very fast with it. It's like how they now play electronic games on the computer. That was my electronic game, but I made money from it.

Q: What was your scalping strategy?

Davide: I scalped the market for four to five years, using the order book extensively. Then, in 2005, I created a software – initially just an Excel spreadsheet, but by 2007, it evolved into a full-fledged software that others could also purchase and use.

This software included formulas that I later patented. Today, using horizontal volumes and volume profiles on charts is very popular. I patented some unique methods specifically for Italian stocks. I couldn't do the same for US stocks due to the numerous electronic communication networks in the US, which makes collecting granular market data difficult. However, this approach is feasible in Italy, making my software particularly effective for Italian stocks.

This software helps you understand if the big players are buying or selling stocks. Typically, 70–75% of the time, when there are buyers, the stock price increases, and when there are sellers, the stock price decreases. These big players have a significant impact on the market – they're like elephants in a crystal shop. My software can detect their presence, which is crucial because they aren't in the market every day. Most days, you see small traders and speculators, but the big players enter only when necessary to make substantial trades.

Q: Did you scalp multiple stocks at once, or did you focus on just one?

Davide: During the day, I could trade 10 or more stocks, but I focused on one at a time to stay concentrated. I used the book, no charts, because in Italy we didn't have Level 2; instead, we had a vertical book similar to a depth of market. I would scalp and every time I'd see a potential, I would enter many orders, canceling them, and placing new ones as I saw potential opportunities. This strategy was really successful until 2011. That year, the algorithms became much faster and smarter. They moved their black boxes closer to the market servers, reducing latency and increasing their speed and efficiency. But the strategy is no longer usable.

Q: How did your trading change after that?

Davide: Transitioning in trading is a gradual process. In 2011, especially in August, I was still very successful, but I noticed that things were changing. My strategy wasn't as effective as before. It's not like you go from 100 to 0 overnight. You might drop to 80, then 50, then 40, and you realize you need to make a decision. I decided that after years of success, the algorithms had become better than me, so I needed to change my trading style.

I added new features to my software and shifted from scalping to day trading. I reduced my trades from 100 or more executions per day to 30, then 20, then 10, and sometimes even just 5 round trips per day. This transition took until 2015.

From 2015 onwards, my approach changed further. As you get older – I'm 58 now – your experience helps you avoid many trades, even if they might be successful but yield very small gains. When you're young, you're more aggressive in trading. It's like running a bar and selling hundreds of coffees; it's profitable but very stressful. Switching to day trading is like going for one trade that is worth 100 coffees. It's less stressful and more efficient.

Q: What was your secret to successful order book trading in the beginning, when you were constantly adding and removing orders?

Davide: In the beginning, the secret was understanding that on the other side of my trades were other people like me. It was a chess game, and I had to think like my opponents. Later, the opponents became software programs, and I focused on understanding their behavior. These programs made money by creating micro volatility while avoiding real volatility. When there's significant volatility, these programs exit the market to avoid losses, as they usually operate on both sides of the market. They tend to leave before major economic data releases at 8:30 a.m. or 10 a.m., like gross domestic product or consumer price index reports, to avoid getting caught in large market swings.

The software programs currently active in the market places and cancels a huge number of pending orders to influence other traders or algorithms. They create the illusion that a stock will move in a certain direction. For example, they make it seem like the stock will go up, but when you execute your trade, you find out it's actually going down because the software was working against you.

Q: How do you take advantage of the fact that algorithms set pending orders to mislead other traders?

Davide: Algorithms don't like it when a human trader goes against them, and they'll punish you immediately. They also try to push you into making wrong moves. It's a very strategic game. The real issue now is that they are so fast that by the time you understand what they're doing and react, it's already too late. That's why scalping the market is no longer viable.

One of my key strengths over the years has been my ability to adapt, like a chameleon, whenever my current strategy stopped working. I navigated through the dot-com bubble, 9/11, the Lehman Brothers collapse, the rise of algorithms, and I'm still here. I continuously adapted my trading style to fit new market conditions.

After the COVID-19 collapse, I had the opportunity to buy stocks at significantly reduced prices and engage in some buy-and-hold activities. Now, while I still do a lot of day trading on certain days, my primary focus has shifted to swing trading. I take a few positions at a time, analyze fundamentals, and look for potential arbitrage opportunities when the market misprices stocks based on my 25 years of experience.

So, my strategy evolved. I started determining whether it was one of the 2 days out of 10 when it was advantageous to stay in front of the market, as most days the market doesn't move in a way that's easy to trade. My software helps me identify those optimal days, and I trade accordingly.

With my software, you can identify the different market players: the piranhas, the sharks, and the big sharks. These players are typically active in the market every day. For example, private traders and software-driven speculators are like piranhas. White sharks (mid-level traders) are present most days, while blue sharks (large institutional traders) only appear occasionally.

I categorized the market this way to help see what the small fish (retail traders) are doing. These small players often make the wrong moves, typically going against the main trend, which can be valuable information. They tend to act contrary to the market over 80% of the time.

The software provides real-time, live updates during the market session. I developed and patented an indicator called the TWbook Indicator. This indicator looks at trading volumes, the average value of individual orders, and other metrics like the up-down ratio (how many stocks are rising or falling). These elements combine to create a proprietary calculation of trader sentiment. I gather information from different trading providers to form a comprehensive perspective on market movements.

Q: Do you rely on volume as well?

Davide: Yes, absolutely. I base my trading on volume. Vertical volumes tell you when the activity happened, while horizontal volumes show you where it happened and how much. I really trust both horizontal and vertical volumes. These are the only indicators I use in my charts.

Q: Can you walk us through how you use your indicator?

Davide: Let me give you some perspective on that. The market provides information primarily from the viewpoint of liquidity providers – those who place orders in the order books. However, my software focuses on the perspective of liquidity takers – those who buy from sellers or sell to buyers. My algorithm reengineers the order book, time and sales data to recreate the viewpoint of those entering the market, rather than those waiting to be executed.

What I can share with you is that my algorithm, which could be considered a form of artificial intelligence today, generates alerts. For instance, this morning at 10 a.m., I received an alert about the Italian stock of Sipem SpA. The alert indicated that if the stock behaved a certain way by 10 a.m., it would typically close below its current price. The system ranks these alerts with one to four stars. By looking into the historical data since 2014, I can see that this strategy has a 53% success rate and a 1.4 profit factor.

This is based on years of data collection, which I've been doing daily since 2010. The historical equity line is quite interesting, which is why I use this data for day trading. My platform generates trading ideas calculated by my algorithm using this extensive historical data.

For today's market, I can provide insights such as a 15-day market profile. This equity line, based on historical data, is really interesting and forms the basis for my day trading.

Q: Once you have the trade ideas, how do you determine your entries and exits?

Davide: In the morning, I assess the market scenario. If the scenario is neutral, I simply say, "Bye, see you tomorrow." But if the scenario indicates a medium, moderate, or strong risk-on environment, I look for real potential opportunities based on the rankings, which includes an increase in volume.

Then I need something to support my decision. Algo stats might indicate a buying situation, but if the day is categorized as risk-off, whether medium or strong, I won't go long. It's completely against my strategy. I need a combination of factors that suggest a strong opportunity. For example, if there's a potential breakout to the downside, I will go short. Alternatively, if there's an upside breakout of a dynamic or static trend line, I will go long. This is how my approach works.

To be honest, I've found that short trades are generally more successful than long trades in this strategy. Day trading with this perspective tends to favor short trades because they are quicker and often deeper. When the market goes down, it's common to see drops of 1, 2, 3, or even 4%. However, market rises are usually more gradual, often around 0.7% on a good day. So, to make real money day trading, it's often better to go short. Only about 2 out of 10 days present a strong opportunity for long trades.

When I'm in a position, I no longer need to refer back to charts; I manage my position on the individual stock itself. I don't usually set a fixed target. I have a target in mind, but I don't place an order at that target. Instead, I trail my profit. If the market moves as I anticipated, I follow the trend with a trailing profit order. This way, if the market continues to rise, I let it go. If it reverses, that will be my signal to close the position.

Q: Where do you put your stop?

Davide: Over the years, I've learned that if I can keep my losses under €400, I can usually recover during the day. However, if something unexpected happens, like bad data at 2:30 causing the market to drop significantly, and my losses exceed €400, it affects my confidence.

In such cases, I push myself to close the position because staying in might lead to more mistakes. I'm very good at managing my positions as long as my loss doesn't exceed €400. If it does, I immediately close the position. For this reason, I don't use automatic stop orders, because the market can sometimes spike unexpectedly, as it did right after COVID.

Q: Do you have a daily profit target?

Davide: No, let me explain. I've done this many times, and here's how it works. Some days, you're perfectly in sync with the market. On those days, if you could trade 20 out of 24 hours, you should. But there are also days when you're completely off, and after two trades, you should just call it quits and say, "Okay, not for me today."

I don't have a fixed trading profit target. Let me give you an example with Caterpillar stock over the last five years. I'll add CNH Industrial to the chart, which is a competitor of Caterpillar. CNH was an Italian company that expanded globally and is now listed only in the US.

Historically, the performance of these two stocks was very similar. However, in mid-2023, CNH's CEO announced that the company would no longer be listed in Milan and would be listed only in New York. Despite the growing market and Caterpillar's continued rise, CNH's stock went the opposite way. Italian investors, wary of having stocks listed in a foreign market, sold off their shares. By the end of November, CNH's price-to-earnings ratio was below 6, which is very unusual.

So, I bought CNH heavily and recently sold it about this level. I held this position for about a month and made a substantial profit. During this period, I was also short on another stock and wasn't day trading because these two trades provided great returns. Now, I'm more focused on finding trades like this rather than day trading every day. I still day trade when there are great opportunities, but otherwise, I look for different types of trades.

Q: Can you tell me about some of the trading competitions that you've participated in?

Davide: I've won 10 trading competitions and placed second, third, or fourth in 14 of the others. Except for a three-month-long competition, all of them were invitation-only and different formats. The Italian Top Trader competitions spanned three months, while the Salon du Trading Paris competition in Paris was particularly tough, where I tied for first place.

Competing in Paris is like playing at Wimbledon. These are one-day events with judges, whom I call referees because they wear referee-like T-shirts. Each time you open a new position, you must raise your hand and announce, "I'm long on this and that." The referees then come over, check your account, record the details, and write them on a board. This process, although interesting, is very slow and feels like going back years in technology.

The competition starts with about 16 traders in the morning. After the first hour, the number is reduced to eight, then four, and finally to two for the final match. In 2011, I became the champion, and in 2012, I was the vice-champion, losing to Rob Hoffman in the finals. Despite the tough competition with traders from around the world, finishing second was a gratifying experience, and I felt truly satisfied.

Q: Did the organizer decide the instruments traded or could you trade anything you wanted?

Davide: For the Salon du Paris competition, initially, you could trade anything you wanted within a budget of €50,000. However, some traders, especially those from Australia or Asia, would fly in on Thursday, participate in the early morning trades, and get disqualified if they didn't make it into the top eight. They often complained about spending money to travel and then being eliminated quickly.

In response, the organizers changed the rules. They decided that if you participated, you could trade the entire day, but in different sections. For example, in the early morning, you had to trade stocks – European, French, Italian, German, whatever you preferred. At lunchtime, you switched to trading currencies. Then, about 5 p.m. European time (11 a.m. New York time), the final session required trading futures. This could include futures on indices, commodities like crude oil or gold, or other assets. This format aimed to determine the overall best trader.

Eventually, the rules changed again. Now, there are separate champions for stocks, forex, and futures, and an overall global winner is determined at the end.

Q: Did your approach to trading in the competition differ from how you trade in real life?

Davide: When trading in a competition, it's like driving a car on a racetrack. On the track, I can push the limits more and more because the goal is to win the competition. During the competition, I go all out, aiming for either a big win or a stop loss. This approach is specific to the competition; it's a duel. Like in car racing, you might drift or drive like in a rally – it's a different approach and strategy just for the competition.

This is not the way I would drive my car in a city and not the way I typically trade. In a competition, you're constantly on the edge, but my regular trading approach is different, even if the underlying strategy is the same.

In my typical trading, I aim for the best performance possible, which isn't just about strategy but also about my emotional approach to the market. I plan my stop losses and how to react to different scenarios, whether the market goes in my favor or against me. I focus on protecting my portfolio with stop losses and careful planning.

Over the years, my trading style has evolved. When you're younger, you take more trades; as you get older, you make fewer trades but with a broader 360° vision. I study inter-market connections and correlations. I enjoy spread trading, like trading one stock against another or one sector against another. In my trading, volumes, charts, and market conditions are all important. I like to use the horizontal volumes for swing trading to identify potential areas for reversal and targets.

Q: Do you use a different chart time frame in competitions compared to your day-to-day trading?

Davide: Yes, I lower my time frames when participating in a competition. Personally, I prefer daily and weekly charts, but I am also good at reading five-minute or one-minute charts. There isn't just one way to be successful. You can excel in different areas, and I enjoy approaching the market in various ways. Lately, I've been focusing on enjoying my life, so I reduce the number of trades or switch to longer time frames. However, if there's a competition tomorrow, I can easily switch back. I've done this type of trading for many years.

When day trading, I focus not only on price breakouts but more on volatility breakouts. This happens when the market accelerates, and the number of trades per second or minute increases, often coinciding with a price breakout from a resistance level.

For day trading, if you use tools like standard deviation with volume-weighted average price (VWAP), you need to be skilled in mean reversion strategies. Sometimes, the price moves to the first standard deviation and then reverts, so you must be prepared for this. Other times, it breaks through and accelerates to the second or third standard deviation. My charts typically show three standard deviations plus the VWAP.

When considering volumes for day trading, focus on the visible range of the last 4–10 days. It's important to understand where traders who bought two or three days ago might be feeling pressure if prices drop. If prices recover, these traders are likely to sell quickly because they are no longer aiming for profit; they just want to break even. They see a black hole below them and will escape immediately once prices recover.

That's why you can often identify resistance levels where there has been significant volume over the past 5–10 days. Swing traders usually don't hold positions longer than that, so when prices recover, many of them will sell simply to break even. So it's relatively straightforward. You have tools like the VWAP and standard deviation, but trading also has a huge emotional component. If you ask traders how much emotion affects their trading, most would say at least 80%. In reality it's likely closer to 90%. How do you manage that?

Think of the famous soccer player Diego Maradona. Imagine being a Maradona in technical analysis, stock picking, or market timing. Even with those skills, if your trading is more than 80% affected by emotions, it won't matter. You need to minimize emotional influence to let your skills shine. How can you do that? You can train for it.

First, do not paper trade because it doesn't involve the emotional connection to real money. Instead, start trading with a small amount of money and gradually increase it. This will help you manage your emotions. Over time, add more money to your account. There will be a point where you realize you can't keep from checking your positions constantly.

If you're waking up at night to check the market, you've likely surpassed your limits. The emotional impact is directly tied to the amount of money you have in the market. For example, buying a single $100 stock might not affect you emotionally, and you could easily ignore it. The same might apply to $1,000 or even $3,000. But at some point, the amount will start to affect you.

Everyone's threshold is different. Most people put more money into the market than they can mentally handle, which is why they lose. They can't manage the emotional side because the stakes are too high.

I recommend increasing your investment gradually, say by $1,000 increments, and observing how it affects you. You'll likely find you can handle only a small amount of money comfortably. If you stay within your limits, you can trade successfully. Trading below your limit isn't effective either because it won't engage you. Find the right amount for you, and you'll be able to trade effectively.

Q: Can you explain your strategy in more detail?

Davide: After my period of scalping the market, which was based purely on intuition, I started incorporating charts to aid my day trading. I began with the VWAP and standard deviations, later adding horizontal volume to my analysis. It's important for me to compare what's happening with the stock I'm trading and the overall market, including futures.

For instance, is the market trending up? Is the stock I'm trading also trending up? Am I on the right side of the market? If I plan to go long, I check if the price is above the VWAP, as this indicates that the stock is more bought than sold by the big players. My goal is to "copy-paste" the actions of the big players because they have the power to affect the market. If they're buying, the market will likely move up.

Standard deviations can act as support or resistance levels, and when combined with horizontal volumes, they provide interesting levels for trading. In my intraday trading, I achieve a success rate of more than 8 trades out of 10. However, the downside is that the two losing trades can wipe out more than a week's profits.

Before exiting a position, I always know where my stop loss should be, but I want to be absolutely sure I'm not making a mistake. It's frustrating to place a stop loss, only to see the price hit the bottom and then move in your favor. This hesitation often makes my losses slightly larger than my wins, but that's normal in day trading.

Q: What is your favorite time frame for day trading?

Davide: I typically trade using a five-minute chart, which I find works best for me. If there's low volatility and I need to trade, I might drop down to a one-minute chart, but that's usually too aggressive for my style. However, a 15-minute chart tends to be too slow and boring for day trading. So, from my perspective, and this is very personal, a five-minute chart is ideal.

Q: What is the number-one trading tip you can give to a new trader?

Davide: First, avoid paper trading. As soon as you gain enough confidence with the market, start trading with real money.

Next, plan your strategy. This isn't about deciding to buy or sell under certain conditions. It's about planning how much money you can afford to lose. You need to decide what you'll do if the market moves in your favor: will you sell at a target, trail your profits, or maybe sell half your position and move your stop to breakeven and let it run?

All these approaches can be effective. There's no single superior method; the key is to have a clear plan. Money management is the cornerstone of trading. Once you start trading with real money, focus on developing a solid money management plan. With good money management, even a coin flip can be profitable. The specific strategies for buying or selling come later, but many people mistakenly start with that. This is a real problem.

Q: If you think traders should avoid paper trading, what are your thoughts on back-testing?

Davide: Back-testing is bullshit. If you test your strategy on historical data and find it's not successful, you might tweak your formula and retest it. If it then shows positive results, that's great! However, what you've done is align your strategy to fit past data rather than create a genuinely successful approach.

This means your strategy is adapted to historical prices, but it may not work well with future market conditions.

Q: Do you recommend starting with a small account, making changes in live market conditions, and continue trading that?

Davide: To be honest, I don't believe there's a Holy Grail in trading strategies. However, you can find your own version of the Holy Grail in effective money management. It's like a marriage, where both partners promise to be faithful for life, but we know that's not always the case. Similarly, with a money management strategy, sometimes we aren't as faithful to it as we should be.

If you want to be a successful trader, planning is crucial. You need a plan, including contingencies for when things don't go as expected with your money management strategy.

For instance, let's say we agree that $500 is our stop loss. If the market is highly volatile and hits that $500 loss, you might hope it turns around and decide not to apply your stop loss. By the end of the day, you find yourself down $900. What should you do? Many people freeze in this situation because they didn't plan for it. They get dragged around by the market, unable to take decisive action.

You must have a plan B for when things go wrong. If you exceed your limits, have a strategy in place to address it. The goal is to avoid a catastrophic loss that wipes out your capital. If you save some money, you can start trading again and rebuild. But if you lose all or 90% of your capital, it's almost impossible to recover.

Consider this: if you lose 50% of your capital, you need to make a 100% gain just to break even. I know many traders, but very few ever achieve a 100% performance. It's something you need to keep in mind and plan for accordingly.

Q: What do you think is the biggest mistake that people make in trading?

Davide: Not applying the stop loss when it was something manageable is a common mistake. Sometimes traders are in sync with the market and very successful because they are confident and trust their decisions.

I recall a time when I was speaking at a conference and mentioned that I had just shorted Fiat (now Stellantis). A man in the audience responded, "Wow! You did a great thing because I just bought it, and whenever I buy a stock, it goes down." This man clearly didn't trust himself.

Why be insecure? If you don't trust yourself, why are you trading? Maintaining self-confidence is crucial for success. Without it, you will likely fail.

To sustain that confidence, you must adhere to your money management strategy. When creating this strategy, be honest in evaluating yourself. Even the best strategy is useless if you can't follow it. Your strategy should suit your abilities and temperament, like a well-fitting coat.

Q: What do you think is the right risk to reward or money management?

Davide: It depends. If you are day trading, aim for a closer risk-to-reward ratio, about 1 : 1. For swing trading, you should look for a larger risk-to-reward ratio because the market opens and closes, creating gaps. These gaps mean you can't always control the situation.

In day trading, you can always close your position. However, if something changes overnight, like a geopolitical event, your stock might open 10% lower the next day. You need a plan for this. Therefore, having a risk-to-reward ratio greater than 1 : 1, such as 1 : 3 or 1 : 1.4, is beneficial.

The key is avoiding the black hole of big losses. This is something we all need to understand clearly. Trading involves small losses and small gains – everyone experiences these. The difference lies in occasionally achieving big gains and, most important, avoiding big losses.

If you can avoid big losses, which comes down to effective money management, you can survive as a trader. Over time, you may learn how to achieve significant gains. However, if you experience big losses, it's only a matter of time before you're out of the game.

So, the first priority is money management. The primary goal of money management is to avoid big losses. Normal gains and losses are part of daily trading. The aim is to eventually achieve substantial profits while minimizing losses.

DAVIDE'S TRADING TIPS

1. **Watch the 4–10 day range with VWAP.**

When day trading, focus on the visible range from the last 4–10 days. This time frame helps you understand where recent traders might feel pressure if prices drop.

Use tools like VWAP and standard deviation to identify key volume levels when traders entered the market. When prices recover, these traders often sell to break even, creating resistance levels.

Swing traders usually hold positions for up to 10 days, so when prices bounce back, they're likely to cash out. By considering this dynamic and incorporating VWAP with volume analysis, you can better predict resistance levels and make more informed trading decisions.

2. **Ditch paper trading and identify your emotional threshold.**

Avoid paper trading, as it lacks the emotional connection to real money. Start trading with a small amount and gradually increase it to help manage your emotions. Over time, add more money to your account until you find your emotional limit. If you're waking up at night to check the market, you have too much at stake.

Identify your threshold. A $100 stock might not affect you, but $1,000 or $3,000 might. Many people put more money into the market than they can handle emotionally, leading to poor decisions and losses. Increase your investment gradually, in increments like $1,000, and observe how it affects you. Find the right amount for you – one that engages you but stays within your emotional limits. By managing your emotions effectively, you can trade successfully and let your skills truly shine. Remember, the key to mastering trading is not just technical skills but also emotional control.

3. **Always have a backup plan.**

There are countless trading strategies out there, but the real secret to success is putting just as much focus on money management. This focus is what truly determines your success. Forget about obsessing over perfect entries – they don't exist! Instead, plan for the end result and manage your trades like a pro. Planning is key to winning the trading game.

Always have a backup plan for when things go offtrack. For instance, if you set a $500 stop loss but decide not to apply it, hoping for a turnaround, you might end up down $900 by the end of the day. Many traders panic in this situation because they didn't have a plan. If you exceed your limits, have a strategy ready to deal with it. Avoid catastrophic losses that can wipe out your capital. By saving some money, you can bounce back and rebuild. Losing all or 90% of your capital makes it almost impossible to recover. If you lose 50% of your capital, you'll need a 100% gain just to break even.

CHAPTER 5

John Bannan

John Bannan is one of the world's top futures traders, earning third place in the Robbins World Cup Championship for Futures Trading in 2022. Early in his career, John was determined to leave his 9-to-5 job behind.

Driven by his passion for financial markets, John immersed himself in trading and became self-taught. His distinctive approach to cycle-based forecasting is the cornerstone of his trading strategy. With over 20 years of trading experience, John transitioned to full-time trading in 2009 and became a commodity trading advisor (CTA) in 2022, managing millions in assets. He specializes in swing trading Nasdaq and E-mini S&P futures (ES) using his innovative market-timing techniques.

Despite his success, John has not lost sight of his beginnings in teaching retail traders. He remains committed to helping others by keeping his programs accessible to smaller accounts and welcoming new clients. Through his CTA, John continues to refine his strategies and share his expertise with the trading community.

    Q: How did you get into trading?

 John: I was in a long-term relationship until my late 20s. Coming out of it, I found myself questioning my path and future. I noticed while working as a market analyst at McCurrach that many of my colleagues one tier ahead of me, managing multimillion-dollar retail accounts, were burning out, working like dogs and not getting paid much more than me. It made me wonder if I really wanted to continue that path.

Fate intervened when I was considering a fresh start in Australia or Canada. I met Anne Marie, my future wife, who was Canadian and traveling to the UK every two weeks for her business. We hit it off instantly, and our relationship quickly blossomed. Feeling ready for a new chapter in my life, I decided to quit my job and move to Canada, despite knowing the immigration policies would prevent me from working for a while. While her business was thriving, and I helped a bit, it wasn't my passion.

With my background in numbers, I turned to reading investing books. Initially, I wasn't thinking about trading, only investing – the Warren Buffett way. Investing felt like a tried-and-true path where a newbie could reasonably succeed. I discovered Phil Town's book, *Rule #1 of Successful Investing*, which became my focus for the next couple of years. I adopted a buy-and-hold strategy, and my investments were successful from the start. The idea is that if the market's general trend is upward, it meant that if you've got a basket, you're probably going to do reasonably well even if you've got a couple of dogs in the portfolio.

Q: When did you make the switch from investing to trading?

John: The problem was that investing really wasn't that exciting. It wasn't successful enough to change my life. Value investing, while solid, takes a long time to yield significant results. In addition to this you also have to deal with some pretty big drops in value in bear phases, which is hard to time and to stomach. That's when I started to look into trading books and courses, both online and in-person in Florida, California, and Toronto. I must have spent tens of thousands of dollars on trading courses.

Q: Did you focus on equity indices or also dabble in forex, options, and commodities?

John: Coming from an investing background, I initially focused exclusively on stocks. This was about 2006 and ETFs [exchange-traded funds] weren't really a thing back then – they were brand new. So, I started with individual stocks, then moved to small-cap stocks where I saw more opportunities. By 2009, I had developed my own trading system using small-cap stocks. It was always stocks for me – I never really ventured into forex, even to this day. In 2011, I transitioned from stocks to ETFs, and since 2014, I have been primarily trading index futures.

Q: What types of strategies did you use? Did you experiment with various methodologies in the beginning, like trend following, momentum breakouts, or picking tops and bottoms?

John: Picking tops and bottoms was never something I believed I could do precisely right. No one can, of course, but now we do a pretty good job of catching more than we don't. I would never have tried to do that 10 years ago because I didn't have the tools. I was always obsessed with getting as close to the bottom as possible in order to buy, but I would wait for a bit of strength in the market as my signal to enter. I used indicators, which have a lag, but when building a mechanical trading system, you have to rely on them. My goal was to get as close to timing the bottoms as possible, not the tops. Tops are tougher to pick, but bottoms are easier to catch in stocks and ETFs due to indicator exhaustion and the long bias of the market. For a long time, I focused on long-only systems. Now I look to go long and short in the indexes, and I focus on timing the turns well ahead of time.

Q: When you were trading long-only systems picking bottoms, what time frame was it on?

John: For quite some time, I focused exclusively on daily charts. Even now, the main swing trading system we use at my company, Comhla, is based on daily charts. I believe that the higher the time frame, the easier it is to identify clear trends. So, all my long-only systems are based on daily charts. When it comes to swing trading, I initially used trend-based strategies; now, we're focused on timing the market before it actually turns.

Intraday trading is a whole different ballgame – it's more about grabbing opportunities quickly rather than holding on for a trend. In my day trading, I have a target and aim for a high win rate, rather than trying to capture a larger move, but daily charts have been my main focus for the last 20 years.

Q: Did your trading style change from trend following to picking tops and bottoms?

John: Absolutely 100%. I now have two long-only systems – Prophetick, which is based on catching bottoms in Nasdaq and is pretty aggressive, and Safara, which is ES only and less aggressive. I also created a system that marries the two together for a bit of a smoother ride, called Artemis. It is generally always in the market long or short the ES and long only the NQ [e-mini Nasdaq-100 futures], only going flat for risk management purposes.

Q: Initially, you explored different instruments and stocks, but do you believe that over time, concentrating solely on ES and NQ has been a key to your success? Does knowing these instruments well help you avoid distractions from other markets?

John: Yes, coming from a background in stocks, then ETFs, and now futures, I've stayed with indexes because it feels like home. There's plenty to focus on without needing to venture beyond them. The idea is that if you have a 20-year history with an instrument and your equity curve is reasonably straight – though never perfectly straight – you can be as certain as possible that it will continue to work going forward. If it doesn't, then it's time to revisit your strategy.

For me, it's always been about chasing certainty. In fact, if you can prove to yourself that you can trade one successful system on one asset, you wouldn't need to do anything else. Having been involved in the markets for 20 years now, it's about consistently narrowing down to doing just one thing well on as small amount of assets as possible.

Q: Have your money management techniques changed through the years?

John: In the beginning, it was always about maintaining and building systems with a 3 : 1 ratio of wins size to loss size. In that way if you have a system that wins only 50% of the time, you still end up making money. However, my money management is now more focused on matching my trading size to the worst possible drawdown historically. In other words, if I know my system has historically a $10,000 drawdown per ES contract, then I have to determine what my size is to walk forward with. So for every $50,000 in my account, I could be risking a 20% drawdown if history repeats and my equity curve comes down to match the worst-case scenario of the past. If I allocate a higher amount, such as $100,000, then my drawdown would only be 10%. This is how I think in terms of system building and matching size to risk tolerance. If it goes beyond a historical drawdown, then that would be the new level to manage risk from. So, I size my trades based on the drawdown or the percentage loss I can handle in my account. The question is: Is it 5, 10, or 20%? Can you handle a 40% drawdown knowing it will eventually recover? While no one wants that, you have to consider it. It's all relative – how much money do you want to make versus how much you are willing to risk.

Also, as a swing trader, especially in futures, having a successful system means you're looking at a lot of ticks. In the ES, a system with an average win size across all trades and history of $1,000 per trade represents a significant number of ticks and would allow for sizable negative slippage before the system would fail. I also look at the win rate because the higher it is, the easier it is to trade. That is why I like to share the long-only side; people following any system prefer to win more, it's easier to stay the course, and it's what I share in the strategies for our retail clients.

Bottom line, a higher win rate makes it easier for the people to follow a system. I aim for a 70–80% win rate for long-only trades. The market tends to have a long bias, making it easier to catch bullish moves. As the saying goes, "the bull walks up the stairs while the bear jumps out the window." It's much harder to catch the bear as it's falling, but easier to catch the bull as it walks up the stairs.

Q: Did you always use stops and do you prefer single entry/single exit or multiple entry/multiple exit?

John: I always used hard stops. I always had one entry technique and about five or six exit techniques using different indicators for different scenarios. It was never about hitting a specific target; it was about trend following and letting the trade run as far as it could. The obsession was trying to get as close to a bottom as possible and then exiting as close to the top of the trend as I could. Now, I am more technical in my stops. I no longer use hard stops but rely on my cycles not only to get it right, but to tell me when I am wrong and determine the exit. For additional risk management I also step out of the market for hedge-known risk events, like CPI [consumer price index] reports and Fed rate announcements, for example.

Q: Can you describe your strategy and how it works?

John: Basically, I have a forecasting-based system. I know what I'm going to do next Tuesday and the week after, right down to the day. It's a very unusual way to trade, but when you look at pioneers like W. D. Gann, who was making yearly forecasts over a 100 years ago, you realize it's been done before.

My system is based on market cycles that repeat over time. The further out you look, the easier it is to see these cycles over the past 100 years – roughly for the sake of example, 20 years of sideways movement, followed by 20 years up, and 20 years sideways, and then another 20 years up. It's just the way it's always been. You can dial right into that and forecast moves with reasonable success. If I was perfect at forecasting, it would be amazing, right? But obviously, I'm not right all the time; however, there are periods where my accuracy is high, which makes a significant difference. Overall, we are right 70%+ on long and short now.

Q: If a trade is losing, do you still exit based on a specific calendar date, regardless of the outcome?

John: If by Tuesday my trade is still underwater, I have another technique that allows for a bit more time before deciding it's time to take the loss. This method gives the trade just a few extra hours to recover, but not much more.

By doing this, I increase my chances of turning a losing trade around. My win rate with this strategy ranges from 70 to 80%, so allowing that small window of extra time can make a big difference. While I'm not right all the time – I wish I were – I do stick to a time-based exit strategy. So, yes, even if a trade is losing, I still follow my calendar-based exit plan. Ultimately, it's important to stick to the system and take the loss. This is a mechanical process there is no time for thinking when trading this way. If you don't like the outcome, you need to go back to the drawing board and fix it for next time. But for now, no thinking allowed.

Q: Does that mean you will not take partial profits early?

John: That's right, I don't. While there might be advantages to doing so, and I regularly go back to consider it and retest it, as a swing trader, I am committed to executing my strategy correctly. It's a reflection of my diligence in following the system and not being swayed by the moves in between.

Sometimes it's heartbreaking because I can be up 75 points and end up with just a 15-point winner, or even a loss. But I've tested this approach extensively, going through history over long periods of time and looking at many, many years of this method. It really makes sense to wait until the trade is over and do nothing in between. Trying to be clever in the middle of the move usually doesn't work out.

Q: You describe feeling heartbreak at giving back profits and that's a feeling many traders can empathize with. What emotions do you experience in those moments, and how do you overcome them?

John: I'm almost always in the market, so I tend to be less emotional about it. I sleep well at night knowing that, over time, I'll do well. However, I don't like trades going against me; I still feel that emotion. It's a horrible feeling to be underwater, especially knowing others are following my trades. It makes it even worse, but even from my personal perspective, seeing my account go down is always tough. Watching a trade go down is a horrible feeling and it always will be.

Curiously, one of the worst feelings is having a massive win and resisting the urge to take profits prematurely. It's particularly challenging in trading because you never want to look like an idiot to the people following you. They see the high gains and if you give it all back, you look like an idiot. They know that you had this much, and you gave it all back – you look like a complete fool. But then there's the balance that I talked about; if you've tested not to do that, in time it will balance out.

Sometimes I'll watch TV to turn it all off. I've got two boys who are into virtual reality [VR], so I put on the VR and play some video games. I am blessed. We do fun stuff together. Saturdays are sacred for me, since the futures market closes at 5 p.m. on Friday and reopens at 6 p.m. on Sunday. I rest and do very little on Saturdays.

I can't say I always follow my trading rules, but I do 99% of the time, which is my saving grace. The only times I've truly beaten myself up is when I've deviated from my system. That's when the really big stick comes out, right? The worst part is that you really don't have a plan at that point.

With a trading system, you have a plan. It sucks when it's not making money, but you know it will balance out over time. You just have to endure the stress and emotion without acting on them. If I didn't have my trading system, I don't know how I'd handle losses. I'm a systematic trader; I need a reason to be in a trade and a reason to get out.

Q: Would you say that having a trading system and trading rules has made you a better, less impulsive trader?

John: It certainly made me a better human to be around. It's the only way I know how to win. In my opinion, trading without a system is like driving at night without your lights on. Not only will you scare the hell out of yourself, your chances of getting to where you want to go are slim to none.

Q: You focus on swing trading but do you also day trade? How is that approach different?

John: Day trading is the most emotionally draining for me. When I'm in the chair, I'm fully focused – don't talk to me, I'm just there, in and out, and then I'm done. Swing trading, however, is more relaxed for me, even though it doesn't always win.

One of the most challenging aspects of building a day trading system, and I've built many over the years, is that the average profit size is quite small. No matter what you do, you have to factor in losses, slippage, and trading costs, making it nearly impossible to create a consistently winning system. It's very difficult and has taken me a long time to become proficient.

In day trading and scalping, you have to be right far more often than you're wrong. You need a really high win rate. By contrast, with swing trading, you can get away with a 50% win rate and still make a lot of money on a trend. You can have five losses and one big trend that covers all of them.

Q: How many trades do you typically make each day?

John: For day trading, two or three trades. Generally, my preference is one and done, trading only one instrument at a time. With something as liquid as the S&P, you could probably drop a lot of contracts on it, but the bigger the size the more your emotions will get you. I trade relatively small and have a target; once reached I am done, and the best days are when I get it done early. This morning, for instance, I traded for 15 minutes about 10 a.m. and was done, but, my average holding period is 1 or 2 hours.

My day trading is really market dependent. There are cycles within the intraday that we follow based on our proprietary research around where we think the turns will be every day; sometimes that works, sometimes it doesn't but we get a profit most days so it's a great little system. I'm usually done in the morning. If I'm still in trade at noon, it's really quite unusual.

My swing trading continues separately because it is managed mainly at the close of each day. For example, today I don't have to do anything because my current trade lasts until Tuesday, so I'm just holding the long position and waiting.

When my trading day is over, I'm in research most of the time. I look at how we can continue improving. I look at where we're at with day trading or swing trading, and whether the swing trading is aligned with my research.

We brought in a new programmer this year who specializes in machine learning and AI [artificial intelligence], and that has been an exciting development for us validating our previous research with the use of thousands of computers in the cloud through machine learning techniques.

For 12 years, I worked with an in-house coder who handled all my coding while I generated the ideas. Sometimes I think I've become a bit more of a dinosaur in the office when it comes to the pace of research, because I don't know AI, and I know very little code. All the foundational work still comes from my work in the last 10 years, but AI is a really exciting field. Having seen what it really can do, it is amazing me daily how much closer we're getting to knowing for sure, without any human bias, that what we do really works walking it forward.

The research around cycle technology is powerful and it's not just a trading system. I see it more as my legacy beyond trading. Can I really prove without a shadow of a doubt that the market can be seen ahead of time 70%, maybe 80% of the time? I don't know yet, but I do believe it's possible, based on what I've seen in the past, because there are pockets of time where we're almost perfect for months at a time, picking turns in the S&P 500, which reflects in other indexes too. If we can do it some of the time, and even a lot of the time, what is it that stands in the way of doing it all of the time?

It's a very powerful possibility, that's why we built a company on it, not just a CTA fund. It's not just a trading system, it's a whole field of research with wider impact than the stock market, but that is an entirely different conversation. Of course, for me, cycle research fits well with my love of trading. That's what's really driving the bus for me because it's keeping the corporation afloat and making it money as we endeavor to increase our understanding and accuracy.

Q: Is your AI machine learning focused on swing trading?

John: For now we use the results purely on swing trading. I believe there's potential to improve day trading using this technology, but there's only so much you can work on at once. Ask me again in a year from now!

Q: What do you like about having both a day trading and swing trading system?

John: As a trader, it is about generating cash flow. Swing trading is not cash flow.

I don't know any swing traders who can rely on it for consistent cash flow. While big wins can happen, so can significant losses, making it challenging to manage daily life around swing trading. Over a longer period – like a year or six months – you'll generally make more money with swing trading than day trading.

That has certainly been the case for me and now I'm getting more confident in my day trading, so my size is going up – not out of greed, but because I've become accustomed to it. The larger the trade size, the more potential profit, but also the greater the potential losses, which adds to the stress.

Q: Day trading for cash flow is important if you have regular obligations. Can you elaborate on that?

John: Exactly, because swing trading might involve sitting through weeks or even months of losses and drawdown before the gains come. During that time, how do you cover your rent?

When it comes to my day trading strategy I have not, and will not, share that. That belongs to ComhlaTech and its shareholders and employees. I have something that works for me, and I'll find other ways to help people beyond that. I've made my other strategies available for clients through my CTA because I know they work. Making money for others and seeing it genuinely improve their lives is incredibly rewarding.

This conversation reminds me of a time in 2015. We were at my wife's family cottage on Lake Erie, a beautiful place her grandfather built. We vacationed there often. We had taken a break from trading stocks in our signal service because something happened to the market in 2015; it was all about to go haywire according to our indicators at the time, so it signaled no trading for a while. This lasted for a couple of months. Meanwhile, I was still trading for myself and doing other things. Then, I closed a massive win to the tune of six figures, which was a really big deal for me at the time, but I had no one to share it with. It felt flat. Making money for yourself is great, but making money for others feels amazing. Maybe it's an ego thing, but it just feels really good; it's hard to explain and probably doesn't even sound true unless you have experienced it.

Q: What can you tell us about the trading competition that you participated in?

John: I've only participated in the World Championship Futures, Robbins World Cup, the longest-running and, in my opinion, the most prestigious futures trading competition in the world. It's the one that Larry Williams won and is a full-year live trading event. When I first heard about the competition, I thought, "One day I want to be good enough to compete in that."

In 2022, everything aligned, and I decided to enter. I was in first place for most of the second half of the year. However, when the CPI report came out in November, I ended up on the wrong side of it and finished in third place for the year.

Q: What type of trading strategies did you use? The same ones that you trade today?

John: I essentially traded the contest the same way I trade every day, though I might be a bit more aggressive with sizing because it is a competition. The starting amount was relatively small, about $10,000.

Q: In this competition you're given the choice to publish your trades? Does sharing the trades affect your trading behavior?

John: Yes, you can publish your trades and allow others to follow you automatically, similar to how a commodity trade advisor works. People pay a fee to mirror my trades. I'm Commodity Futures Trading Commission and National Futures Association registered, and my CTA offers two programs: a more conservative program for those seeking about 1–2% a month, and another for investors willing to take on more risk looking for higher returns. These can be followed, but the competition is a competition.

In a competition, you need to push it to make it, aiming for 300–400% returns to win. That is very difficult to do consistently with a nice straight curve, which is what you want but competition trading is much more aggressive. I can deal with my own emotions. If I make a bad trade that drops 20, 30% in the account, that is going to feel absolutely terrible if I have people following me. I don't want others to experience that. I can handle the stress of competition trading, but I don't want anyone else to have to deal with it.

Q: It sounds like you're managing no less than three different portfolios at one time – two CTA programs and the trading competition account. How do you handle it all?

John: It's actually a few more. On the retail side, I have strategies where I contact the broker I'm working with, and he places the trades, handling all the allocations. There are hundreds of accounts following me and millions of dollars are being traded in these accounts, but he takes care of the allocations for everyone following the programs. This simplifies my life significantly. There are two strategies there and they only trade a few times a month, with a general hold of a few days to a week. The amount of trading isn't aggressive – maybe 30 trades a year for each program.

The CTA program is more hands-on for me. While there is some day trading, it's only for specific positions. Managing other people's accounts as a CTA requires skill and a focus on making money with less volatility, which is mainly achieved through swing trading. The hardest part is managing the allocations – keeping track of everyone's accounts, figuring out the sizing, and then buying as one big unit in two different instruments (ES and NQ) before distributing the allocations to various brokers. There is some math behind that. Besides these, I also trade the competition account, the corporate account, and my personal accounts, but it's really only eight accounts in total, so it's manageable.

Q: As a systematic trader, why do you choose to execute trades manually rather than automatically?

John: Over 12 years, my programmer and I built a complex, indicator-based system. This was in 2016 or 2017. At its peak we had 10 day trading systems for NQ, 10 for ES, 10 long-only swing trading system for ES, and 10 swing trading systems for NQ – 40 systems in total, all running simultaneously.

I needed at least $100,000 to manage it because there were so many trades. It was reasonably successful, but we ended up paying the broker a lot and it ate into the profits too much. We even built an application programming interface to automate the trades directly through the brokers, which was fantastic.

The problem is that technology fails. With such a complex setup, I was always paranoid about potential issues – computers freezing, some unexpected forced Windows updates, or having to switch to Linux, which is a real pain. Watching all the machines used to keep me up at night.

When I started focusing on time-based analysis and strategies, I realized I didn't need all that complexity. Our current approach, using time-based strategies, is far superior. So, I decided to focus on that and simplified it all. Now we make more money with less effort. I also enjoy pressing the buttons myself. Being in charge gives me a reason to be here, and I don't fully trust technology for everything. I use it for data analysis and setting limit orders, but I prefer to handle market exits manually. I like trying to grab that one extra tick – it's something I just can't help.

Q: What can you share about your time-based forecasting strategy?

John: It all started in 2013 when I became interested in forecasting markets. I met someone from Florida who had been trading for about 50 years longer than me. He was in his late 70s and mentioned that his former business partner, who had recently passed away, was the last person taught by W. D. Gann before Gann died in 1955. This trader was quite eccentric and casually mentioned one day that he had a lot of Gann's original materials and he believed that markets could sometimes be predicted to the pip, to the penny.

If you look into Gann's material, he was very mathematical and believed you *could* actually predict a market to the pip, to the penny. It was based on some "woo-woo" mathematical model. I never really uncovered a lot of it because all of my predecessors in this area were very secretive, but that's what got me into it. I thought, "Wait a minute. How is that possible?" and then I fell into the rabbit hole. For many years I dove into the world of cycle analysis, exploring whether it could be done.

Then the deeper I fell in the rabbit hole the more I realized it was possible. I don't know what the turning point was, where I really started to see it but it was about 2014–2015 that I really started to see the success of it. I'd been trading cycles for a couple of years sporadically here and there, supplementing what I was doing, and by the end of 2019 I was thoroughly convinced.

In early 2020, we recognized a shift and decided to transition from trend-based trading to forecasting. Having had considerable personal success with various models, we launched a new company dedicated to this research – ComhlaTech – with a group of family, friends, and longtime business associates.

I informed my clients about this shift since I was stopping the signal service entirely. We sent out emails with predictions for different market events. Many of the forecasts were accurate, and even those that weren't perfect still yielded small profits through our techniques. This success impressed our clients, who appreciated the new approach.

We really had seen it work well, and it continued to work until sometime after the nineteenth of February. I did one more trade in Nasdaq Futures and we ended up taking a loss just as the coronavirus epidemic was starting to really kick off, shortly before lockdown. My trend-based system stopped me from finishing out those dates because something different was happening. We had a loss where I shouldn't have been wrong because the news interrupted the cycle. We were expecting an uptrend because everything lined up but the market moved down and we took a loss. We were left scratching our heads, wondering what went wrong.

When that first change happened, I realized something was off. We didn't take any more trades because our trend indicators advised against it. We also advised our clients that it was not advisable to trade.

Q: Your technique is based on past cycles repeating themselves but what happens when you have a huge event like coronavirus that has never happened before? How do you have the confidence to know that this is a completely different scenario from anything that we've ever experienced?

John: I didn't trade again until April. It was too scary; I didn't want to play the game. In hindsight, I look back at my system, and it nailed the bottom of the market. It was picking tops and bottoms all day long for hundreds of points, as the market was violently ripping up and down. But I didn't want anything to do with it because I was just too scared, and more focused on keeping the family safe than making money. I had money, it was fine, so I just watched it work.

Q: Does that mean that when there are big unknown events, you will step aside and let the market shake out before coming back in?

John: COVID was a once-in-a-lifetime event. Short of a something disastrous, like a terrorist attack worse than 9/11, I will continue trading. Even during the banking crisis, there were no signals to stop trading. It really took a global pandemic for me to step back and think, "Whoa! What was that?" Was I right to stop trading then? Perhaps. But now, with more confidence in my strategy, I might handle it differently because my system proved itself during such a significant event.

In 2022, I made more money going short than long, which almost never happens. The banking crisis didn't bother me at all because my system was working so well. It was just ping, ping, ping – 300 points over three days. The timing was impeccable, and the system worked flawlessly.

So, I don't worry about market fluctuations anymore. To be honest, I think the pandemic aside, which is fair to call a little bit different, if another crisis happens, I'm hoping to take full advantage of it. That is not to say that there are not times where we are simply wrong. As much as our goal is 100% accuracy, 100% of the time, we are not there yet!

Q: If you had to give one trading tip to a new trader, what would it be?

John: Learn how systems work, learn what makes a good system. Learning to code would be beneficial, too. If you can't, find someone to help you. Find a platform that you can code on; start building a system that can help you even if it's just on paper. Prove it to yourself by back-testing and forward testing. Trade as small as you can to learn because you'll behave differently in live trading compared to demo trading. Live trading is the best way to learn. Or find someone with a good system and just follow them.

Q: How far back do you recommend back testing?

John: It depends on your strategy. For swing trading, you should go back at least 10–20 years to cover all the bull and bear cycles and see how your strategy performs under various market conditions. However, you're often limited by the data available from vendors or your charting package. For day trading, a couple of years is usually enough because it's more active and short term.

Still, you won't really know until you code it. I've had many great ideas that looked promising visually, but once I coded them, they turned out to be garbage. Coding helps eliminate human bias.

Q: What do you think is the number-one skill it takes to be a successful trader?

John: Emotional discipline. Everyone feels emotions, but the key is not to act on them. You must stick to your plan. Emotions are the hardest part of trading. Also, being part of a trading room is helpful. Trading can be a very lonely business, and a trading room allows you to share ideas with others. While I rarely act on the information I get from there, I enjoy the camaraderie and learning from other traders.

JOHN'S TRADING TIPS

1. Focus on learning to trade very few instruments well.

Focus on mastering one or two trading instruments well, and you won't need anything else. For John it's always been about chasing certainty. When you start with 10 stocks, and then go to 5 ETFs and then end up with 2 instruments, if you can prove to yourself that you only trade that one system and it was a really successful system on one or two assets, you wouldn't need to do anything else. This approach simplifies your trading strategy and enhances your expertise. Many traders start with multiple stocks or instruments, but over time, narrowing down to one or two instruments can prove to be the most successful strategy. After 20 years in the markets, it becomes clear that success often comes from concentrating on doing just one thing exceptionally well. Mastery over one or two instruments can provide the certainty and consistency needed for long-term trading success.

2. **Don't break your trading rules.**

John finds that his biggest regrets come from trading outside his system. It's crucial for traders to follow their system consistently, as deviations often lead to significant losses and regrets. While it's challenging to adhere to the rules 100% of the time, maintaining discipline most of the time is essential. A trading system provides a structured plan for entering and exiting trades. Even if it's not always profitable, it stabilizes performance and helps manage the stress of trading losses. Without a system, handling losses can become chaotic and much harder to manage. Stick to your system to better navigate the ups and downs of trading.

3. **Use day trading for cash flow.**

If you love swing trading but need reliable income, consider using day trading to generate cash flow. Swing trading often involves big wins and significant losses, making it hard to rely on for day-to-day living. Over time, swing trading can be more profitable, but it requires patience and the ability to withstand drawdowns. Day trading, however, can provide regular income to cover living expenses. As you gain confidence in day trading, gradually increase your trade sizes based on skill, not greed. Remember, larger trades can mean bigger profits but also bigger losses. Use day trading to manage immediate financial needs while pursuing long-term gains with swing trading, but only when you are ready and have a proven system and the discipline to follow it. The difference between success or failure in the markets is how certain you are that your system works.

PART II

PROP TRADERS TURNED FUND MANAGERS

CHAPTER 6

David Floyd

David Floyd landed his first gig in the trading industry in 1993. With more than 30 years of experience in technical analysis and global fundamentals, David's passion for the markets ignited early during his college years. Trading is in his blood and has been his day-to-day focus ever since. His career began on the FX and fixed income desk of Standard Chartered Bank, and by the age of 24, he had become a prop trader on the Pacific Stock Exchange. He later founded his own private fund, which quickly grew to over $7 million.

David's approach is highly specialized; rather than aiming to be a massive total return fund, he prides himself on consistently grinding out profits in both up and down markets. He focuses on positive convexity, performing well when the market is down, which is particularly attractive to investors seeking diversification.

Specializing in trading futures, David focuses on key price levels while integrating multiple time frame confluence, order flow, and option volume. He loves the flexibility of being a full-time trader, with his trading day typically done by 8 a.m. Pacific Time (PT).

Q: When did you become interested in trading?
David: I studied economics at Northeastern, a great school in Boston. I was clear on what I wanted to do. I got an economics degree and was the president of the economics club. I knew I wanted to be in the investment industry by the time my junior year rolled around. It's been in my blood and my day-to-day since then.

My first job out of college was not actually trading related, but it was at an investment firm. At that time, I really wanted to get on a trading desk at a bank. Back then, I didn't really understand the difference between being a sales trader and actually trading firm capital. But it wasn't important because I wanted the buzz of being on the desk. A colleague of mine recommended I read *Market Wizards* by Jack D. Schwager, a book I'd never heard of. I bought it that night and was done with it the next morning. That was the catalyst. It showed me trading was exactly what I wanted to do. So I got a job at Standard Chartered Bank and was on their FX and fixed income desk. That was my first taste of how markets move and how big orders get done. I wasn't a trader in the traditional sense; I was a sales trader, but nonetheless it was a great experience. I stayed there for a year until they wanted to relocate all the West Coast operations to New York. I had moved to San Francisco as I'm originally from Boston and I wanted to keep the West Coast lifestyle.

So oddly enough I left Standard Chartered and became a prop trader on the Pacific Stock Exchange electronically. I was one of the first 20 people in the country to have an electronic terminal on my desk so that I could execute orders directly with the specialist on the New York Stock Exchange. That's real trading because you're risking your capital, and my income was completely derived by trading. The first year was a grind. I didn't lose very much money, but I didn't make any money either. I had a part-time job in the afternoon. Given that it was West Coast hours, I was done with trading every day at 1 p.m., when the markets closed. In the afternoon, I was a cold caller at Merrill Lynch in Berkeley, California. It was a miserable job, because I'm not a sales guy. Smiling and dialing was just awful. About a year later, I started getting the hang of short-term trading and here we are today, 20-odd years later, and I'm still doing short-term trading. I'm doing it in different asset classes now, but I've been in trading by and large since I got out of college.

Q: Is that all the education you got in order to make it in trading?

David: It was for the time being. Later on in my career, I decided to go back to grad school. At that point, it wasn't really to learn new things. It was really more to build my network. To get together with people who were driven, had connections, and tap into that. Of course I learned a few things, no doubt. I did my MBA.

But looking back, it's exactly what I thought it would be, which was an amazing way to build connections. That is why I chose a school with a really strong alumni network. Everything else has been learned on the job. Trading is a job where you never, ever stop learning. Jared Dillian, a trader and author, often says something like, "As a trader, you always have a position on whether you're flat or not. You're always ruminating on what could have been, what should have been." And that can be a tough way to live at times.

Q: What was your first experience with trading firm capital like?

David: I wasn't trading in my first job at the bank. I was taking orders on behalf of institutions as a sales trader. I started trading actual capital in 1995 and at that time I was trading New York Stock Exchange stocks through what they called the DOT machine. DOT stands for designated order turnaround, which was an order routing system that linked directly to the specialists on the trading floor in New York. Similar to today, I had a narrow focus. The stocks I traded back then were Citigroup and Telmax, which was the Mexican telephone company, and it was always just one or two at a time, never more than that. And that was by design. You had to get really good at understanding the stock movements, not the fundamentals of the stock, not the business model, none of that stuff mattered. You had to understand the tape and how the order flow is happening.

Even though my order was going through electronically, that order was still being handled at the other end by a person, the specialist on the New York Stock Exchange floor. He's got people out in front of him, floor brokers buying and selling shares, and then he's got these orders coming in electronically. He's still making a market. He knows that at this price, Goldman wants to sell 100,000 shares of stock, and Morgan Stanley wants to buy half a million shares of stock, or whatever it might be. So this guy, in making a market, is taking risks. It was the reason you focused on one or two stocks at a time, because you could read into what was happening if you looked at the order flow long enough. Looking at his bids and offers, their sizes, how they were changing, you'd understand what he was trying to do. Human beings do the same thing over and over again when confronted with different scenarios. If you could understand that, you could have that slight edge.

If you were just trading off of prices or, "Oh, that stock's in the news, I'm gonna go trade General Motors," you haven't even looked at it the way I have or somebody else has for weeks and months on end, which means that I have an advantage over you. Because I'm able to look into what the order flow is doing and understand what the specialist is trying to do. And that was a huge edge! The other edge we had at that time was an audio feed piped into the office from the S&P pit in Chicago, because since we were trading really big liquid stocks, everything was driven by the S&P futures. If the S&P futures were rallying, your stocks were rallying and vice versa. So we had our audio feed in from the S&P pit and that was immensely helpful because you could hear what was happening in the pit. And there was a gentleman, a floor trader, on the ring of the pit calling the action.

Think about that, a person calling the action in the S&P pit: "Morgan Stanley on the bid for 100, we got Goldman on the offer . . . ." You start listening to all this stuff and hearing the crowd noise. This gives you an edge. It lets you know when things are about to accelerate or hit the downside. That's a huge edge. And we rode that from 1995, probably up until 2002. About 2002, a lot more algorithmic trading was coming on the scene and basically the edge got ground into nothing. I would say that one of the big mistakes I made in my trading career was not trying to adjust into that new market environment.

Rather than trying to figure out how to make the adjustments, I said, "Well, you know what, I'll push out my time frame and start trading FX." Not that it didn't work out, but I can tell you that I would have been better off if I'd just tried to figure out the new game here, because the game clearly had changed. I could have surrounded myself with other traders who've succeeded during the last 7–10 years, and we could have put our heads together and figured it out. So not doing that was my mistake. I probably spent at least a year and a half trying to transition to trading FX on a swing trading basis. It worked out, but ultimately I made that turn back in 2018. So I definitely spent a fair amount of time doing FX and it worked out really well, but I knew deep down my temperament suits short-term trading much better. It's just where I wanna be.

Q: Did anyone introduce you to trading or did you go into this all by yourself?

David: That's a great question. When I was at Standard Chartered Bank, the vendor we had for the quote machines on our desk was a company called Track Data. Back then, they were the cutting edge quote provider in terms of latency and all those things that were really important. The sales rep knew that our office in San Francisco was due to close down. And he told me about a group of guys over at the Pacific Stock Exchange, who were starting to trade upstairs electronically. You put up a little bit of risk capital and get access to margin. I was 24 at the time and I had this idea in my head that you could take advantage of intraday price movements. I didn't know if it was true or not, but something told me that I could. So when the sales rep from Track Data told me, it sounded right up my alley. I went over and met with those guys, and I didn't even give it a second thought. At 24, you don't have a lot of responsibilities other than rent and even that was pretty marginal at the time.

I figured I had a severance package coming from the bank, I had unemployment, I could do part-time work. What was the worst that could happen? Maybe I'd blow through my risk capital. But again, at 24 you don't really have a lot of downside. So that's how I got into it. There were only five of us in the office, and the other four guys were all traders who had been on the floor of the Pacific Stock Exchange for years, and they were trying to transition to trading for themselves. That was really hard for them. They were used to being floor traders, reading the crowd, having a built-in edge with the bid-ask spread, and all that kinda stuff. They couldn't make the adjustment and very few did make the transition. But we all traded along and tried to figure it out. It took me about a year.

Quite honestly, I was having a hard time pressing the button to place a trade, because I was worried about being wrong. I didn't want to lose money; I'm a human being. And I do tend to be more risk averse than other people. So what would happen is that the move would start, then I'd be a buyer. By then you've given up a little bit of that edge. And sometimes that could be costly. That was the difference between making money on the trade and scratching or losing it. It was due to a lack of confidence, nothing but a mental roadblock. I wasn't believing in the process I had set in place. I didn't believe in it at my core, so I wouldn't execute it with conviction.

Maybe 10 months into my "career" as a real trader, this other guy joined the office. He just started making money trading and was doing really well. One day I was looking over his shoulder and I noticed he was doing the same type of trades that I was thinking about doing, but he was doing it with conviction, and I saw him make money. So I connected the dots there. Suddenly I was like, "Oh, it's about getting the proper game plan. Then the mindset comes." It's not the mindset, then the game plan. I don't believe it works that way. First you need to have the right game plan, or trading approach, trading style, or trading technique, whatever you wanna call it. By watching this guy, Bob, execute with conviction, it gave me permission to do the same thing. And to be honest with you, that was it. I never looked back.

I went from my account flatlining – making nothing in the first 10 months of trading – to it starting to take off. So I think you've got to get the order right. You've got to have a game plan that you feel confident will work. That doesn't mean just back-testing it. You have to live that game plan, watch it in real time, feel the pain, feel the joy of placing a trade. Once you get conviction on that, then you can start really building on that foundation.

Q: Did you ever blow up an account or lose a big chunk of it?

David: No, I never did. Sometimes people ask me, "What's your biggest trade ever? What's your biggest losing trade?" I never had those. I was a grinder. I might go into a drawdown over a period of days but I never had a trade where I was like, "Oh, my God, I just lost." When I put my money up to be a prop firm trader, I put up $25,000. My money was on the line. And that gave me access to leverage. You could buy 1,000 or 2,000 shares of a stock that's really expensive. Might only be in the trade for a minute or two. Your risk, if you were disciplined, was usually an eighth or a quarter point. It was 250 bucks for every 1,000 shares traded, not huge amounts of risk. I never had a big losing trade because I was never in a trade where the stock got halted and it opened lower or I made a big bet expecting one thing and another thing happened. I never did any of that. If anything, it was my drawdowns that were my "worst trades ever," but actually that would be a "worst phase." I just went into a period where I couldn't see straight.

And that's a really important point. Trading at any level, especially on a shorter time frame, requires so much mental focus that after a while, you just have to walk away from the screens for a day or two. When you get into one of those drawdown periods, walking away is the hardest thing to do. You're thinking, "I wanna get my money back." But what you're going to end up doing is losing more money. So yes, I never had a big losing trade or a big winning trade. And that's still how I am to this day; I grind it out. I don't have any great stories to tell on the summer barbecue circuit about how I bought Google and it gapped up 50 points after earnings. But I can tell you about how many times I ground out five points in an S&P trade after it went against me 10, or something like that. I could tell you those stories all day long. People are like, "That's really boring, David. I don't know what on earth you're talking about." But it's the reality.

Q: What is life like as a full-time trader?

David: There are a lot of ups and downs, no doubt about it. You're never going to be perfect. You're always going to be learning. The markets are always going to be changing. For me, the lifestyle is not necessarily about the income per se, although that's a good thing. It's the flexibility. I work my tail off from about five in the morning until about 8 a.m., when it's lunchtime in New York. And then I've got a natural break for the next two hours. I might casually look at the close for another opportunity or two, but the big opportunities are in the first 1.5 hours of trading. I do my prep work from about 5 to 6 a.m. The market theoretically opens at 6:30 a.m. PT, although the futures are already open. But I usually only do my trading during the pit session hours. So I have a very flexible day. If I wasn't doing this interview right now, I'd be off, maybe getting a coffee, running some errands, doing some business-related things. But not trading. If I have a position open, I'll be more involved, but I'm not looking to build new trades late in the day.

Q: Are you trading your own capital or managing investment capital at this point in your career?

David: Both, actually. I still, to this day, trade my own capital. It is definitely a source of my income. About two years ago, I decided to start a managed account program that basically mimics almost everything that I'm doing in my own personal account. So that's been a lot of fun. I wanted to get a two-year track record under me and now we're kind of at the point where I start to get more aggressive about going out and marketing it. That in itself is a challenge. I've got two other guys with me who are on the marketing and sales front. That's a full-time thing. Even with a good track record, it's really hard to raise money because I'm relatively unknown. I might get a lot of allocations from individuals, which is great, but Goldman Sachs or some hedge fund is not gonna allocate an unknown guy $10 million, even though I'd probably handle it with no issue.

I'm also very specialized. I'm not trying to be a massive total return fund, I'm trying to be a grinder, making money in up and down markets. So maybe a term that a lot of people aren't familiar with is *positive convexity*. I keep track of my P&L as a percentage of my accounts, whether it be my account or the total assets of the fund. I try to see on any given day when the market's up 1% or down 1%, how am I performing? When the markets are down 1% or more, I'm usually up on average half a percent, and that to me is really important. It's meeting a need in the marketplace where people should have it as part of their portfolio. I'm not the core of their portfolio by any stretch, but when markets go into phases when total returns are hard to come by, I'm the guy they can rely on to be non-correlated to the S&P 500.

I'm negatively correlated to the tune of about −0.3, and I have positive convexity. That becomes very important to a skilled investor. They might say, "I need 10% of my portfolio in something like that to give me actual diversification." That's how I'm aiming to trade. I'm not gonna be the guy that's up 30% in a year.

Q: How much capital are you currently managing for the fund?

David: Very small at this point and I'm not ashamed of it. It's a hard process. Right now, I'm managing just a little over $7 million. That's investor capital. We could probably scale this to 85–100 million before we would have to get really good on order flow techniques and figuring out how to execute larger blocks of orders without sacrificing fills and quality of execution, but we'll get there. That's a problem I'm more than willing to get through at that point in time.

Q: You currently trade full time. Give me an idea of your routine to manage it all.

David: It's not perfect, but it's all about lifestyle choices. At this stage of my career, every incremental gain I have makes a difference. Becoming a better reader of the tape, having better focus, keeping that mental acuity, and so on. That requires good sleep, nutrition, and for me, a rigorous workout routine. That helps clear my head at the end of the day. I can go mountain bike riding, snowshoeing, skate skiing, trail running, and so forth. Those are all things that give me the ability to get out of here and think about nothing else. Oftentimes I do think about trading, but in a good way. Things like "If only I'd done that today, it would have made my trade a little bit better. Or I should really have thought about how I phrased that line in the research report to clients this morning. I think that could have been better." I think about those types of things.

I believe that, especially as you get older, you can't really maintain your edge as a trader if you're trading and then living a crappy lifestyle. It will not translate into doing something really solid the next morning. It's impossible in my mind, at least in the long run. Because at the end of the day, the guys I know who succeed at this and continue to succeed, they are diligent about their game plan and how they show up each day. You can't do that unless you're living a good, clean life. It doesn't mean I don't have a beer and a glass of wine now and again, but during the week I have to show up fresh. Especially for me: I'm on the West Coast, my day starts early. I get up at 4:30 a.m. So you have to be very disciplined.

Q: How many hours do you typically trade in a day?

David: I trade the opening for 90 minutes, maybe 2 hours. I rarely execute a trade after 8:30 a.m. PT in the morning. I'll usually be around for the close to see what's going on. I keep track of every single trade and have it logged in my software. I know that in the closing hour I'm much less effective than I am in the first 15 minutes of the day. So why fight that? I'll show up and make a decision if something unusually good appears, but otherwise I'm just an observer, taking it in, not forcing anything. This doesn't mean I'm not doing a lot of work outside those hours. Like today, I have a trade on, but I'm not trading. I'm just managing it. That's very different.

Q: How would you describe your trading style?

David: It's very short-term scalping. I trade S&P futures, the 10-year note futures, as well as euro and yen futures. With the euro and yen futures, I might be in those trades for several hours, maybe a day or two, or maybe a little longer. But for the S&P, most of my trades are minutes, maybe an hour or two at most.

Like today, I've been in this trade since about 7:20 a.m., and here we are at 9 a.m. So that one is a little bit of an outlier. But on the open, trades are normally very quick, usually anywhere from 5 to 10 minutes, sometimes less than a minute; it just depends on what's happening.

With shorter-term trading, you're usually trading with bigger size because you're trying to take advantage of smaller moves. If you just go in with one contract and it moves, that's great, but it doesn't move the needle. Given that I use this to drive my portfolio, I need to trade at a size that makes a difference. Yes, I'm trading a lot of contracts, but I'm not sitting there with a 20-point stop loss. Not even close.

Q: What are the patterns you look for in the markets?

David: The core of it is support and resistance, sometimes mean reversion, sometimes trend focused. A great example was yesterday. We've had a big support level for several days. Late in the afternoon, I was just sitting at my screens, nothing was really happening. All of a sudden, the market just fell out of bed. In 10 minutes, it went from $5,270 all the way down to $5,247. Not only was that a big support level I was aware of, but a move that fast felt kind of weird. The market held it and started to rally back, dipped a little bit, and then rallied again. That was all I needed to know to get in. That's what I call a good support or resistance because it happens so quickly.

Q: What other techniques do you combine with support and resistance areas? Do you have any other things you look at?

David: The price levels are one thing. I look at support and resistance as an area where there's the potential for a trade to develop. So it's an inflection point. Something will happen potentially and I want to be aware of it. I may want to act on that. But a lot of other things have to come into play. Multiple time frames, when the higher time frames and the lower time frames are coming together. I might execute my trade on a 1- or a 5-minute chart, but what does the 30-minute chart look like? What's the 60-minute, what's the 4-hour chart like? Are they all kind of coming together? Because it's so important to get that confluence. Looking at the option flow is another huge factor. Is there a lot of call volume, a lot of put volume? What type of volume is coming in the underlying instrument you're trading?

If you're looking to go long and put volume outweighs the call volume by a decent margin, do you really want to be trying to go long? The answer is no. So you've got all these inputs where you're either checking the box or you're not checking the box. I also look at what related markets are doing. What are the big hot-and-heavy markets? You know, tech has been that way for a while. What are 10-year notes doing? What's the price of gold doing? Those all factor in to some degree. You gotta have a pretty wide berth in terms of understanding what the market is doing. It's not just about the support and resistance level. That's kind of step one. Now, let's look at option flows, the time frames coming together, and what related markets are doing. One of the things you learn as a scalper is to read the order flow. You start to get a feel for the market. I know that's not a very absolute concept, but if you look at the tape, you can get a sense. I can tell when the market doesn't seem to want to take a move.

That's part of the reason why I'm long in the S&Ps here. I had a level at $5,296, we got down and just kept doing this for the last 90 minutes. The market didn't want to go below that. Now this doesn't mean that it ultimately couldn't have broken down lower, but while I'm in that trade, I'm checking if the market is respecting the support level. I'm gonna be an observer and follow along. I'm not trying to make any forecasts. I'm trying to get in sync with what the market is already doing. I'm not saying, "Oh, I'm gonna go short here because I think this level won't hold." Well, maybe it holds or doesn't, but I need to see some evidence. Will I always get the best price? No, I'll never sell the absolute top tick or buy the bottom tick, but I'll get in at a price where I've got a little bit of reassurance that I've made the right decision. Doesn't mean I'm right, but I'm not just jumping in blindly.

Q: Do you pay attention to the news when you trade this sort of strategy?

David: I pay attention so that I don't get into trades right before the news. If I have a trade that's been on for a while and it's working, I'll suffer through the news. Unless it's really bad news, it's usually going to fit with the current trend. The market typically discounts this stuff all in advance. Tomorrow, for instance, is the nonfarm payrolls job report. I will not be looking to see if the payrolls are great or they're bad. It doesn't matter, I will not be placing a trade based on that, absolutely not. Five or ten minutes later I might, but for me to go, "That's bullish or that's bearish," it's really stupid. I don't know how the market is going to interpret it. The headline may look great, but could have people concerned about inflation and higher interest rates, therefore the S&P would move lower.

So even though we created a ton of jobs and I went long thinking that's great, I would end up losing money. That to me is avoidable. It's too much of a binary outcome. I might make a point, but I might lose a point. I'm not interested in that. I want to make a point and lose a quarter. So I always trade after news events, I give the market time to digest how it feels, and then go back into the same process. Are we holding support? Are we holding resistance? What are the flows looking like, and so on.

Q: How do you manage risk? And what are your favorite ways of managing a trade?

David: For swing trades, I always use fixed targets, and I aggressively move them higher as the price moves in my favor. On the shorter term scalps, like in the S&P, it's all based on what the market is doing. The market either respects what I thought would happen or it doesn't. Now, you have to give it a little bit of breathing room. You just can't say, "I got in at $5,290 and if we go below $5,287, I'm out." Because the market will very often just whip below $5,287 like it did this morning and come right back up 10 points. So if you had fixed stops in there, you would have been stopped out and you would have missed this good run.

You have to take it in the context, and that requires a bit of judgment and quite honestly, it requires experience. There's a young kid in town here who's doing an internship with me. He's 20 years old and absolutely loves trading. That's the same question he often asks me. "Where's your stop at?"

I'm like, "Well, it's gonna be in here somewhere."

"What do you mean by in here somewhere?" he goes.

I'd say, "Yeah, it's right around $5,285."

He'd ask, "So $5,284?"

I respond, "I'm just gonna see what the market's doing when we get to that level and I'll make a decision."

And I laugh, but I understand where he's coming from. It's not necessarily knowable in advance. You have to evaluate it in real time and that's really hard for people to do. But when you get to that point, you have an edge. I have a way of seeing the market that very few people have, because I've put in the hours. If you don't put in the hours, I don't know how you can expect to do this job, or any other job for that matter, very well. It's not about getting some setups and saying, "Hey, if you buy this *x* percent retracement off a resistance into support, that's the trade setup."

Sometimes it might be, but I'm not interested in "sometimes." Whereas anybody who's just looking at that setup will execute that trade every single time, which is not appropriate. There's times to execute your trades and there's times where you pass. This morning was a great example. It seemed like the right thing to hold onto that trade. Whereas the casual observer wouldn't have held as that support level was being tested and broken through and then coming back and then breaking again. People would get frustrated. I'm looking at that going and I like it. That's a good sign. I look over 20 minutes later, and it is 10 points higher. But it's that level of experience and intuition you develop over years that can really help you on a day-to-day basis.

Q: How do you know when it's time to close the trade and take profits?

David: That's the one area that I'm a little bit more deliberate on, only because over the years I've noticed that the market goes to levels and usually it gets stuck there. Just like the market got stuck at $5,296 today. That's a good level to be a buyer. Or if you were short, a good level to cover. I had an upside target of $5,309 to $5,314. Well, we got up to $5,308 and we pulled off a little bit. That's why I paused and said, "I'm gonna take a little bit off here." I already knew what my target level was. Let's say I looked over and we just kept pushing through $5,309. We go to $5,310, $5,311. Yes, it's hitting my target, but I'm not going to take profits off because the market's just bulldozing right through those levels.

The reason I took half the trade off is because we went up for nearly $100 over 35 minutes of being bullish. We get into $5,309 and we immediately reverse. The market's respecting the level that I thought would be an upside target, I'm closing half. I'm not going to close the whole trade because the market is clearly strong right here. Now, maybe it comes all the way back and it stops me out of breakeven or wherever I adjust my stop loss. But the opposite would have been true if we carved right through $5,309, went to $5,310, then to $5,311. I'd just be sitting there and let the market tell me when it's done. Yes, my level's there, but the market's going to go where the market wants to go, not based on what my level is. The market doesn't care about my level. Sometimes it does, but not all the time.

Q: What's a typical reward-to-risk you like to aim for?

David: It's one of the things people really need to think constructively about. I would love to tell you, "Hey, it's 3 : 1, man, I make three times what I risk." That's not true. It's also not true for most professional traders. I'm lucky if I get 1 : 1, 1.2 : 1 over a period of time. That's still a winning combination, especially when you combine that with a high win rate. There's other traders out there with much better reward-to-risk. But they're also the type of traders who probably take a lot of small losses and then have the ability to really stick with that winner and just milk it for all it's worth. That's not me; I'm not that guy.

If you told me I had to go out and manage a portfolio tomorrow and hold on for months and years, I'd tell you, "Nope, you got the wrong guy for the job." So you really need to align your temperament and your risk tolerance for the style of trading you're doing. Risk management for me is real simple. Peter Brandt says this a lot, even though he does more swing and position trading. He has the same philosophy as me. When I get into a trade, I'm expecting the trade to start working nearly immediately. If it doesn't, that means I'm wrong. It's okay to be wrong, but it does mean that I'm wrong and I'm already starting to think about closing this, stepping back, reevaluating, and maybe getting back into the trade at a later time. The market clearly said no. I don't try to rationalize a bad decision.

You have to give it a little wiggle room, but I'm usually out pretty quick. The one thing my peers over the years have never accused me of is lack of patience. I've got the patience of a saint in terms of waiting to execute a trade. I've also got the ability to say I'm wrong and move on. Every once in a while, I'll be a stubborn meathead and let a trade go against me but by and large you have to get out and just move on to the next trade as painful as it is.

Q: What's a book you'd recommend every aspiring trader to read?

David: That would be *Best Loser Wins* by Tom Hougaard.

Q: Do you use any specific software or tools for journaling, for charts, or anything that might help people perform better?

David: There are a lot of tools out there that are marketed toward inexperienced retail traders, who often have very unrealistic expectations, and those are tools that you will never find on my desktop or any desktop at the professional level of trading, such as banks, prop desks, hedge funds, and so on. I have nothing against the trading platforms that brokerage firms give you, but I'm not gonna trade on those. The execution is gonna be wretched compared to what I'd get on an institutional-level platform. You can get institutional-level platforms even as a retail trader.

If you're getting something off the web for free or super-cheap, it's like a carpenter showing up with a set of plastic tools they used as a kid versus the guy who shows up with the toolbox full of high-grade craftsman tools. Who's going to do a better job at remodeling your house? Pretty straightforward. So for me, I use professional-grade tools. I use MotiveWave for my charting software. And I also have a professional data feed so that there's no latency, there's quality of the data. These things all cost money. So if you're the casual guy who's managing his 401k and wants to make a trade here and there, basic platforms will work just fine for you. But if you want to make a career out of trading, you need to have a robust platform and a high-quality data feed.

Q: What made you decide to start a fund and manage other people's capital?

David: A lot of it came from demand from my existing clients. I've had a morning note that goes out to my clients for years. And a lot of them have been at this game a long time. They know my style, and they're not as passionate about what I do. So they said, "Hey, why can't you just execute the trades that you're doing for me? When you tell us about it in the notes, it still relies on me to actually take the trade. That's kind of annoying given my schedule. Is there a way that you could just execute the trade?" And I said, "Yeah, of course there is." That started the wheels turning.

And quite honestly, I want to manage a fund because I think I've got a skill set to bring that is very valuable. Again, I'm not in there to be the stars' fund of the month because they had a great total return. You know, anybody can get a great total return. I want to be one of those guys that you look at and say, "That guy knew how to grind it out and provide a very specific piece to my portfolio that really helped it perform better." That's what my job is and I'm determined to do that. I've done it over the last two years. If you had taken a 10% or even a 20% allocation of my fund, a couple of amazing things would happen.

Your total returns are better, your volatility is lower, your draw-downs are lower, and your internal metrics are better. Your Sortino ratio is better, your Sharpe ratio is better. Why wouldn't you want that?

Now, do you want my fund as your only investment? Definitely not. That's not what it's designed for. But when you insert that into a traditional portfolio mix, boom! I want to be known as the guy who really knows his craft and does it extremely well. I'm very niche oriented. I know it doesn't appeal to the masses, but I'm not trying to do that. I want to appeal to the people who know what they're looking for. It's like wanting to put my stamp on the marketplace so people know what I do. A little bit of ego, yes, but there's nothing wrong with that.

Q: What makes raising a large amount of capital for a fund so difficult?

David: The big banks and institutions look at it like this: Does the trader, in this case, me, have the infrastructure in place to take on a $10 million allocation? And they might say, "Okay, yes, it looks like he does. He's got all the clearing arrangements, the technology, everything's in place." But the bigger thing they're looking at really boils down to something simple, which is being known with a proven track record. If they decide to allocate $10 million to me, versus let's say $10 million to Warren Buffett – of course that's two different strategies – then what is the upside for them? If it's a great year, it will be easier to justify their decision.

But let's say I didn't have a very good year. I didn't do badly, but I didn't have a very good year. And at the end of the year, the powers that be in the organization are looking at the portfolio and saying, "Why did we allocate to Aspen Trading again? They were down a couple percent last year and S&P was up 7%. The track record doesn't look so good." Whereas if they allocated to Berkshire Hathaway and they lost 2%, they'd say "Ah, but it's Berkshire Hathaway." That's the difference; they are covering themselves. I've talked to enough people in the industry who have really good track records, even better than the big institutions, but in the end it's about name recognition. It's a career risk for somebody allocating to a lesser-known fund and having it not work out so well. And that is why it's difficult to get a big allocation.

Q: Do you manage your risk differently when trading for the private fund compared to your own trading?

David: Oddly enough, when I'm managing my own capital, I'm more risk averse than when I'm managing the client's capital. That doesn't mean I'm reckless by any means. My brain is wired in a way whereas most people would be just the opposite. I tend to be a little bit less emotional when I've got the investor capital on the line. I'll usually give it a little bit more room to run. I don't want that to be taken in a bad way, because it's not like the metrics between my personal account and the managed account are radically different; I'm still very prudent. But there are times when I won't be comfortable in a trade, but I'll give it a little bit more room in the managed account. Sometimes it works, sometimes it doesn't.

Q: What do you think are the top skills people need to succeed in trading over the long run?

David: Having very realistic expectations. That's not really a trait, but you've got to start there. Patience. It really does boil down to that. But managing the expectations is really where you start from. You have to start with the expectation that it's going to be really hard and will always be really hard. You'll get some winners, but it's a grind. You need to really love it. I was reading a great article the other day about the difference between discipline and motivation. Discipline is like "I have to go to the gym, I have to eat well, and so on." But if you're not motivated to do that, the discipline will fall off and you're not going to follow through.

I can't think of any other profession I'd rather do. And I've had a couple of my buddies – since we're all in our mid-50s now – ask me, "Hey, what are you thinking about looking ahead to retirement?" And I'm like, "Retirement? I love what I do." You have to really love this because it's going to kick you in the ass every single day or at least once or twice a week. You have to love it, you have to live it, you have to breathe it. It needs to be ingrained in you, but if you're just doing it because you wanna make some extra money, it won't work. Now you might have to try it at first to develop that passion and that motivation, but most people know they're drawn to trading like it happens with any other profession. There are people who are drawn to be writers, surgeons, or whatever it is.

Q: Does managing a fund bring on a new workload?

David: I'm at the stage of my career now where I realize that I have to continue to do what I do. I don't know much about marketing a private fund. Yes, I can contribute, but I'm delegating that stuff to other people. That's how any smart business should run. I stay in my lane. I realize that in order for my fund to work, I have to bring in other people who are really smart and can leverage what I'm doing. We're coming together as a unit to try to create something really good. I still work a lot. But when one o'clock rolls around, I have the afternoon off. I can take a nap and go work out. I can run errands, do boring household chores. It's a nice change of pace.

I'm not getting home from work exhausted and then looking at a mountain of tasks in front of me. I'm really fortunate to have a degree of freedom that most people just do not have. It comes with a price, though, which is that you're always on. Your income is highly variable and that can be really unsettling. Trust me, I've had years where I've made very little money, and that's not good. But I've chosen that path.

Q: Is there anything you'd tell new aspiring traders who want to get to where you are today?

David: Trading is non-stop learning. Ten years ago, I could never have contemplated starting a fund and having it be serious. I might have done it, but I think it probably would have flamed out. I'm at that point in my life right now where this is what I want to do for the next 5–10 years. So take your time to reach your goals, but don't stop learning.

Q: What do you think is the difference from 10 years ago versus today? Have you become a better trader? Do you have more time or a better idea of what you want to do?

David: One kid is off to college, the other one is at the tail end of middle school. So our household is less chaotic. I also gained a lot of maturity and clarity in the last five years. Even in your 40s, you're still certainly wiser than you were in your 30s. There's something about your 50s when things just start to kind of come together. I have gotten really clear on what I want to do and what type of person I want to be. I've done a lot of spiritual and personal work, quite honestly. And when you combine those things and start becoming really deliberate about what you want and don't want in your life, suddenly things open up for you and you can see where you really want to go. Of course we all have our mundane problems to deal with. But you start to get a little bit sorted out and I am really determined to do this. The two guys I work with are in the same boat.

I wasn't even thinking about a fund 2 years or even 10 years ago. I was thinking about how do I continue to trade? How do I continue to attract customers? How do I maintain a household with two kids, a wife, and two dogs? A very different mindset than where I'm at right now. It's also different financially. A lot of my financial goals have been met. So everything's a little different. My advice is: don't feel pressured to reach your goals now. It's all about timing and giving yourself the time to get there.

DAVID'S TRADING TIPS

1. **Grind it out.**

Having big winning trades sounds exciting, but it will also mean longer drawdowns. By grinding it out like David, you're gaining more consistency in your equity curve.

2. **Find your specialty.**

David trades only a handful of instruments and sticks to a very specific style of trading. It allows him to master his craft and stand out from other traders while trading according to his natural personality.

3. **Listen to the market.**

As David said, there's no point in closing a trade if the market is "bulldozing right through those levels." Let the winners run and take profits when the market pauses.

4. **Treat trading as a real career.**

If you want to be a full-time trader, view it as a profession. Use professional tools, organize your finances better, and build a strong routine. Those who succeed are not treating it like a hobby.

5. **Give yourself time.**

Whether you're at the beginning of a prop trading journey or already profitable, give yourself enough time to reach the next level and have realistic expectations.

CHAPTER 7

Sunny Harris

Sunny J. Harris has over 40 years of trading experience. With a background in mathematics, she built one of the leading computer graphics software and retired at 30 to start her trading career.

Sunny ran a hedge fund for several years and was rated the number-one trader with under $10 million by Stark Research for two consecutive years, achieving impressive profits of 365 and 178%. She has been a full-time trader since the 1980s, employing dynamic moving averages (DMAs) in combination with the average true range. Sunny has consistently observed that the market tends to rise by 1.2 average true ranges before pulling back, and then again by 2 average true ranges before another pullback.

As the author of over seven popular trading books, Sunny is a respected mentor to both individual and institutional clients. Her trading style is based on pattern recognition, using custom tools she developed with her expertise in mathematics and programming. In this chapter, she shares her decades of trading wisdom, offering valuable insights and strategies honed over her extensive career.

Q: Sunny, where did you grow up and what was your life like before trading?

Sunny: I grew up in Appalachia, in the mountains of North Carolina and Tennessee. I believed the only way out of there was to get an education, so I went for it. I finished high school at 17 and earned my first college degree at 20. After that, I started working, but continued going to school.

87

Q: When did you finish school?

Sunny: I'm taking a Java class now, so I would say I never really finished. The most fun thing in life is learning.

Q: Did you come across trading in school?

Sunny: No, I came across trading later. I finished my bachelor's degree in math and started a master's degree. One of my professors, whom I got along with really well, said that he was interested in Fibonacci numbers and asked if I'd do my master's thesis on Fibonacci numbers under him. I was just barely 20 years old at the time and told him, "I have no interest in Fibonacci numbers."

And he said, "Well, you should, you can use them in the stock market."

I responded, "I have no interest now nor will I ever have any interest in the stock market."

That's how much you know when you're 20. So I did my master's thesis on something entirely different, but it's something I use to this day in my SunnyBands equations.

Q: What was that master's thesis about?

Sunny: It was about the least squares method, specifically least squares curve fitting with a digital computer. At the time, curve fitting with a computer was a big task because computers were new. It's nothing now; you can just run it in Excel. But back then it had problems. In fact, all least squares formulas have problems at the turning points. Whenever you have a change from up to down or vice versa, they have trouble figuring out the equations for the trough in a way so that they will also fit the trend. That's where my DMA comes in. I created a way that's still used to this day to do better least squares fitting.

Q: What did you do next?

Sunny: When I finished my BA, I got a job at Lockheed, working in an engineering group with a top secret clearance. We were doing prototypes for the space shuttle. I don't think Lockheed got the contract for that, but it was fun working on it. I liked the programming part of what I was doing much more than the engineering part, which is why I asked to be transferred over to the systems programming group, where all they do is program. I spent the next several years doing systems programming using Fortran and assembly language.

And then I left Lockheed to join a company of three guys founded in San Diego. I took a 25% pay cut to start this little company that didn't even have offices. The four of us ended up working out of my home and by that time I had my son, who was one year old. We just worked all the time and created the world's leader in computer graphics software. I was the vice-president of operations and in charge of leading the place. It was a lot of fun, but I also worked all the time so I decided to retire in 1980, when I was 30 years old. We'd gone from the 4 of us to 105 employees.

Q: What was it like to retire at 30 and what did you do?

Sunny: I traveled all over the world. I took three or four trips a year, usually three-week trips to different places. I still love to travel and do photography.

Q: Did you find it boring to travel and not have a job?

Sunny: It took me nine months to get bored. That's just my personality; I have to do something big. I always say, if you're not living on the edge, you're taking up too much room. I just like to stay on the edge and lead the edge if I can, which I've done a few times.

Q: What brought you to trading in the end?

Sunny: After retiring, I gave my money to money managers, who said they were going to increase my investment by several million. All I had to do was invest in this thing called commodities and let the commodities trading advisor (CTA) do the trading for me, which I agreed to. Unfortunately, within three weeks they had lost $75,000 and I said "That's it . . . I'm not gonna risk more than that. These returns all look negative." So I took my money back and learned to trade it myself. I figured I could do that poorly on my own, so I decided to go for it.

Q: Do you know why they lost that money so quickly?

Sunny: They were trading pork bellies futures. It was an up market and they were shorting. Now I know that. Back then, I had no idea what long or short meant or what pork bellies were. That's how I got into futures trading.

Q: How was the learning curve when you started trading?

Sunny: In 1981, I was trading stocks and mutual funds, corporate bonds and municipal bonds, investment diamonds and real estate. So I was managing a large portfolio. I began specializing in the S&P 500 when the Chicago Mercantile Exchange started trading futures based on it. That was in 1982 and back then it was the "big boy." It was a $50,000 margin, not $5,000. You had to call the floor on a real telephone, since we didn't have cell phones. They'd pick up and you had to say your name and what you wanted real fast. They'd hand signal the order into the floor.

Somebody there would hand signal back. Then they'd tell me what they got. All this took three to five seconds.

When I first started, I would say something like: "This is Sunny Harris, account number such and such, BUY 20 S&P front month at the market."

Soon they said to me, "You don't need to say any of that. Just say 'Sunny BUY 20' and I'll know exactly what you mean."

I said, "How do you know that?"

They said, "You're the only woman who calls the floor."

I used to go to Chicago three or four times a year and talk to my guys on the floor. I had my own two brokers, who I always went through. I called them directly instead of calling the general number. So that was a cool time.

Q: Did you get profitable quickly?

Sunny: I didn't lose money at first, which was probably a bad experience. When I was trading mutual funds and stocks, I had a stock broker call me every day with recommendations. He was good. At one point in 1987, he and I had a little disagreement, but he'd been my broker since the 70s. He's called them all right, except this one. I told him, "I'm gonna go to Europe, I wanna sell everything I hold in stocks and mutuals."

And he says, "Oh, no, this is the biggest bull run in history. We haven't seen anything yet, you just wait."

I said, "No, my charts are telling me that we're at a peak and we're gonna go down. I think we're gonna have a crash."

We had lunch, I showed him what I saw and he's like, "Nah, charts don't mean anything."

I said, "Well, it's my money and I'd like to sell everything."

He responded, "Okay, if you think so."

I sold everything and went to Europe. I watched the market crash on television in London. I watched the Dow Jones 30 go down 105 points on Friday. And then I told my travel buddies that it's going down 500 points on Monday. And it went down 506 points. And with that, I was hooked. Trading with charts is my thing now; 1987 was the cement to it all and I've been with the S&P 500 index ever since.

Q: What type of strategy were you trading back then?

Sunny: I see patterns and formations. Not only on the charts, but everywhere. In fact, after I retired, I got an associate's degree in film and photography. If you're able to see patterns, you can take a good photograph without cropping and that's what I did. So I see patterns on the charts, but it took a long time to get to the point that the charts had moving averages on them. They were just charts. And they weren't even candlesticks back then. In fact, they weren't even reporting the open; it was just high, low, and close. I would see patterns on the charts and decide to buy or sell.

Q: So you sold everything, went to Europe and what happened next?

Sunny: So the Dow was down 105 points on Friday and 506 on Monday. I called my stock broker on Tuesday morning and said, "Buy everything you can get your hands on." The market made a pullback, but for me, that was a million dollars. No loss, buy again lower and watch it go back up again. That was my biggest trade ever.

Q: What was your worst trade?

Sunny: My worst trade was when I lost $13,000 in two minutes. Which was a lot more money back then. We were in a war with Iraq at the time. Scud missiles were flying everywhere and every time there was a report that they hit Jerusalem, the market went down. I watched all this happen and I was long. Then James Baker came on the television and said that the market dropped precipitously. I called my floor broker like crazy, "Get out of the trade, get out of the trade."

He said, "Not held, not held."

I said, "What does that mean?"

"I don't have time for this," he said and hung up on me.

So I had to ask my trading friends what "not held" meant. I found out it meant he's not held to a specific price, because the market is moving so fast. I can't give him a limit price he needs to hit. So I called him back and got out. By that point it was minus $13,000. I've learned to hold on to losses a little longer. I could have just waited. If I had weathered the paper loss for a little while, it came right back up. But you have to be willing to read the charts, so you'll know where these things are going.

Q: You mentioned that you started making money from the start and that was not necessarily a good thing. Did you eventually lose money or have big losses?

Sunny: No, I've got a lot of mathematics to throw at what I see in the market. I really have never lost big, but I do have two losing years in my record. In 2001, I lost when the Nasdaq [National Association of Securities Dealers Automated Quotations] crashed in the dot-com bubble. I had a lot of investments in Nasdaq at that point. In fact, I was trading my hedge fund. So I lost 11% that year, when the market lost 76%. That's one losing year. And I don't remember what the other one was, but I know I've had two losing years. I don't keep very good track of my statistics.

Q: How did you recover from those losing years? Because I'm guessing that takes a big hit on confidence.

Sunny: It's hard to do. When you have a loss like that and the whole year adds up negatively, it's pretty disheartening. So usually when that happens, I'll go somewhere, take a trip, take a break, come back fresh. I feel more confident just from having a good time somewhere. And I take more photographs.

Q: You've been trading for 43 years as of January 1, 2024. In those 43 years, did you mostly trade your own account? Have you ever thought of setting up a fund?

Sunny: I did have a hedge fund for a couple of years. And I realized I don't like managing other people's money. They call you every day and ask a lot of questions about the performance of the account, how much money was made, what was traded and so on. If you have many of those people, it can get to be a very busy day. I just don't need it. I've got plenty of money to trade on my own and I would rather just do that.

Q: Would you say that fund did pretty well?

Sunny: Yes, I was the number-one CTA at that point. They called me up because they wanted me to keep my statistics and send them in every month and show my trades. I didn't know what they were doing with any of that information, I was just required to do it. Then they called me up at the end of the year and said, "Congratulations!"

I said, "For what?"

They said, "You're number one."

I responded, "Number-one what?"

They said, "You're the number-one CTA. Haven't you seen the rankings yet?"

I said, "Where would I see the rankings? I didn't even know I was being ranked."

So that was kind of fun.

Q: Tell me about your current trading style.

Sunny: I'm a technical analyst, so I see chart patterns and things that I know from the 746 books I've read. It's partially intuitive because my brain is feeding off of information that I've absorbed over the last 43 years. I trade three to five times a day with the little swings that go on intraday. I use my custom SunnyBands indicator for everything I do. I trade e-mini S&P 500 futures on a five-minute chart, bonds on a 45-minute chart, and stocks on a daily chart.

Q: So you have a good mix of time frames here. How do you manage all of this? Do you have a routine of what to look at and when?

Sunny: I've got computer screens all around me and I know what's on each one of them. I do different projects on different computers. I run TradeStation on a solo computer. I don't run anything else on it. I'm always doing visual checks back and forth, on five monitors.

Q: How did you go from calling on the phone to place trades to now trading on a five-minute chart? It's a big gap.

Sunny: It is a big difference and it went slowly. I learned daily charts and weekly charts first. And then from there, I progressed to the 15-minute charts on the S&P 500. I did those for many years until they added the overnight session. And once we got Globex and then started trading 23 hours a day, things had to change. That 15-minute chart didn't work as well anymore. So I went down to the five-minute chart and I've been there for many years.

Q: Do you plan to trade the one-minute chart eventually?

Sunny: I always have a one-minute chart on one of my monitors and I watch it, but I find that it is too fast and too shallow to actually get any good profits out of. By that I mean that it jerks back and forth, but with each jerk it's only moving a point or two. So the little pivot points are a point or two apart, you can't catch that. So I don't trade it.

Q: How did you come up with that SunnyBands indicator you are now using for all your trading?

Sunny: The DMA came from my master's thesis. It was about how to fit curves to something that has inflection points. So I had the mathematics already available. When I began trading, I was using moving averages and I found out that this is a really quick way to give money back in whipsaw. I didn't like that too much. Then I started using the MACD [moving average convergence/ divergence]. It was better, but not what I needed yet. So I added an ADX [average directional index] filter to it, so that it would take the MACD trades only when there was a very short-term trend. I think I was using ADX of five periods. I did that on 15-minute charts with the MACD and the ADX. I got that idea from something Jake Bernstein published back in the day.

Of course now I test every concept I come up with or read about in TradeStation, but at that time it was primitive compared to what we have now. But I was still able to test concepts and I've done that ever since. I have eight banker's boxes full of research that I did to get to the DMA. And then the SunnyBands are just an extension of the DMA. The upper inner band is 1.2 average true ranges from the DMA. And the outer band is 2.0 average true ranges from the DMA. These outer bands give me an idea where the market could go next. Since the DMA is recalculating its lengths internally with every tick of the market, it's self-adjusting and very dynamic. So it knows when to get out of the way of the market and when to follow it closely. This way, it avoids most whipsaw. I use the SunnyBands indicators to trade extremes all the way back inside the bands.

Q: What's the logic behind the 1.2 and the 2.0 average true ranges?

Sunny: I found over and over again that the market will go up 1.2 average true ranges and then pull back. And then it'll go up 2 average true ranges and pull back. Initially, I just eyeballed that. And then of course I had to code it and optimize it to see if there were any better settings and there weren't. That was right where the sweet spot was. That's what I mean about seeing patterns.

Q: You use that tool to trade both the trend and reversals. How do you play both scenarios?

Sunny: The DMA tells me the direction I should trade in. When the market's trending, the two DMAs will stay close together. And they'll go up. And when the market's making a saddle (i.e. going neutral), that's a period of sideways action. The DMA moves out of the way so that we have to get a true turn before they'll cross over. It's kind of a weird concept, but that's how they work. It gets out of the way of the whipsaw. The key is having an indicator that's recalculating based on what the market is doing.

Q: Are you looking at any kind of zones for your trading or is it only based on SunnyBands?

Sunny: I do look at the open of the day, the low of the day, and the high of the day, or of the session. I only trade the day session. I know exactly where the SunnyBands signals are. They call out to me after 37 years of trading with them.

Q: Your trading is very mathematical and systematic, but I'm guessing you've added your intuition and discretion over the years, too?

Sunny: Of course, how could I not? After this many years of watching the same thing over and over every day, you feel the rhythms. I'm by no means R. N. Eliot, but he saw the waves in the ocean and got attuned to the waves in the market, and I can feel the waves in the market now. When you shoot baskets enough times, you're gonna get good at it or give up.

Q: Are you using any kind of robots or automated trading or is it all manual?

Sunny: It's all manual. I worked for two years on trying to get an automated strategy made out of SunnyBands. It was good, but it wasn't as good as I am, so I don't need it. It wasn't as good because of the intuitive part. I see things that I can't program.

Q: So in a typical trading day, for how many hours do you tend to be at the charts?

Sunny: I don't like to trade the open. I'm at the charts from 7 a.m. California time to the close. I usually close out of my trades by 1 p.m. I don't like to go into the extended session. So I trade from 7 to 9 a.m., and then do a live trading room where other people can watch me trade. That's over at 10 a.m. and I have to take a little break. Then I come back and trade until the close. And at the same time, I write books, code, work on my website, and so on. I stay very busy.

Q: You mentioned that you take about three to five trades a day. How long do you hold them for? Is it a few minutes, a few hours?

Sunny: It depends on the trend. If the trend is like it was this morning, that short lasted for about 45 minutes. And then it reversed and went long and it lasted the rest of the day. So I didn't know beforehand how long it was gonna last. I just follow along.

Q: Do the SunnyBands give you a target for the trade or is it just giving you the entry?

Sunny: It gives you the entry, but let's say we went long at the bottom SunnyBand and now we're going up and it hits the top band but it doesn't turn red, it stays green. No reason to get out of it until it turns red. So usually it'll turn red above the SunnyBand and then come back inside and that's when I go short.

Q: Tell me about your money management. How do you manage your trades? Do you scale in, scale out, or have any kind of stop loss?

Sunny: I have a spreadsheet called *Ultimate F* and it's a derivative of Ralph Vince's work *optimal-f*. Ralph and I became friends after I found some errors in the mathematics of his book. We talked about it and I gave him what I had done to fix it and he allowed me to call mine *Ultimate F* after his *optimal-f*. I changed it so that your equity curve doesn't have the deep retracement that it does with his *optimal-f*.

His system makes a lot more money than mine does, but it's way more dangerous. So I've been building a spreadsheet to find out how many contracts I should put on a trade based on my *Ultimate F* compounding. I don't ever let it go above 20 contracts, but that's the way I maximize my profits with a simple spreadsheet. I don't scale in or scale out. I just put that many contracts on, and then I take them all off.

The formula is based on the profit-and-loss stream you have to put your trades in. So you enter the profit or loss from your past trade and it will give you the next number of contracts to trade. When you have a series of losses, it lowers the contract numbers until you start winning again, and then it starts going back up.

Q: What's your typical win rate and risk-to-reward ratio?

Sunny: I've got a 78% win rate and 2 : 1 on the reward to risk. So it's pretty good.

Q: Where do you keep everything you've learned over the years?

Sunny: I put everything I want to remember or be able to look up quickly on my website, http://MoneyMentor.com. So if I want to know when the Fed meetings are, I can find it under "Resources." And if I want to know what the symbols for the next contract are, it's under "Resources." And earnings reports and the Chicago Mercantile Exchange calendar, I link everything in there. So this is my own personal resource.

It started with me having a little black book and keeping everybody's names and phone numbers and addresses and it branched out from there. It became my magazine, "Traders

Catalog and Resource Guide," which I published for eight years. And then it went into MoneyMentor, which I opened up in 1995.

Q: If you had to give any advice for newer traders who want to be at the level where you are now in trading, what would you tell them?

Sunny: Read, read, read. And trade in sim mode until you've got a string of profitable trades. Don't trade with real money. You can and will lose it. Everybody loses, even I lose. I had a losing week last week, I lost $40. I was really disappointed. So we all experience losses, and it's better to experience those losses while you're still in simulation mode.

Q: Don't you feel like real money makes you take it more seriously than sim trading?

Sunny: You should see me in my live trading room. I get just as worked up about a simulated trade as I do about a real one. I think for most people, as soon as you go into trading real money, you will have losses, because you're going to be scared. I had one client tell me he was gonna go out of sim and into real money. I asked him not to do that. He then lost $1,200 and called me up, almost crying. He was just brokenhearted. I told him to not trade any more real money. Go back into sim mode and let's see where you get from there.

Another week later, he called me up, saying "I've lost $4,500 now."

I said, "Are you in sim mode?"

"No."

So I highly recommend simulation mode for a long time so you get really good. There will always be another trade. There will always be another crash. There will always be another run up. So I think the best skill a trader could have is patience.

Q: How do you know when you're ready to trade real capital?

Sunny: If you have a month of positive trades that would be enough to support you and your family, then you can go live. But if your positive streak for that month was $50, you can't live on that. So keep going till you get really good at it.

Q: You seem to integrate trading really well into your life, and I think that's also by choice. How do you see trading and life working together?

Sunny: I wouldn't do anything differently, I love what I do. When the market closes on Friday afternoon, I have a little letdown because I can't trade anymore. I'm married to a physician, so I have a lot of time to trade. They're busy people. We've been together for 33 years and we're used to each other. So the doc does the doc's work and I do the trader's work and never the twain shall meet.

Q: Do you feel like there are any personality traits that helped you as a woman succeed in trading?

Sunny: I think women are more patient than men. Men want to get right in there and fight the fight. And women are like, "Let me learn a bunch of stuff first. Let me sit and look at this and do some analysis and then see if I want to do it." In my experience, men jump in with both feet for the most part. Obviously most of my clients are men. It used to be almost all men and now I have about 10% women. It's not a lot, but it's a lot more than it used to be.

Q: Why do you think women are less likely to get into trading?

Sunny: Women are more risk averse, I think. I'm not, I'm atypical. I like the risk. That's the part I enjoy. But I do think women are a little more risk averse, and they want to wait and see things work. I would say that a lot of women would wait for the trade and let it develop, whereas the men will jump at it. That's the problem I see with the male clients I have.

Q: You said that you have read 746 books so far. Do you have any recommendations of books that traders should read?

Sunny: An absolute must-read is John Murphy's *Technical Analysis of the Financial Markets*. It's been around a long time and it's been updated several times. When I first decided to learn about trading, I was just newly retired – this was in 1980 or 1981 – and I went into the bookstore and found this book. It was $50 and I thought, "Oh, my goodness, I hope this thing's worth it." So I read it and highlighted it cover to cover. And I went out and bought another copy so I could highlight less and just focus on the really critical things and read it again. And then I had lunch with John Murphy one day when I was at a Technical Analysis Group seminar and I bought another copy, so he could autograph it for me. So now I have three copies.

Q: What do you get out of books as a full-time trader?

Sunny: I always hope that I will find something, but I'm often disappointed. I read them anyway. I have a little page on my website called Book Club, where I talk about the books I'm reading and I love to have comments and corrections. As I told you, I keep a lot of stuff on that website.

Q: What do you think are the most important skills for a trader?

Sunny: Patience, fortitude, and persistence. You've got to stay after it for a long time before you get good at it. So you've got to have patience; you've got to have persistence and the fortitude to keep going through the losses.

SUNNY'S TRADING TIPS

1. **Look at patterns in the market.**

As you gain trading experience, you start to notice patterns in the market. Sunny's passion for photography helped see patterns in the market. It's what made her sell her stocks before the crash in 1987.

2. **Have a mix of instruments and time frames.**

Sunny developed a style of trading that works across a wide variety of time frames and instruments. As a result, she can diversify her trading by trading markets that are not correlated. She also mixes day trading with swing trading.

3. **Focus.**

A good trader wouldn't perform as well trading too many styles. Focus is important both while trading as well as for the big picture. Sunny decided to focus on her SunnyBands technique, and that's what made her successful.

4. **Stay busy.**

While retiring and traveling the world might sound inspiring, Sunny quickly found out she had to have a bigger purpose. That's when she got back into trading. Through trading, Sunny stays curious and keeps learning. It gives her a chance to use her skills and see good results.

5. **There will always be another trade.**

The market will always be there. Missing a trade isn't a big deal. Traders like Sunny who are doing it full-time aren't pressured to enter a trade they aren't certain about. They have the willingness to wait for a better trade setup to come.

CHAPTER 8

Ali Crooks

Alistair (Ali) Crooks, a full-time trader based in the UK, is known for his extensive experience in trading forex, commodities, and index futures. As a prominent trading coach and the founder of Traders Support Club and Trader Coaching Academy, Ali has made significant contributions to the trading community. In addition to his coaching endeavors, he has successfully managed a regulated fund, applying his trading strategies and expertise to achieve consistent returns. His approach to fund management is characterized by rigorous market analysis, back-testing, and live trading, ensuring high standards of performance and risk management. Ali's private fund management showcases his deep understanding of market dynamics and adaptability to various trading environments. He frequently shares his insights and techniques for managing a fund through various chapters and talks.

Ali's trading career began at the age of 25, and now at 47, he boasts nearly 22 years of trading experience. He spent 13 years day trading, during which he was profitable for 11 out of those 13 years. For nearly two of those years, trading was his only source of income.

Ali grew up in Amersham, a town about 45 minutes from central London. Although Amersham is a wealthy area, Ali's family was very middle class. His father, who worked hard for everything in life, instilled a strong work ethic in Ali from a young age. Motivated by a desire to make money, Ali took on jobs like delivering papers and cleaning cars as soon as he could start working. He attended university in Newcastle, in the north of England, where he developed analytical skills and a knack for statistics, which later proved invaluable in his trading career. Although Ali found university too theoretical and lacking in practical application, these skills became beneficial to his future success in trading.

Q: How did you get into trading?

Ali: Before trading, I was a bit of a serial entrepreneur. I originally thought that I was going to go into sport management. The idea was that I was going to work for a big corporate marketing agency. While I was at university, I ended up being placed with Nike. I got to the end of my degree realizing this isn't for me. This is not what I want to do. So I left university and started my own business, which went very well. We were renting out cars and four-wheel drive vehicles to film sets and big companies. I did that for about two years and then sold that part of the business. I then went head-first into health and fitness with a training product my friend came up with and our intent was to revolutionize the industry. We brought the product to market, but that didn't go very well. So I ended up having one successful business and then one unsuccessful business with a lot of debt. But throughout it all, I'd always had an interest in investing and making money.

And at the time, I was part of what was called the Investment Club Network. We used to meet once a month and discuss different stocks that we were going to invest in. I did it because I wanted to have money working for me, but I hadn't really ever thought of pursuing trading itself. I found it very frustrating, because we would sit there for two hours and eventually pick one stock. Then that stock would go sideways for who knows how long. There was a guy there called Tim from Australia. He worked part-time at Microsoft as a programmer and spent the rest of his time trading. I just got really excited by it. My business had failed because my business partner didn't want to continue investing money into it and I couldn't do it on my own.

This is when my interest for trading started, because I felt like this was something I could do that was completely under my own steam. I wouldn't have any staff. I wouldn't have all the challenges that go with a normal business. I wouldn't have such big overheads, and at the time I thought it would be easier to control with less external factors to deal with. Trading would be purely down to me. The idea of having that freedom and being a trader who didn't have to worry about all the business things really appealed to me. Obviously at that time, I was being very naive, looking only at the upsides. Tim was really my first coach and mentor who helped me. But at that time, there wasn't an abundance of training in the UK and we didn't really have resources like YouTube. So I flew out to Las Vegas for a three-day training where I learned about options. I came back and within about six weeks, I'd blown the £5 K I had left.

Not a huge amount of money, but at the time it was all the money I had. I felt sort of lost for about a year because I liked the idea of trading, but I was primarily trading based on greed. I thought about it and eventually told myself, "No, this is too risky, I shouldn't be doing this." But after about a year and a half, I got drawn back into it by a friend whom I knew through another trader. He was a lot more focused on technical swing trading, rather than trading call and put options on the short term. That was a real eye-opener because the challenge when you're trading options is, yes, you can get the direction incorrect and still make money if you are trading the right option with the right variables, but primarily you've still got to get the market direction, timing, and so many other things right.

Essentially he was trading a contract for differences (CFD), which really appealed to me because it was much more about technicals. For the next two to three years, I was on and off, until I decided to get really committed. What I did was interesting. I got myself a fairly boring job working in a factory packing boxes, just doing anything I could. I was on a shift, Monday to Friday from six in the morning all the way through to 1 p.m. UK time. And then I would come home about 2 p.m. and trade the US session. Despite learning more about swing trading there was still that greed-based part of me that wanted to day trade. Looking back I think it had a lot to do with my age and a newfound desire to make trading work.

Q: You went from having different businesses to working in a factory. How did that feel?

Ali: Especially at the age of 20–23, my ego didn't like it. What was driving me was this idea of having an income that wasn't beholden to anyone else. At the start, I wasn't passionate about trading, but I was very goal-oriented. I see this with a lot of the traders I talk with now. They're in it because they want to get away from something that they're doing. They don't like their job, or circumstances, or simply want an additional income.

I set myself a very simple goal when I started out: I wanted to earn enough in one month to pay my rent for that month. Now I realize looking back, it was actually a stupid goal because I was trying to fit my trading results into a very short window, in the hope that I would hit this arbitrary goal, which didn't really mean anything. As a result, I would still over-leverage. I was still a greed-based trader. I hated the fact that I was working in a factory, because I knew I could achieve more.

Q: When did you become profitable? And how did you make it happen?

Ali: I started to fall in love and became fascinated with charts, the challenge, strategies, and my own performance. That's when it really changed. I stopped trying to trade to make money and got curious about why I had been stuck at breakeven. Slowly, I was able to understand what I was doing wrong. And with the help of another trader mentoring me at the time, I started tracking my trades and journaling in great detail.

I would log down about 15 data points for each trade, as well as track my emotions at specific points through each trade. Everything was being tracked! Soon enough I realized that if I had two or more losing trades in the morning US session, my average number of trades that day went up to nearly five. Obviously, on some days, those trades were legitimate because there were more trade opportunities during that afternoon session. But what I noticed is most of the time I was revenge trading. Those losing morning trades were the trigger for me to take poor setups. Instead, I was trying to make back the losses I had that day. These were not huge rule-breaking trades, just subtle changes or observations I was choosing to ignore, just so I could be in more trades than I shouldn't have been. I don't think I would ever have noticed that if I hadn't had somebody there to coach me and I hadn't been tracking my trades.

Q: What kind of strategies were you trading as a beginning trader?

Ali: I was day trading. I would come home and trade the US morning session, which was my afternoon in the UK. In short, the strategy was trading trend pullbacks on five-minute entries. I would look for a lot of trend confluence across multiple time frames. Then once I got consistent, I started fading my chosen markets at the end of the day if they met my reversal criteria. I really enjoyed the intensity of day trading when I started out. I did that for about 13 years. I was very quick to lose a lot of the indicators. I know they can work for some traders, but for me it was very much price and moving averages.

If we're looking back to 2006, when I was really getting into the flow of it, I would be at the charts pretty much every weekday. If I was going into London to meet a broker or friends, I would almost have a sense of anxiety about leaving the screens, because back then, you would have probably two, maybe even three days a week where the euro or the pound would trend extensively, often all day. It would move very smoothly. I was only focused on a few markets: euro, pound, possibly yen, and the US indices. Once I got to trade full-time, I became more focused on a few more currencies in the morning using a specific filtering process so I didn't end up trading too much. Then I would look at the US indices in the afternoon.

Q: What kind of money management did you have in place?

Ali: The one thing I've been pretty solid on since the beginning is risk management. I only ever blew that first account trading options. I learned very quickly that the only way I'm gonna stay in the game, even if I'm not making money, is through risk management. So I would be looking at losing no more than 0.5–1% of my account per trade when I was day trading. In the beginning, I would scale in and out of trades, but I quickly realized looking at the data that I would have been better off getting in with two partial entries and then running the entire trade rather than fiddling around with my exits. This can work for some people but not for me.

In my early days of trading, I felt as if I had to have something to do. So I would exit a third of my trade at one point, and then a third of my trade further on, and another third somewhere after that . . . and actually, I would usually have been better off holding the trade until the latest exit. So that was something that I learned quite early but it takes time to emotionally be able to hold positions longer. These days I'll scale into some of my positions, but I'll hold the entire position until it reaches a predesignated target.

Q: How did you feel blowing up that first account and how did you recover from it?

Ali: It made me realize at the time how risky trading can be if you don't know how to manage your trades properly. In fact, I walked away from trading for nearly a year. So it meant I didn't really deal with it straight away. My perception and as such my belief about trading at the time, despite my ignorance, was "this is too risky, I'm not doing this," and I went off looking at other ventures. The truth is, I had to go do something else because I had no money. Then eventually I started learning about risk management and came back to trading. If you are a trader reading this and you have been aggressively blowing up a trading account, make sure you take the time to analyze why. Or find someone who can help you find the reason(s) why. In my case, I was trading options and was way over-leveraged. Even though I knew which contract to buy, I didn't know how to deal with the amount of losers at the level of risk I was taking. It didn't take much of a move for me to lose too much on each trade. A lot of traders want to get straight back in because they want to recover their losses; I also did this at times but once there was no money left I had no choice but to stop and reevaluate properly.

Q: What made you go back to trading a year later?

Ali: Seeing somebody else competent and successful at trading is what brought me back to it. I met a trader named Kevin. I can remember when I first saw him trade and I was thinking, "He's just got that laser-like focus and confidence. He's diligent, patient, and not chasing trades." That got me motivated to start again. I got to visually see somebody doing it the right way, and he had the results I wanted trading a style I liked. He wasn't driving around in a Ferrari, but was living life on his terms. He had a nice car. He had everything I was looking for. So I was able to tap into that.

Q: And this is the guy who coached you to become a profitable trader?

Ali: Yes. Tim helped me understand the basics of options and I had to then take a course in the US. Kevin helped me quite a bit. He was working with a small group of traders and that was really useful. It's important to have someone who can hold you accountable because it's easy to learn something and apply it incorrectly. If you do it all yourself, it is very hard to self-evaluate and know exactly when you are doing something well or not, and as a result of that what needs working on and when. What happens when you have a losing run? Are you able to stick to the strategy? Or what if you go through a really good run . . . do you unknowingly get too cocky, take poor setups, or start to over-leverage? In the end, I didn't trade exactly the same way Kevin did, but I took a lot of the core elements of his analysis process. But more important, I applied his focus, discipline, patience, and how he dealt with losing periods.

Q: How long did it take for you to get profitable from trading?

Ali: From the very start when I was trading options, it took me about four years to show a good six months of consistency. But there was an entire year there where I wasn't trading.

Q: Tell me a bit more about what you've achieved so far in terms of funding and lifestyle.

Ali: I started trading at 25, and I'm 47 now. So I've been trading for the best part of 22 years. I day traded for 13 years and was profitable for 11 out of those 13 years. For nearly two of those years, trading was the only income I had. Then back in June 2020, I set up my own fund with a company that's regulated by the Financial Conduct Authority. I'm one of only a few traders who were chosen to do it. Now, I think there's only three of us who are still trading profitably. It's interesting how a lot of the guys who became money managers at the same time as me blew up their accounts or are no longer doing it. Those of us left have over seven figures of assets under management. It wasn't something I thought I would ever do, and I had the opportunity to do it six years ago, but it's only in the last four years that I realized, "Yes, that's what I want to do next." Trading other people's money and taking on a new challenge helped me see my own trading and my students' trading journey in a different light as well. It helped me become a better coach.

Q: You've evolved from day trading. What is your trading style these days?

Ali: Yes. It's a similar process, but I don't go anywhere near the five-minute chart. I'm primarily a position and swing trader. I do have intraday swing entries. So I will use four- and one-hour charts to scale into some of the positions. I still trade with the trend, but I also trade reversals, which make up far less of my overall number of trades. I keep it fairly simple. Support and resistance with moving averages are the main elements I use to determine the market condition. I don't trade the common moving average cross-patterns. Instead, I'm using moving averages for confluence and momentum. I spend some of my analysis time looking at the retail sentiment, but that's more to manage my trades and hold them to longer targets. I'm primarily looking at a basket of about 25 markets, including US and European indices, major currencies, a few minor ones, and a couple of commodities. I don't trade anything exotic or with low volume.

    In terms of strategy, I have a process called the *market condition formula*. I start by filtering only the markets that are in the relevant conditions. Out of those 25, I might only have two or three markets where I'm potentially looking for trend setups. And then I might have another two or three where I'm looking for reversal-based setups. I also have very strict criteria in terms of entries. I think that comes from being quite loose with my entries when I first started trading. If the market I'm looking at is in a good condition, but doesn't meet my specific entry criteria, I won't trade it. Often I'm right about the market condition, and price does head off in that direction, but doesn't give me the entry I want and that's all right. I'm very focused on a specific entry criteria because that allows me to continually collect data and measure my performance. I want to know over the weeks, months, and years that what I'm trading has an edge. You can't have that kind of consistency unless you always trade a clear setup.

Even though I trade 25 markets, I'm never in more than five trades and very rarely in more than three positions. It comes down to good risk management. The only thing that is different is that I don't trade my trend and reversal trades with the same risk profile. I will run my trend-based setups for longer and use sentiment for my exit. I won't use sentiment when I'm trading a reversal. So there are these subtleties that the data I track help me understand and implement over time.

Q: Do you pay any attention to news or fundamentals?

Ali: For me, news is more about seeing where potential sentiment is. I'm looking at how retail traders react to news and I very often do the opposite. I don't use the news as a method of entry, but sometimes to scale into a position further after a specific news announcement. What I've noticed over the last couple of years is that the market has become very news centric, obviously because of what we've seen with inflation and interest rates, and often there's a lot of quiet periods prior to those announcements. Very often I am back in front of my screens, not to trade that news announcement, but to see what effect that has on the market. Frequently, that will then allow me to take the trade that I'm looking for because I'm seeing the move. For example, the market's been quiet for the whole morning and then a period of time after the news comes out, I get the breakout and the move I want. Now I either wait for the specific entry criteria to take the trade or scale further into a trade I am already in.

Q: When you say you're a swing trader, how long do you typically hold your trades for?

Ali: The average is about two to three weeks, but I sometimes have setups that are entered and closed in a day if there's a fixed smaller target. I've got one strategy where I trail my stop loss and another where I hold to further predetermined higher time frame levels or moving averages. That will often mean being in those trades for longer. I've had some of these positions run for two to three months if not more.

Q: Are you using any automations like robots?

Ali: I prefer manually trading through my analysis. I like the feel of it. I think it's because I've been in the game for a while. I was around before you could automate anything. So I think there's an element of old habits die hard. That being said, I have robots for one of the entries, because I've been able to optimize it down to the 60-minute and 4-hour time frames. I don't want to be staring at my screens all day, so I only really use robots to get into trades so I don't have to sit there. The analysis, conditions, and filtering that I use for those setups are done manually. The robot just does the entry for me.

My belief is that if you're going to automate stuff, you need to have the data to back it up and faith in that system. A lot of people I speak to want to use a robot because they think they don't have to get involved. But you can still turn a robot on or off and react to the trade results. You still have to deal with the ups and downs of it. So trading a robot isn't a way out, but it can be a really useful tool if there are setups and strategies you want to trade, but don't want to be glued to your screen.

Q: How many hours do you spend on trading on a daily basis?

Ali: I spend about an hour in front of my screens on average, per day. It's not a huge amount of time and I would say that only a fraction of that is physically trading.

Q: What does a typical day look like for you?

Ali: I'll get up around 5:30 a.m. or 6 a.m. I tend to wake up feeling like my brain switches on very quickly and I'm thinking about things I want to do. Then I can quickly go into schedule or to-do mode. So before that, I try to have 10–20 minutes of either breath work or meditation, just to get my mind focused. I have this thing where I write down all the things I'm thinking about, including thoughts that I've had about trades or things that are coming up later that day. I call it my think box. Then I will go straight to my screens and go through my process of looking at potential trades. I won't just randomly go and look at different markets or look at news announcements. I will only look at the possible trades that I've got on my focused watchlist. That will take me about 30 minutes. After that I see what the day ahead has in store regarding news and if any could be relevant to my live or potential trades. I make any notes I may need and then move onto other things.

Usually in the morning, I do some form of exercise. We'll walk the dogs. I'll reply to any of my clients or host a trade analysis session with my students. Then I'm back to my screens about 1:30 p.m. to see what happens around some of the big CPI [consumer price index] or inflation numbers. I'm never staring at my screen waiting for trades, but I'm using those times to adjust stops or place orders after the news announcements. I designate certain times during the week, usually midweek and weekend, where I go back through my entire watchlist just to see if there are other markets that have moved and are now meeting my market condition formula and would go into my focused watchlist. I'll spend a little bit more time on the major currency pairs and the indices because I like to get an idea of where they are in comparison to retail and news sentiment.

On Sundays, I will read a couple of articles from sources I follow because I like to get an idea of what people think the market is going to do. It doesn't necessarily mean I'm going to trade in the same way. Very often, I'll end up trading the opposite. I will update all of my spreadsheets and my data, so I'll make sure that's all up to date and review my journal. Then I'm ready for the coming week.

Q: What would you consider to be your best trade so far?

Ali: My best trade was in April 2023. It was the most amount of cash I ever made on any one trade. So I was in a position that I had built over two months, which ended up being a 13.5 : 1 reward to risk. I'm not necessarily looking for those trades all the time, but the other reason it was the best trade is because it took a while to reach target and I added further to the trade in May. So it ran from April through to the end of May and it was quite challenging. I needed a lot of faith in the system because as I built the position, price wasn't going the way I wanted. I was getting my triggers and then price would go the other way. Then I was getting another trigger. So it really challenged me mentally and it was all about waiting and waiting and waiting. I also had a very quiet February and March that year. It would have been easy to get out sooner to cover up those slow months. In total I made £71,000. So I was really pleased with that one.

Q: What about your worst trade?

Ali: I can remember plenty of times when I might've had a good Monday and then a bad Tuesday, and then the rest of the week I would be revenge trading and getting what I call the red mist come over your eyes when you go into a bit of a blur. I never was the sort of trader that would go, "Right, I'm going to risk 5% to try and make my last three trades back." But I would let little things go, and by the end of the week I'd be really frustrated with myself. I think the one trade that was my biggest individual loss was being long on one of the Swiss franc pairs, when the Swiss National Bank decided to unpeg themselves from the euro. The euro and the Swiss franc used to be pegged, so the currency exchange could only move between certain levels. Then it happened completely out of the blue.

I remember sitting in front of my screen. I thought something had gone wrong with my charts because it fell so quickly. The chart couldn't keep up. I was actually running a live session with my day trading students at the time. Quite a few of us were in that position. So the market's falling away and I went straight to my broker and noticed I'd been taken out of the trade at my stop loss. I remember saying to the guys in the room, "There's no way that we are going to get our stop. The market just moved too quickly. We're going to get requoted by the end of the day." In the end, I got a requote from my broker, and for that trade I had a 1% risk on, I ended up losing 5.5%. That was a really good lesson for my students. I said, "Imagine if you had over-leveraged at 5, 6, or 7% on that one trade, where you'd be right now."

We were fortunate in that scenario to be requoted at a 5.5% loss, when there were other brokers giving 10 or 12 ratios. So if the client risked 1%, they were losing 12%. So imagine if they had been risking a higher amount. Obviously, that's a black swan event that's not gonna happen very often, but it wiped out a lot of traders and I think two brokers here in the UK. So I always use that as a lesson as to why risking less than 1% per trade is important. Something could happen and you want to be in a position that if you do get slipped, you'd still be okay.

Q: That's a crazy one for sure. Tell me about how you manage your capital currently. What's your trade management process?

Ali: Yes, so everything I do is with a fixed stop. Just because I have 20 years of experience doesn't mean I have a crystal ball and know what the market's going to do. On two of the three strategies I trade, I will scale into a position. It happens more when I'm trading counter-trend. If I'm trading with the trend, I go pretty much all in on that position. As I said earlier, I don't scale out of positions anymore. I'll have either a predetermined target or I will be running a trailing stop on a higher time frame. One of my strategies is always a fixed 2 : 1 target, because that's the best data we have on it. Another one uses a trailing stop. The third one uses a higher time frame discretionary exit. So it's usually a higher time frame moving average or support/resistance and my average reward to risk is about 3.8R on that particular strategy.

Q: How does the scaling in work? Do you have specific levels or conditions to scale in or do you go with how you feel?

Ali: The first entry is near a support or resistance level. I will never get in exactly at that level. If I'm trading counter-trend, I will wait for the price to move off the level to some degree. My initial entry is when I get a certain set of criteria set up on the one-hour chart. And then if price moves in my direction, the next entry is on the four-hour chart. So it's slightly later. Essentially I'm scaling in when price proves itself relative to those time frames. I'm splitting the position in half rather than getting all in at the first point. I have some traders I work with who are slightly more aggressive. They will take a partial entry right at a level. But for me, I like the price to show its hand a little bit before I get in. It doesn't guarantee a win, obviously, but that's how I like to do it.

I think it's very important that you try to maximize profitability, but you have to weigh up profitability against what you're able to trade. You have to enjoy the way you trade and make it personal to you. Inevitably you're going to hit losing periods, drawdown periods, and if you own it, and know that it's profitable over the long term, you're far more likely to stick to it through those bad periods.

Q: Do you have any favorite tools or resources for trading that you'd like to share?

Ali: That's a good question. Because I teach people, one of the things that I see a lot of is an information overload or an overuse of too many things. And I think as a result of being successful with a few tools, I've sustained that. So if we're talking technically, it's price action and moving averages. In terms of indicators, I will look at sentiment. I will gauge the sentiment fundamentally from reading different sources, primarily online. I have three or four sources that I'll look at. I'll use a sentiment-based indicator that you can get on MetaTrader4. I would say that sentiment is probably my favorite indicator because it isn't a simplistic two lines crossing. I will also use divergence on my counter-trend, my reversal positions.

Resources wise, maybe it's because I'm a bit more old school compared to some of the traders who are coming through now, but I try to keep the amount of information sources to a minimum. I like Forex Factory, because I look at the calendar and see what the key news items are that day. I don't study the impact. I don't go anywhere near any of the forums, because all I'm looking to do is see what that news announcement is. And I have the experience of trading around that. So for me, I keep it fairly minimal because I have done better when the amount of information sources I have are high quality, but kept to a minimum and used in the right way. I think some traders can get to a point where they have too many things going on and it's now difficult to make a decision.

Q: When did you decide to start trading a private fund?

Ali: It was one of these things that aren't part of a plan. I got approached by this regulated company in the UK that wanted to expand the number of retail traders they had on board. They were offering to trade a fully regulated fund. Initially, I said no about six years ago, and then just over three years ago I said yes to it. I did it for the challenge. It's a different thing to trade a fund rather than trading your own money. I'm so used to going through inevitable drawdowns that they don't affect me, but going through a drawdown, knowing that it's other people's money, challenged me a little more than I thought. So I've learned a lot from it.

Q: Did you have to make any adjustments on your trading when trading for the fund?

Ali: Yes. The main one was risk. Ultimately, it's all about risk, whether for prop firms or a private fund. I don't want my clients to have 20% drawdowns. The simple solution is to trade in a very similar way, but with a lowered risk and I only trade two of the three strategies I trade for myself. That means the clients aren't going to get the same level of returns, but they're not going to have to deal with the same drawdowns I deal with. That not only allows them to sleep at night but it also allows me to sleep at night.

Q: What can traders do to make getting funded easier?

Ali: The first thing I would say is take your time. So imagine I was coming to you for money, you didn't know me, and I'd only been trading consistently for two months. Would you give me your money? How would you feel about handing over £200 K of your cash just because I had made 10% in my first-ever two months of trading? I suggest traders to become consistent and have owner-ship of their own strategy first. Out of all the people I've worked with over the last three years, the ones who have been consistently successful with getting funded and staying funded did it trading with their own strategy and money first. The ones who have struggled are the ones who have gone straight from learning to trade to then trading a funded account. The key measurement variable is trade adherence. Some traders will trade for two months, show they're profitable, and will attempt to fund that account.

But what if they're profitable by over-leveraging and doing a million and one things wrong, and they're just showing a random profit at the end of the two months? You need to show you have a high level of trade adherence, that is, you're sticking to your rules. Because if you don't have high trade adherence with your own money, it's highly unlikely that when you put more capital in the mix coupled with predefined drawdown and target, your adherence will get better. If anything, it might go down because you have all these additional pressures. For a lot of traders, that's not what they want to hear. But I think you need to find your worst-performing period for the last one or two years and make sure your funded account risk profile works for that period. Or at least have tested and traded that strategy for a while. Don't focus on the profit that you could make from a funded account; focus on being able to manage the drawdowns.

And go for one that doesn't tie you in to making a certain amount of profit in a certain period of time. So they all have their specific parameters, but if you need to make 10% in one month, that completely changes the way that you look at the market. But if you have six months or an unlimited amount of time to make that 10%, as long as you stay within the drawdowns, it's much easier to manage your risk and emotions.

Q: Do you feel like there's a trading style or risk profile that's better for a fund trader compared to other styles?

Ali: One of my key principles is risking an amount that makes you feel uncomfortable. And I don't mean risking more. This is counterin-tuitive, as what I mean is risking a smaller amount where you almost look at it and go, "How am I going to actually hit the profit target because I'm risking so little?" The great thing is that you're doing what everybody else isn't doing. Most of the people who go into a prop firm challenge are focused on hitting the profit target and getting to the next level. It's better to keep your risk lower once you start trading for a prop firm or a fund, because if you hit a tough run at first, you're in the red right away. Keep the risk low until you've built up a good return, and then you can increase slowly. Yes, you can wipe out and start again but psychologically it's a big fail and a lot of traders have a hard time getting back on track. Plus, the irony is, when I speak to traders who tell me they don't want to, or struggle to, find the money to trade for themselves first, they are often the ones who have spent thousands on multiple failed funded account challenges.

Q: What do you think are the most important skills a trader must have to trade a fund successfully?

Ali: I think resilience is number one. You can have a trader who's technically gifted and can read the markets extremely well. But if that trader has no resilience, as soon as they have three losing trades, they will start questioning what they do and changing risk parameters. That trader is going to struggle. I would also add the ability to expand your time horizon. It's natural for humans to do something well and expect a result now. Currently in society, if we want something, we can order it, we get it very quickly. So we tend to want the result of our hard efforts quickly. In the short term, the market will test you, tease you, and punish you. But in the long term, the market will reward the trader who has, not just the right skills but also the right attributes.

And then, lastly, another one is self-awareness. It's the ability to reflect on what you have done or haven't done and change it for the better. So for me, it wasn't until I was able to accept the fact that I was actually trading overly aggressively that I was able to then make changes. There are a lot of traders who will brush their misdemeanors and their bad trades under the carpet. So I would say resilience, long-term thinking, and self-awareness are key. Obviously, you need to have a decent level of technical skill to be able to execute the trades.

Q: Is there any specific indicator you recommend to traders?

Ali: Five years ago, my immediate reaction would have been "You have to focus on price, because it's the leading indicator." And I still agree with that. But I think it's important to have your own tested system. If somebody comes to me and says they use whatever the indicator is, I don't judge that trader based on the fact they use that tool. But what I want to be able to see from that trader is that they have the data and confidence to apply that system. It isn't really about one tool or indicator, but it's about your own tested system kept simple. Certain things work better for certain scenarios, so I wouldn't say there was one overriding tool. You just need to own it and understand it.

Q: How has trading changed your lifestyle?

Ali: In so many ways. If we're talking materialistic, I'm earning and have way more money than I ever thought that I would have. When I was at university, I thought I could do quite well, but I didn't think I would have the amount of money, the choice, and the freedom that I now have. Trading has given me a lot of time to do other things. It's allowed me to travel and teach. Funnily enough, when I was at school, one of the things I wanted to be was a physical education teacher. But the thing that I battled against was the amount of money a teacher earned, because I loved the idea of teaching, but there wasn't much money in it. Now I get to be the teacher, but in a different environment. And I would say it's given me friendships as well. My best friend is a trader. Traders like talking to other traders.

It's not something most people's wives or friends from school understand, so having a closer friend who understands it is great. And it's given me plenty of challenges along the way. Today I feel challenged and stimulated by the markets as I did 10 or 15 years ago. And I would say it humbled me as well.

Q: I know some traders have a bit of trouble with their partner who doesn't understand trading or isn't really keen on it. How do you manage trading with your wife and your relationship?

Ali: I'm fortunate that Sarah sees how much I enjoy trading. She sees me on the good days and on the bad days when things haven't gone my way, but she knows that it's part of who I am. What's nice is that she doesn't ever ask about results because she understands that she's going to have a short-term focus and the short-term results don't matter to me. So she lets me get on with it, which is nice. I've had a previous partner who would ask me how I'd done every day and it made me feel a certain pressure, even though financially there weren't any issues. I ended up being in a position where I didn't want to actually say anything. My wife Sarah is great because she knows it's important to me, but she doesn't get involved in it. I think you should have no expectation your partner is going to get on board with you being a trader, because the stats show that 80% of people who trade the markets lose money.

So chances are that your partner is going to feel some stress about you doing it. They will usually think it's some sort of gambling and the overriding stats of how most traders behave back that up. So what I always say to people is don't argue. If your partner says it's gambling and it's risky, say, "Look, I'm learning to do this properly. You have to give me a long-term outlook. I'm not doing this to try and make money in one month." But also as the trader, don't expect your partner will understand. Make sure you don't let hours and hours in front of your screens jeopardize the time with your partner. I fell into this trap before when I would say, "I'm only gonna be there half an hour" and 90 minutes later, I'm still sitting at my screens. That's going to negatively affect your relationship. So make sure you give them quality time, so they don't feel resentful toward you and your trading.

Q: Why did you decide to stop day trading?

Ali: Into my early 40s, I could feel myself wanting to do more swing trading. I started swing trading while I was still trading intraday. And obviously the size of my own accounts had grown such that I didn't need to be trading at high frequency to get the same returns. Now, I can be in trades for longer. I'm looking for those two or three positions that could end up being 10 : 1 or 12 : 1 winners. I find that more of a challenge than being in front of my screens every single day. It's where I've wanted to go personally. It wasn't that I didn't enjoy day trading, but 13 years is a long time to be in front of your screens from Monday morning through to Thursday afternoon each week.

Q: What lesson do you want people to take away from this?

Ali: I talk to a lot of the traders about recency bias, because people can understand when you say to them you can remember what was in the news last week but not six months ago. People understand that they have a short-term focus, but I think they underestimate how much that is affecting their decisions as a trader. I know that if I'd learned this earlier, I would have progressed more quickly. You need the ability to execute and do everything right short term, and have acute focus on that one trade at that specific time because you have to take every trade setup that meets your criteria, but you have to let go of wanting a reward right away. In most other areas of life, if you're successful short term, you will get a reward. One of the things that has separated me from a lot of the traders out there is not intelligence, but my resilience and perspective. I know and accept my process and strategies are going to have bad or quiet periods over the short and sometimes medium term. But it doesn't change the way we think, act, and operate.

Whereas a lot of traders will then try to change the strategy when they should instead look at the data. So for me, being more data oriented – which I first avoided when I started out – has actually helped me become more resilient. Resilience is something you have to build. And I think that more traders should take the long-term view, despite the fact that a lot of these prop firms and challenge accounts are, without the trader knowing, getting them to think short term: for example, "Can I get to the end of the month and pass the challenge?"

The market rewards traders who manage that long-term perspective, while doing everything correctly consistently over the short term, regardless of the short-term result.

And lastly . . . have the awareness to be able to see if you are trying to find a technical solution to what is actually a psychology problem.

ALI'S TRADING TIPS

1. **Have a long-term view.**

   In the short-term, the market will test you, tease you, and punish you. In the long-term, the market will reward the trader who can apply the right skills and attributes.

2. **Back it up with data.**

   Ali is a big believer in relying on data for trading decisions. Even during slow or losing months, it's easier to have confidence when you have data to rely on.

3. **Don't be afraid to hold winners.**

   Ali's best-ever trade came from building a position over two months that ended up being a 13.5R win. He resisted the urge to take quick profits and it led to a much larger profit.

4. **Resilience is built over time.**

   Sticking to a strategy is tough, but it gets easier once you do it for a while. In the end, a technically gifted trader won't succeed without resilience.

5. **Risking so small that it's uncomfortable.**

   It's easier to stick to a strategy when you're not afraid to lose. You can always build your risk up over time once your experience catches up.

CHAPTER 9

Aatu Kokkila

Growing up in a small city in Finland, Aatu Kokkila started trading forex in 2012. In 2016, he began managing funds, and as of 2024 he manages over $32 million. His trading strategy focuses on fundamental events and news. He spent years analyzing the potential for continuation and mean reversion moves for many pieces of data. This unique systematic approach to fundamental events earned him the title of Best Performing Currency Systematic Strategy over five years by the *Hedge Fund Journal* in 2022 and 2023. As a teenager, he was one of the top-ranking World of Warcraft players globally. His background in gaming taught him the importance of dedication, strategy, and teamwork. He invested over 10,000 hours in gameplay, a commitment he carried over to trading where he spent nearly three years studying markets and analyzing data before perfecting his strategy.

Q: How did you get into trading?

Aatu: When I was in the army, a friend suggested I explore trading as he thought there were many parallels to gaming. He recommended I read *Market Wizards*. The book inspired me to delve into trading, and I realized I wanted to do this full-time after gaming.

Q: Did you start with paper trading or did you live trade right away?

Aatu: I live traded. I never thought paper trading had any value, because emotions play such a large role in trading, and you are not going to realistically feel them in paper trading.

Q: What instruments did you start with and how did you trade it?

Aatu: At the time, I only traded the EURUSD because I understood it best. This coincided with the European debt crisis, which created a lot of volatility in the pair. I realized that factors like yield movements in Italian and Greek bonds and the European Central Bank commentary were driving the market movements, which I found fascinating. I would then take directional swing trades depending on where I thought yields were going based on news flow.

   Back then I wouldn't even have a proper headline tool and would just read the news from any source I could find. I would form a view and swing trade with wider stops. I don't think markets were too efficient at the time reacting to yield movements, so you could make money off that.

Q: How long did it take you to become profitable?

Aatu: I became profitable almost immediately thanks to sheer luck and favorable market conditions. You had quite sharp directional movements in EURUSD during the time based on prevailing news flow. About 90% of my trades were on the EURUSD short side and especially after Draghi's "Whatever it takes" speech to the long side, which worked because there were decent short-term trends.

   When the market direction is trending and volatile, a common way for novice traders to make money is to pound on the short-term trend. It's like the early days of the crypto markets when having a long bias would have worked well, even if you didn't fully understand what you were doing.

Q: Did you blow up any accounts before turning profitable?

Aatu: Not really, but I would frequently have sub 20–40% drawdowns because of leverage. Looking back, I was lucky I never blew up any accounts when I started out.

Q: How did you get the money to trade?

Aatu: I made money by teaching people how to play World of Warcraft.

Q: How did you become one of the best players in the world for the World of Warcraft?

Aatu: World of Warcraft started out as an item-gathering game for me, but I was quickly hooked by the player-versus-player element. I was a teenager and unsurprisingly found it more exciting to play the game than go to school. I would pretty much skip school to play the game all day from 2005 to 2009.

I felt I had nothing better to do than play video games because school and grades in Finland didn't matter until you got to university back then.

In any case, when I first started, I never imagined I would spend so many hours on the game. The competitive aspect of playing against other players really captivated me. Although I was terrible initially, I improved by watching videos of better players and adopting their techniques.

I became good enough and surpassed those players I originally modeled. I started figuring out strategies on my own and got to the point where I released videos myself, which became quite popular. The videos surpassed over three million views in total on `http://Warcraftmovies.com` and our team was the highest-rated team in the world in the 2v2 and 3v3 brackets.

Ultimately, I started losing interest in the game. I wanted to do something else with my life than play video games. Back then e-sports was not considered a realistic career choice.

Q: You were part of the number-one team in the world; how did you find your teammates? Did being part of a team make you a better player?

Aatu: It did. I would say the main reason I was so successful was that I played with the best players at the time.

We met by pure coincidence. My teammates were about the same age as me living in totally different circumstances in Dubai but were all equally driven to become number one. We became close friends and continue to stay in touch.

In 2022, we even tested the game again if we "still had it" and made it to the top 50 with all of us managing tough jobs, kids, and so on, having only a couple of hours to play evenings. That was pretty cool considering the players are much better nowadays and many play the game for a living.

Q: Would you attribute your success to practicing before the competition?

Aatu: Actually, we never went to a competition. We won the qualifier in Europe for the first Blizzcon, which was the biggest competitive event at the time, but we never went there. My uncle had passed away at the time and I was very let down by that. My mother encouraged me to go, but I guess I was also a bit socially awkward as well.

Q: How do you think being a top-ranking gamer made you a better trader?

Aatu: If you want to be good at something, you need to have a lot of determination and the drive to build skill sets. Being a great gamer definitely gave me confidence that I could become good at trading as well. You need both the determination and confidence to push through.

However, the big difference with trading is that it forces you to educate yourself in various valuable areas of life such as psychology, economics, and communication skills in case you want to become a money manager.

Even if someone tried trading for a year and didn't make any money, they would still learn a lot about themselves, their emotions, and how they handle pressure. It has a lot of beneficial carryovers to other areas of life such as enforcing discipline and being mentally sharp, which provided you with the opportunity to exercise introspection.

Q: Is the feeling of loss in gaming different from trading?

Aatu: It was a relatively similar feeling for both. If I did a great job playing and still lost because of being unlucky or something, I wouldn't feel that bad at all. Likewise, I never felt the losses if I did my best job and followed my rules.

What always has been painful are the losses from breaking my rules like overtrading. It was the same thing in gaming; if I felt I played terribly when I shouldn't have, I would be extremely self-punishing.

Over the years, I've learned that being too hard on yourself for mistakes is counterproductive. You draw the lessons, stop dwelling on them, and move on. It's a skill you learn over time.

Q: How did you get to managing $30 million?

Aatu: In 2014, I had a lot of success swing trading the USDRUB. After the first Ukraine war broke out it virtually went from $35 to $50 in a straight line, but then I encountered a large drawdown when the central bank sharply raised interest rates and I was short. I thought the ruble would go to freefall regardless of what the central bank does, but that day I really learned that my opinion was worth nothing without risk management. I can have a good angle, which is right or wrong, but if the risks are not well managed, it doesn't matter.

Although I made good money trading the Russian ruble still relatively speaking, I realized I would never be able to market this track record as I was well cognizant of the fact that fund managers get paid for managing risk, not making highly volatile returns.

I had already built a lot of research in 2013–2014 on events in general, so at the start of 2015 I made the conscious decision to only focus on central bank events and news data because I saw they moved the market most. I had also studied by that time most of the relevant books and analyzed my trading to come up with an effective set of rules for trading events.

Event trading worked wonderfully from 2015–2017 in the high-volatility and deflation regime, and we already grew to over $30 million AUM [assets under management] in 2018. At the time we had an account at Darwinex, a UCITS [undertaking for collective investment in transferable securities] fund, and managed accounts, which in retrospect was not a great setup because it caused major performance differences across the platforms.

In terms of performance, the writing was already on the wall in early January 2018 when I made 6%. At the time I had been profitable for 16 out of the last 17 months. At that point, I thought it was too easy. A good friend told me I should go out there and buy a Porsche with the winnings. Whilst I managed to stay calm on the outside by saying that's the last thing I would buy with the winnings, I also thought it was too easy.

Of course, that marked the highwater mark for performance for the year. By the end of January, I had lost over 5%, finishing the month only slightly up.

Afterward, in 2018 and 2019, volatilities tanked and my trading process at the time wasn't ready to cope with the new market regime. For example, I would still have great entries but would not take profits as markets moved a lot less. I also didn't really know too well how liquidity worked and we would have a lot of performance differences across brokers and fund accounts. We lost quite a bit of AUM as a result and we only grew to similar AUM levels in 2023.

While market conditions never returned to levels of 2015–2017, my trading process has significantly improved over the years and in terms of risk-adjusted returns. For example, I realized event trading works better with a team. Nowadays we know how liquidity works very well and have put an inordinate amount of time into improving our take profits in different market regimes. Moreover, we have realized we can trade even lower risk and have similar returns if we are good at sizing conviction versus low-conviction events. Therefore, we have performed well even in challenging low-volatility conditions like in 2023.

Q: Psychologically, how is it different to trade for yourself versus managing money?

Aatu: I have always been quite detached from money itself and cared more about the process. However, I do feel the responsibility.

What has given me comfort is that I have always had a large proportion of my wealth invested into trading and improving the business in general, meaning, I am the one who takes the biggest hit proportionally.

Nassim Taleb said it well that having skin in the game is like an existential commitment that is very similar to the spartan adage "come back with your shield or on it." I belong to a camp that would never invest in or trust a manager who didn't invest their wealth into their fund.

Q: Did your trading strategy or money management techniques change when you started managing money?

Aatu: Yes, I realized I needed to keep drawdowns lower if I ever wanted to attract investor capital.

Naturally, this has meant a lot smaller returns in turn than I would have probably gotten managing my own money.

Q: You are a strong proponent of back-testing historical fundamental data. How far back do you look?

Aatu: We have researched events sometimes up to 30 years back (in case of Japanese interventions). I have personally traded over 1,000 events, and we have meticulously researched over 3,000 events in our proprietary research library that acts as the basis for our pre-trade planning today.

Q: Do you use any trading robots or are you discretionary?

Aatu: Ultimately execution is done manually, but our decision-making rules are systematic and risk levels are set in stone.

Q: You spend a lot of time analyzing whether you should take a trade. How much thought is put into the exit strategy?

Aatu: As much time as we spend in other key aspects, such as entries and interpretation, which is a lot.

Q: How do you manage your positions? Do you use single entry, single exit, or scale in or out?

Aatu: We always scale in and out.

Q: How many hours a day do you trade?

Aatu: It really depends on how you define active trading. We only trade when there are events, usually about 10–12 a month. The trading day can range from a few hours to 16 hours and we work in cycles if we must monitor prices overnight. Much of our work goes into research and generating trading ideas instead of trading itself.

Q: How many trades do you have on at the same time?

Aatu: For a given event just one, but that position would be fractionated for best possible execution.

Q: How long do you typically hold your trade for?

Aatu: The average hold period is about three hours. The duration is distorted because, usually, we exit our losers within 30 minutes; however, our winners can run up to days.

Q: Do you think having a trading team makes you a better trader?

Aatu: Absolutely. For event trading, I think running a team is a must, or at least you need two persons to bounce back ideas and monitor the news flow. Our approach is very research-intensive and there is a lot to monitor during a trade.

Q: What's your typical trading day like?

Aatu: Usually the start of a trading day is quite relaxed because the trading itself could take a long time; hence, we have prepared our scenarios in advance. We mainly gauge the news flow to see whether that has changed our scenarios, adjust if necessary, and then focus on the trading. The trading itself can take a long while, and we might work in night shifts.

Q: How important is it for your team to meet in person or can you meet virtually?

Aatu: Both have their advantages. While we work remotely most of the time, the "human" element on this job is important as you have quicker interactions and trade preparation for events together.

   However, we are all introverts, and we have discovered trading by itself works better when we all work remotely to maintain the highest possible focus levels.

Q: Why did you choose to manage money through Darwinex?

Aatu: The traditional route is to create your own fund, but what I appreciate about Darwinex is that they provide regulatory backing and the vetting process, saving you significant costs on regulation and time spent on raising assets.

   Having run a UCITS fund before, I find this setup significantly superior. While an earlier majority of our money went to regulation, lawyers, and operations, now I can invest in improving the trading, which has meant building the team, research, and so on.

Overall, I think Darwinex offers a unique and smart platform, targeting a younger generation of asset managers, which I believe will continue to evolve over the years. As trading is getting more popularized with the online prop trading industry, I think Darwinex stands in a unique position as they are genuinely trying to build people in ways to become asset managers. They are also ethical, which cannot be said about all the prop firms in the industry.

Q: What do you think it takes to go from trading your own money to becoming successful enough to manage money?

Aatu: I would start by setting a realistic expectation. It's as in any other craft; for example, a surgeon doesn't start performing operations after one year of studies. Or if they did, it would get ugly.

The brilliant investor Bernard Baruch, who traded during the Great Depression, said that "if you are ready to give up everything else and study the whole history of the market as carefully as a medical student studies anatomy – in addition to having the cool nerves of a gambler and the courage of a lion – you have a ghost of a chance."

I think that anecdote captures well the essence of long-term success in trading. Unless you are willing to commit, you can't expect to perform. Even if you ultimately end up losing money, you will learn a ton about yourself in terms of how you deal under pressure and maintain your emotions.

Q: How high leverage can you use?

Aatu: We can go up to 1 : 5 leverage on high-conviction bets. Most of our positions are not leveraged because they are lower conviction trades. That kind of trading is all about consistency.

For high-conviction trades, we use leverage because the probability of success is higher. Sizing your bets higher based on conviction levels is a good time-tested methodology and is very important for our success.

Q: Do you look at losses or drawdown on a closing basis or intraday basis?

Aatu: Closing basis.

Q: What are some tips that you can give to aspiring traders?

Aatu: The basics, such as finding out a trading style that works for you psychologically, are well taught and documented in trading books. On finding a style of trading that resonates, I believe that creating a process toward executing an edge and being systematic (rules-based) about it is paramount. I would then continue to read a lot of books and test with a small live account to see how consistent one can be with following the process while keeping emotions in check.

Trading works only for a small percentage of people. I think more people can make investing work. People often think trading and investing are very similar, but not necessarily. Of course with investing, if you go down the rabbit hole of trying to beat professionals, again you need similar levels of work as with trading. The paradox of the game is that you can put inordinate amount of time into this craft and still be worse off than just investing passively.

For example, to be a successful investor, you can get away, for example, with a solid portfolio on low-cost index funds and real estate. The only psychological qualities you need are patience and the discipline to stick to a plan of reinvesting your income for a compound return. Again, those are still very difficult psychological qualities to enforce; hence, a majority of people will never be successful investors either.

Another problem is that this will take a lot of time, unless, of course, you have a large starting stake. But there is no other way around it.

Overall, for someone who is very driven, day trading can be a "quicker" way to make money than investing. However, very few manage to because the learning curve is very steep and it still takes a lot of time make really good money unless you get lucky with market selection. Unless you love the process and genuinely find it incredibly exciting even though you get no results initially, I would advise on the passive approach or figuring out something else to do with your life.

AATU'S TRADING TIPS

1. **There's no substitute for hard work and preparation.**

To become a good trader, you must put in the work and thoroughly analyze the markets. Consistent success in trading comes from a deep understanding of market dynamics, which requires dedication and extensive research. Always be diligent in your analysis, study historical data, stay informed on current events, and continuously refine your strategies.

This same philosophy of hard work and meticulous preparation made Aatu one of the top World of Warcraft players in the world. Just as he invested countless hours into understanding the game's mechanics and strategies, he applies the same level of commitment to his trading. There's no substitute for hard work and thorough preparation in both gaming and trading.

2. **Surround yourself with a good team.**

Surround yourself with a good team that you can trade and practice with. Trading with a team allows you to share insights, challenge each other's ideas, and continuously improve your strategies. A strong team provides support, diverse perspectives, and collaborative problem-solving, all of which are crucial for long-term success. This same philosophy propelled Aatu to become one of the top World of Warcraft players in the world. By collaborating with skilled players, they honed their tactics, shared knowledge, and pushed each other to improve.

3. **Clear strategies and calm execution.**

To become a successful trader, you need a well-articulated strategy and the discipline to follow it. Clearly defined rules serve as your guide, allowing you to stay calm and execute your strategy with minimal emotion. This approach ensures consistency and reduces impulsive decisions. Maintaining this calm, focused state of mind is crucial for long-term success, not only in trading but also in gaming and most facets of life. By adhering to your strategy and staying composed under pressure, you create a foundation for sustainable growth and achievement in any competitive field.

CHAPTER 10

Andres Granger

Andres (Andrew) Granger grew up in the vibrant city of San Francisco before moving to South Korea. Starting his investment journey in high school, he quickly evolved from a young investor to managing a multimillion-dollar crypto fund. His deep understanding of market dynamics and trading strategies reflects his passion and expertise in the field. Originally diving into trading to escape the 9-to-5 grind, Andres now manages a crypto fund valued at over $10 million.

One of Andres's key strengths is market-neutral strategies like arbitrage trading.

Andres's trading style has evolved over time. He started with traditional CME (Chicago Mercantile Exchange) futures, like the euro, dollar, and peso. Over time, Andres shifted his focus to trading indexes, particularly favoring the DAX (Deutscher Aktienindex) and Nasdaq.

His expertise in arbitrage and trend-based trading, along with his ability to navigate both active and slow trading periods, highlights his adaptability and skill in the trading world.

> *Q:* Where did you grow up and what brought you to South Korea?
>
> *Andres:* I'm from Spain, but mostly grew up in the San Francisco area in California. It was a great place at the time, but then once I came over to this side of the world, everything was so interesting. I've been living in Asia for so many years now. I first went out to Japan and to China, and part of a trip after college.

129

I wanted to travel to these different places I've been seeing in movies. I was into films a lot and Korea was kind of like the finale of the trip. I got to Japan and liked it a lot more than I thought I would. Then I went to China. People were super-nice and it was a lot of fun.

Finally, I came to South Korea and I didn't like it at first. I really waited for that part of the trip and thought things would be so cool. But just like how people say, it's not like it in the movies, it's not like it is in the dramas, and it definitely wasn't. And I actually really didn't like it at first. I concluded that I should stay here, learn some of the language and find out, because maybe I wouldn't have the chance to come back ever again. After six months and learning a bit of the language, I decided to stay and I've been here ever since.

Q: When did you start trading?

Andres: My first ever trade was at 18. I was finishing high school and had a tiny bit of savings. I thought I was trading, but it was more so investing. I had no idea what I was doing, but got lucky. The real trading started years later, after I moved to South Korea. My schedule would be crazy because I'd go in for a 9- to 10-hour day of working at a hospital and squeeze in trading in the very early morning. After the first year, I started getting serious about it. I knew it was gonna take time. Like a lot of things in life, when you take enough time doing it, you get better.

Q: What was it like taking your first trade at 18?

Andres: I remember that it was hard opening an account at the time. Once I got it running, I opened the platform and all I could see was charts. I started looking at mutual funds. I felt like I should probably learn some technical analysis to understand where the market is going. And then I took my first trade.

Q: At that point you were only investing for the long run. What made you want to jump into active trading?

Andres: I always felt that there's obvious daily volatility. Holding something so long term that could be in drawdown for several months didn't feel good to me. I figured that the professionals out there would move in and out of trades daily and find more opportunities for trade. Nowadays the trades I take can last for up to three months. This got me the idea of moving around faster in a market and not just investing long term. So I became focused on making a little bit of money in and out every day.

Q: Did anyone introduce you to trading or did you come to it all by yourself?

Andres: I had this idea kicking around my head from the very beginning of high school and never talked about it with anyone. I had a statistics teacher, who talked about investing, trading stocks, currencies, and spent entire classes just on that. It makes sense to me now, coming from a stats teacher. But at the time it just blew my mind. The fact that you can work hard your whole life to retire, or you can take like a year's salary, invest it, and it would grow to actually be more money than you could earn in your entire lifetime. It made it a lot more interesting. From there I always thought, "I'll get into it later when I'm in my 40s, maybe 50s." And then at some point I was like, "I don't like any of these other jobs I do. Maybe this trading stuff would be interesting."

Q: What kind of jobs did you have before you got into trading?

Andres: I did a lot of different things. When I arrived in South Korea, I got into marketing. I also worked for an investment firm under the Hyundai company. I was doing small jobs for them but got to see inside the trading world for the first time. Most of my work was in sales and connecting clients with what they needed. I was often flying over to China for a day or two and then flying back to South Korea.

Q: It sounds like some pretty good jobs to me. What was it about them that you didn't like?

Andres: Having to clock in daily from 9 to 5. It's South Korea, so depending on your seniority, you had to be there by at least 7:30 a.m. As you advance, you need to show up super, super-early to show everyone how work is done. This is how we kept our company going. It became pretty exhausting, especially in the winter months. At 3–4 p.m. it's already getting extremely dark. I get out of work, pitch black, I go into work in the morning, pitch black, and the work is very challenging and stressful. Trading is also challenging every day. There's never just a very easy day. But to me it's a lot of fun and it keeps my mind fresh for sure.

Q: What do you find interesting about trading?

Andres: I find it really interesting to see the action. Even now, I'll still trade my own personal scalping account several days out of the week and just do a lot of trades there, in the same old style and way that I've done since the beginning. Of course, on some days you still have bad days, and some days are good, but overall it's still very interesting to me and keeps me sharp with what we do at the fund.

Q: Did you go straight to live capital or did you prefer trading demo for a while?

Andres: I went right to live capital and then back to sim, and then back to live capital. I would go through these periods when I wanted to test out live capital maybe for a month, trying to keep my drawdown low. Then I'd go back to demo, rewatch the trading videos, and then the next month I'd try to do it better. I spent well over a year doing that, but I remember clearly that once I hit the two-year mark, I told myself "No more demo account; it needs to be live." I didn't trade many different types of strategies, only short-term trading. I'm not a fast learner at all and for the first two years it was just drawdown after drawdown. Every time I touched the market. Everything was losing. Constantly.

Then finally, it was right about the two-year mark, my trading started going better. I wasn't losing anymore, but I was only barely covering my commission costs. I couldn't cover the $110 market data feed yet. I was still having to work a secondary job and it wasn't completely covering my lifestyle. But not too long after, things finally took off. My profits were starting to look very consistent on a monthly basis. And once I had that, then each month very quickly increased.

Q: What made you go from losing to breakeven and then to profitable? What was the difference?

Andres: I hate to have the simplest, most basic answer, but realistically my skills improved. I was doing the same things, I knew the same material, but I'd had enough practice of actually executing and reading the order book quickly. I started making better decisions. A huge part of that was completely cutting down the error trades. What I mean by error trades is, say you wanna buy something and you click the wrong thing. You hit it at a higher price than what you wanted. You wanted this trade, but should have actually canceled it, especially in a fast scalping environment. That small difference can really eat up your profits over time.

What really helped me was reviewing the videos of my trades. I'd try to spot the obvious mistakes I should watch out for. This work stopped me from losing on top of being able to spot those days where the price action is bad. I know the kind of price action I can make money in and try to stay away when it's not happening. Once you really get rid of all those errors you're making, then you become profitable and can start to scale it up.

Q: Were you trading the same instruments and strategies back then or did your process change over time?

Andres: It slightly changed over time, but I'm still trading futures with the fund. I started off in traditional futures, trading the CME and Eurex products, and one of my very first markets was in currencies, trading things like the euro, dollar, or even peso. The commissions through the CME are quite high, so you really have to be making a few ticks per trade. And when the volume is strong, they can actually be very interesting to trade, but you can also have those slow days when there's nothing to trade. Over time, I started trading indexes, specifically the DAX and Nasdaq the most.

Q: What was your worst trade?

Andres: This experience is engraved in my memory. I got in a trade on the DAX near the daily high. I felt that I could get a pullback trade off the high, so I went for it. As soon as I clicked my mouse, the market just spiked up. It was a very random large spike of 37 ticks just in a single second. That kind of move hadn't happened in prior months. I always used stops on my scalp trades that were far enough from the market to where I don't want to ever have to use them. But in this case even my stop didn't take me out of the trade. There was no slippage or anything. I still had the trade on and I was like, "What just happened?" It may have been so fast that the software I was using just didn't work, but I was still in the trade.

I was super-nervous about it. It was one of those deer-in-the-headlights situations. I froze for a few seconds and then went to close it. I was in for only 12 seconds, but I knew I should have been out faster. I was really upset with myself. That one trade alone ended up costing me about US $1,300. Back then that was huge. I wouldn't even have a $1,000 losing month. Maybe one month would be down by several hundreds of dollars and the next month would be up a little bit, but that one month was the worst of all.

Q: How was your mindset after that big loss?

Andres: My confidence took a hit. I knew that I wouldn't make it all back in the next trade, so I took things very slow. The market always goes against you the opposite way and just rips. And when it does go in your favor, you're too quick to take profits. It stuck with me and definitely hurt for a few months. It kept me worried.

Q: How did you recover from that? Did you take a break or just go right back to trading the next day?

Andres: After that one trade happened, I literally turned off. Not turned off my computer. I turned off the ability to trade on my platform. I thought, "What's going on in this market? Is it going to have other moves like this? Is today some crazy random day?" No, it was just one single specific move. The market stayed volatile after that, but it stopped. I watched it for a bit. After 15 minutes I said, "Enough of this." I went to the video recording of that trade to understand what happened. There was no real reason why it spiked up exactly at the moment I got into it.

Then I took a big step back for the next couple of months, where I'd only take a handful of trades per day and stopped trading live. But pretty quickly I told myself that I had to get back into it. It sucked, but I was very cautious with my trading after that. I built my way back from there with the same consistent grind, day in, day out. Once I did come back and then had a few more good months, I started sizing up, realizing, "Okay, I can actually make money." It was a great confidence booster once I actually made that money back, but it was an absolutely slow grind.

Q: You mentioned that you record your trades on video. When did you start doing that?

Andres: I had heard about doing that when I first started trading. I looked up things online and listened to podcasts to figure out how different professionals do it. It just made sense, so I thought, why not do it too. I found the videos so much more important than a screenshot. I could play it back at a quarter of the speed just to see how things were going at certain times, and for bad trades I could see what kind of price action was happening. The recordings absolutely helped, without a doubt.

Q: So how long have you been trading for overall?

Andres: It's been nine years since I started actively trading, but much longer since my very first investment trade.

Q: Do you still question yourself from time to time? Do you still feel like it's maybe not the right thing or that you should go back to a job?

Andres: Not at all. I once saw this very old trading video from Charlie DiFrancesca, who was a professional market maker. He traded bonds on the floors of the CME. He was in the middle of a talk about being a trader, and what you really learn from it. He said he's met doctors and lawyers who after so many years want to give up. They want to give up their profession, retire, take an easy life, and just relax after they've made their money. And Charlie said that trading is the one industry where he's met people who never want to give it up.

They want to keep trading for as long as they can, for the rest of their life. Before he passed away, Charlie got a cancer diagnosis. When he was given the diagnosis at the hospital, he said that he's going to invest his money. It was millions and millions of dollars. He would be giving it to the bank. He asked if they could just keep him alive another eight months beyond what he had left, because he wanted to keep trading. That's how much he was into it. I'm the same way. I don't think I'll ever lose my interest in trading at this point.

Q: Tell me more about the crypto fund you're trading.

Andres: I've been lucky enough over the last few years that this fund has been going well. Not so long ago, I was the one losing the money. Right now we're a little over $10 million. So that's actually been really exciting. It's also become a very interesting challenge and I'm liking it a lot. We're getting to a point where we need to trade large sizes and we need to figure out how to do it. Early in the fund, it was hard to even get $100 K from an investor. Now we get people wanting to put in $100 K to test it and by next week they're ready to put in $1 million, and the week after they'll add another $2 million.

There are tricks that you wouldn't really need when you're trading just a few million dollars, but as it grows larger, you need to develop new tactics to get in the market with a larger size. And the biggest thing is, we also don't want people to notice our positions. Because once they do notice, there are some of those predatory funds or traders out there trying to liquidate people's positions by running the market in some way or another. It doesn't happen very often, but we prefer not to be noticed. That has been an interesting challenge.

Q: As someone who manages a fund, how much of your time is actually spent trading?

Andres: I'm the main person who has to be trading, and I set standards for myself. I really like trading manually, so I try to do and keep up as much as possible in order to keep my skills growing and see what I notice in the markets. Sometimes I just observe. There are so many opportunities or strategies that you can start developing, so taking time thinking about what you can improve is helpful.

I generally work a good six days a week, if not seven. At least a couple of those days are 10–15 hours of just straight working. And then the other days are about eight hours, but sometimes I like to take a little time for myself, so maybe it's only five or six hours of work. I've only grown into taking time to relax over the last year.

I can have a little bit of time to myself because I've earned it and the markets aren't going anywhere. Even if I have trades going on, I don't need to keep looking at the charts. We've got alerts if anything crazy happens, which is a good risk management practice.

Q: Tell me a bit more about your trading style.

Andres: What I focus on these days is a market-neutral style of trading. The fund I run has two different offerings. You can invest in the market-neutral or the directional fund. Obviously the directional returns a great deal more than the market-neutral fund when the market is trending. Like last year, the directional was up 75% and we did 27% for the market neutral. I've always really liked a market-neutral style of trading. I don't feel comfortable trading directionally, especially manually.

Instead, I want to come in to work and hopefully make money each day. When you trade directionally (i.e. with the trend), you can go through some nasty drawdowns that I've seen last for a few months at a time. It's soul crushing, really. It's part of my trading but I myself gravitate toward something that's more market neutral, where the returns aren't as great. They aren't as exciting, but it's nice to watch funding come in on a daily basis.

Q: How exactly do you trade market neutral?

Andres: What we do is arbitrage. We make money because of where the spot market is compared to where the futures market is. It works when there's a divergence in price. The idea is to spot when the cash market will either be at a discount to where the futures market is or the opposite way around, and we just play that spread in between. Say the cash market is at a discount, we're buying the cash, and we're selling the future. Those two things don't stay in alignment all the time. In fact, they're often diverged by a basis point or three basis points, and that's great. You're buying up one, selling the other, and as soon as that collapses, then you're exiting the trade.

Good execution is very important with that type of trading. You're not really able to do this when you're executing millions of dollars at once onto both legs. You have to do this over time and bit by bit, because if you want to sell $100 at $95 and there's only 18 on the bid, then you're going to blow right through that market and the price will shoot way down. If the market is going to tick down and now my spread is crushed, maybe I want to execute little bits at a time to get the size I want and let the market naturally move back to an equilibrium of price and then exit.

Q: Do you face similar size problems with directional trading?

Andres: Not quite, but it's still similar. We're always asking how much we can clip in without pushing the market. Then we wait for the next orders to come in and check the volatility. We have many metrics to look over all these things. We're getting limit orders filled, we're also hitting into the market at the same time because who knows where price is going to be in the next 20 seconds. We may lose the price that we're able to enter in right now, which is pretty nice. It could go down again, but our metrics, our trading, our setup is telling us, no, it's more than likely going to go up from here, so we need this trade on. We have 5, 15, 20 minutes to get this trade on in this volume and execute the remainder of what we need done, or we have to wait until the next trade and we missed it.

So it's always a bit of a balance, but it's not so complicated. We have bots to execute them. Because you really don't want these automated bots to be executing something so difficult and complicated that basically all of your signals work against each other and the trade doesn't even happen. But that's pretty obvious. When you're creating bots, you quickly see, "Okay, I put too many parameters on this, that's not working. I need to take this stuff off. What's the bare minimum I need to actually make this work?"

Q: In your trading, what's the balance of robots and manual trading?

Andres: In our directional fund, it's 100% automated. Our market-neutral fund is still automated, but I execute certain things for clients manually. For instance, if a client wanted to move their capital from one exchange to another, that's a lot of volume I have to execute in a very short period of time to close out all trades and then reopen the trades on a new account. I remember trading in Luna as it was crashing. That market would go up and down 2, 3, 4% in less than a minute.

So something you buy now, even without leverage, is already up 4% 30 seconds later. It was insanely volatile, but it specifically got really volatile and really interesting once it cracked below a dollar. It really went wild. It was fun. I'm the trader for the fund. There's safety in having a manual trader to execute if things go wrong even when everything is automated.

Q: Do you trade your own account on top of that?

Andres: I have a test account and I try to match, if not improve, the returns that we're making for clients. That's the place where I go to learn and perform. I'm constantly trying to grow it, but it's great having a place to experiment. So we have different styles of test accounts, some of which are running bots and newer trade styles constantly. The bots will usually run an average of 1500 trades a day in different accounts and strategies.

We also have our own in-house market making system – it's a bit of market making, but in another way, it's actually a bit of a stat arb [statistical arbitrage]. So we're executing into two different legs in two different markets, but doing it very quickly.

Q: Do you look at fundamentals or news to decide what to trade?

Andres: Not at all. I'll know of fundamentals that are happening and because of that, I'll think of what the spread could do (narrow or widen). Recently, there was all this hype about a Bitcoin exchange-traded fund that created interesting conditions in the market. This meant that I was probably going to trade with much lower risk. We don't want to be leveraged in something when it's risky. It's interesting, because other funds that were heavily into crypto didn't lower their risk. They thought, "What on earth are these guys doing?" It would have been a large risk to us if this market went crazy, so we preferred to play it safe. Other than that, I don't look at fundamentals for trade ideas.

Q: Who came up with the logic for the bots?

Andres: The bots are based on the way that I traded manually before. I traded arbitrage for a few years on my own. And then I started working with this guy who previously worked as a coder for Morgan Stanley. He was a directional trader, while I was market neutral. We combined our forces and worked on it for two years. We got to a point where it was working and at least all of our execution was going well, but it would just grind flat, barely making any money. The size that you could get on was so insignificant. Arbitrage trading is always capacity constrained, but the returns are very good. If you have bots running this, you know what the win rate should be. If it doesn't work out, the bot just moves on to the next trade.

Q: What instruments do you trade? Do you have a list you always focus on?

Andres: We trade the top 25 highest-volume markets. So volume in the cash market and open interest in the futures market. Those are the two really big factors that determine what we trade. If it's something where the futures market only has a few thousand dollars of volume in a day, there's no way we're going to touch that. But something that has maybe $5 million of daily volume in a day, we might be able to place some very small trades. We normally look for something that has $20 to $100 million USD value of daily volume at the very least. That really leaves it up into the top 25 markets of daily volume. And then inside of that, we really will work in maybe the top 15 altogether. So we're open to the others, but if the opportunities aren't great, we stick to the top 15.

Q: How long do you typically hold your trades for?

Andres: It really ranges. We usually close trades faster when the market is volatile: about three days. When the market is trending well, we can hold trades for up to three months. The total average would be about one month. We scale in and out of all these trades. That is a massive part of our risk portfolio. We do this without using stops at all because we're always scaling in and scaling out based on volatility targets. If it's highly volatile, we'll keep our position size smaller. If it's not too volatile and trending well, we'll increase our position size to a maximum of 3x. The bots can even go up to 5x, but they're limited by the amount of volatility in the market. Generally, we're in about 1.3x to 1.5x for the directional fund.

Q: Is that based on the asset itself or something else?

Andres: It's based on the dollar amount that we have inside the fund or inside the trade. So for example, we have our 10 different selected markets and for 1 out of the 10, the position says to go ahead. I need to get $100,000 on this and then that puts me at more heavy compared to everything else in the portfolio. This puts my entire position to 1.5x. Even though these markets are very correlated, we may be short in several of them and then long in a handful as well.

So when our positions change over from long to short, they don't all instantly change at the same time. Because of this volatility targeting, it still says, for example, this position is still good for a long trade, until it isn't anymore. This really does hurt because we're never buying the very bottom and selling the very top. For this kind of directional style of trading, you need a trend to develop first. You cannot just be flipped in and out of trades all the time. If movements are choppy, that's the worst kind of condition for us.

Q: What makes you decide to go long or short? Is it based on technicals?

Andres: It's trend-following. We trade based on moving averages. So maybe there's a 30-day and a 5-day moving average on top of several factors we put in our system. We take a long position after the 5-day crosses over the 30-day. Then if they slowly start to diverge and the 5-day is saying no, but the 30-day is saying yes, we start to scale out of the trade. And when things completely flip over then it's a short trade, so whatever else I have on needs to be exited and now a short position needs to be created.

Q: What does an average trading day look like for you?

Andres: Generally, I wake up and look at the different things I have. I really hate looking at my phone or computer first thing, but it's part of life. I like to have some sunlight coming in, drink water, and try to set my head correctly. I try not to be too stressed about anything that's going on. Exercise is really important for me. I'll do a 15-minute home workout, then check how my trades are going. I message the team, talk about anything that we need to go over for the day. But then I actually go out and do a full on workout at the gym. From there, it's always coffee, coffee, coffee. That's what you need to keep this kind of lifestyle going. Many of the cafes around my neighborhood know me well. I try to go to a new one every day, but there's simply not enough.

Then I get serious about trading. It can be a heavy trading day or just a trade study day, when I look at how things have been trading overnight. I might consider how I can improve. Then it's time for our daily team meeting, where we discuss everything we need to do. Once the meeting is done, I continue with trading. I try to cook at home for myself each day. It doesn't happen too often, because of meetings and trying to have some sort of a social life outside of trading. I was an overweight kid growing up and I've learned to diet and exercise over the years. Now I want to be healthy in any way I can.

I try to relax in the evening, but I have alerts on my platform, if anything important happens. Watching YouTube is what keeps me up way too late in the night. I end up going to bed at some ridiculous hour and being too tired the next day if I get stuck on YouTube.

Q: Do you trade from home, an office, or coffee shops? What's your favorite way of getting work done?

Andres: I've checked all the boxes here. Trading from my own place is what I do most. But what I love about this lifestyle is to go trade from a cafe if I want, because not all of it is intense trading. So much of it can be studying and I can take my laptop out and look across different markets, or open up the order book, see how things are going, and take notes. Before I opened up the automated fund, I used to do my scalping at home, take videos of my trades, then go out to Starbucks to review it all. People would watch me sit there and watch order books flash numbers across the screen up and down. I don't think there are many jobs out there where you have that luxury.

Q: You previously told me about your bad trades, but what about some of your best trades?

Andres: When Luna was just collapsing and everything was going to nothing, I was in a spread trade between their spot market and their futures market. The trade needed to be exited because they were going to delist the contract for the futures market of Luna the next day. So our position needed to be liquidated manually. The spot and cash market obviously needed to be dumped for USDT. The spread was already so wide. There was nearly a 1% difference between the spot market and the futures market, so it meant we were going to take a hit. When it was time to exit, I did it in tiered levels throughout the order book like I usually do. I was able to exit on certain sides and saw the price move an extra 5%, which I was able to capture.

I had other friends too doing a similar trade and they made a lot of money. In those situations you have to ask yourself, "Was it the market conditions that made me money? Was my trading good?" That was one of those situations where I looked at it and it went up super-easy. You could make money like nothing. Once you experience what "easy" actually is in trading, it's quite fun, but it's a unique case. It's been over two years and I've never seen that again.

Q: Do you know how much money you made on that Luna trade?

Andres: We didn't have a huge amount of money left in that trade. When I was closing it, we had $35,000 left, but I made $4,500 in less than 30 minutes by trading out of that spread and letting the volatility take parts of the trade out. At points it's going down and I'm adding more to it and taking away and adding more and taking away. Say you take away $5,000, and then put back $4,000. You're always working in and working out. It was like taking bits off to help your overall price. That was just a very fun one. Nowadays we make $100 K if not millions per trade, but to do it on a small account size in one small trade back then, it was definitely unique.

Q: Do you have any favorite resources that are must-haves for your type of trading?

Andres: The first one is an order book. I use Bookmap and Quant Tower these days. They both have their positives and negatives, but using a professional order book is great. Another tool would be Grafana, because you can create alerts and use all kinds of metrics. Another free resource is Coinglass. It has a bunch of information from liquidations, open interest, funding rates. It's one of the first things I check each day.

Q: Do you feel the average retail trader can benefit from having an order book platform or is it only for professionals?

Andres: I would say they absolutely can. After learning and using it for a while, they would become more of a professional. Their work is just more of a professional grade once they incorporate order flow and use it correctly. There's a long and big learning curve, but if you're taking trading seriously or as a career, then go for that. Go for the extra step and do it as professionally as you can.

Q: What convinced you to create a fund and accept investments?

Andres: It really came down to the fact that we have these strategies we've been trading for years and we can put size on them. It was kind of a no-brainer. The other thing was that I was previously trading for a fund. I was getting a nice percentage of what I was making. Then, one of the owners branched off to make his own fund and kind of sniped me. That pulled me to create my own fund. It's funny because it wasn't that long ago that I was just another bedroom trader, trying to make it. I'm definitely not the smartest person. I think anyone reading over this chapter will easily see that. So I feel like if I can do it, then other people can do it, too. In the end, all we're trying to do here is buy low and sell high. Whatever you can do to make that happen can work.

Q: I think a lot of it is connections. How did you meet the people that you work with now?

Andres: That was a really big one. It was a while back in 2020, when Discord was really popping off and people were getting on Discord communities. One Discord group was created by a hedge fund trader who had worked for Goldman Sachs. He created a special group you had to pay to join. He was on Twitter so I thought, "Yeah, of course, why not?" There was no teaching, it was just discussion. I joined that and then after a while, I made a silly video series to show the kind of arbitrage I was trading. It would be like 90% jokes and then information. I just made it for the group and for fun. Yet, they loved it.

Then a guy contacted me directly through Discord and said, "Hey, I'm doing this at a fund, do you want to come trade for us?" I was very surprised, but I soon started trading for him. I met our lead developer in that Discord group, too. He was a quant trader focused on trend following and I was the guy going off about my market-neutral trades, so it was a good match.

Q: If you had to give advice to traders who want to get profitable and start a fund eventually, what's the advice you'd give them?

Andres: It's a bit of a platitude, but if you're not profitable yet, just be disciplined in what you're doing. It might sound ridiculous, but you might need to be disciplined even in your losing trades. Track the trades and make changes over time. That would be the most crucial part for someone trying to get profitable. If you want to start a fund, you need to understand that it's a people business. You could be performing excellently for your investors and yet you make a comment or you don't get back to them on time and they pull their funds. And you think like, "I'm making them money; they should be happy."

I've seen people who don't have good people skills not make it after they start a fund. I'm really busy trading, but I do my best to jump on calls with clients. Jesse, our head of operations, is on calls several times a day. It's often with current clients, but also for onboarding new investors or potential ones. So for someone who really wants to create their own fund, realize that it's not just about the trading side. You need someone who's just as important to be the business manager. There are all kinds of regulatory laws and things that you have to get around. If it were up to me, I wouldn't have ever been able to deal with that. I could never have done it on top of trading.

Q: How did you feel when you first got to trade investors' capital? Was it a big change to go from trading for yourself to having outside capital or was it pretty easy?

Andres: It was pretty easy but I have to admit that I was nerve-wracked in the first couple of months. It was a little bit stressful. But then I quickly saw that my trading actually got better. I'm very diligent and disciplined with cutting trades, but when it was someone else's money, I was even more so. I was taking fewer bad trades and cutting other trades faster when trading for others. Someone once told me, "The first cut is always the cheapest," meaning cutting your trade right away is always cheaper. Then it gets more expensive. It really is true.

ANDRES'S TRADING TIPS

1. **Record your trades.**

   Video record them or, at the very least, have a review process to go back over your trades. Ask yourself, "Was it the market conditions that made or lost me money? And was my trading good or bad?"

2. **Build your team.**

   Andres got to where he is today from the connections he's made on his journey. If you meet new people, online or in person, you can expand your opportunities.

3. **You don't need trends.**

   Contrary to common belief, trading profitably when the market is neutral is possible. Andres uses arbitrage when two assets are priced differently. That gives him better returns when the market is not trending.

4. **Stay disciplined.**

   It might sound clichéd, but being diligent with your process, even if you're losing money, is required to succeed. As Andres once heard, "The first cut is always the cheapest."

5. **It's a people business.**

   Many funds fail, because trading and managing the business and clients is a lot of work. You can set yourself up for success if you bring on help and don't try to do it all alone.

PART III

PROP TRADING PROS

CHAPTER 11

Jean-Francois Boucher

Jean-Francois Boucher, a full-time day trader living in Jasper, Alberta, began his trading journey in the late 1980s. He initially made a significant amount of money through an early initial public offering (IPO) but lost it all trading options. After being diagnosed with leukemia, his inability to leave the house provided him with ample time to focus on trading. Despite the setbacks, he persevered and connected with the right people, eventually finding success in his trading career.

By 2016, Jean-Francois had developed his own unique trading style, moving away from trend trading to focus solely on price action. He started trading prop firm capital, targeting small intraday market moves with tight targets. Over the years, he has built a family office managing over eight figures.

Jean-Francois believes that understanding how to lose is crucial in trading: "Once you know how to lose, money just falls into your lap. Learning to lose and not chasing money is the key to success."

What sets Jean-Francois apart from most traders is his approach to trading as a structured business with clear guidelines. This disciplined methodology makes him a great inspiration for those interested in short-term trading.

Q: Tell me a bit about where you grew up and where you are now.

Jean-Francois: I was born and raised in Montreal, Quebec. As a teenager, we moved to Sarnia, Ontario, and I quickly had to

Q: What made you move to Jasper?

Jean-Francois: I came here as a result of a divorce, propagated from trading losses. You can say that I "lost my way" to Jasper National Park. It's a very similar environment to where I grew up. Small town, countryside, fresh air. I spent my 20s and 30s in Toronto. That city was really killing me. I really couldn't wait to leave such a big city. And finally, I ended up moving back to my roots, going back to an area very similar to where I came from.

Now I have a long-term partner here, and I'm the stepfather to her teenage daughter. While back in Toronto I also have three adult daughters, so I'm a father of four. I love my kids.

Q: How many years have you been trading so far?

Jean-Francois: From the beginning, it's been about 18 years. It was a disaster in the beginning. I don't really count that as trading. It was more learning to tie my shoes. Now I trade for a small family office and for a couple of prop firms. Things are very different, and it has a lot to do with discipline.

Q: What did you study in school? And did you have any favorite subject or topic back then?

Jean-Francois: Through high school, I was really fascinated by science, anything that I couldn't touch. It was as if I had to prove it to myself. I liked things that had to be experimented or tested. Then after college, I leaned toward electronics. I graduated college with a major in electronics engineering. I was hired by IBM Canada before my last exam in 1989 – I started work in February 1990 and worked there for the next 17 years.

Q: When did you get introduced to trading?

Jean-Francois: I came across trading as a teenager in the 80s. My dad was trading in the beginning before computers. He was looking at the quotes in the newspapers and drawing his own charts. I don't know how he was doing it, but he was a trend trader following stocks. I always saw him drawing the charts after getting the newspaper on Sunday morning. It was a routine; he did it for years. Over time, I learned that there's a reason for this discipline.

learn to speak English. Fast-forward to today, I'm living across the country in Jasper National Park, Alberta.

Fast-forward 20 or so years later, I tried it for myself at 35 years old. I had a young family of three kids, a wife, and a fantastic job. I was making more money than you can imagine, and it was too easy for me to waste it. So that was my first experience with trading. If it didn't work, I could just make one more deposit.

Q: What made you want to start trading?

Jean-Francois: I think I wanted to test the unknown, to see what's on the other side. I saw people on TV doing it in the early 2000s, during the internet bubble. It looked so easy back then. I'd even meet people and ask, "How did you make all this money?" And they'd reply something like "Oh, I bought stuff in the morning and I was rich in the afternoon." That got my interest, and I had a pile of cash I could use for it, too.

My very first trade happened when the company I worked for split off its manufacturing from the software division. I was then offered an IPO as an employee. So I participated in the CLS (Celestica) IPO in 1998. We were offered the shares at an IPO price of $16. And before the end of the second year, it had increased to $128. That's how I got my little nest egg. Fast-forward to 2005 or 2006, I basically lost it all.

Q: How did you lose it all?

Jean-Francois: I was working the night shift in an electronics manufacturing environment. At this point, I had been in the same environment for almost 15 years and I had gotten tired of it. I wanted to try something new. I knew trading was going to be my way out. It offered a lot of solutions to my problems. Back then, as soon as you'd deposit money in a trading account in Canada, the first phone call you'd get was, "Hey! Do you want to learn how to trade options to protect your stocks?" So I took a course and learned to trade options. I traded two contracts, made good money, and everything after that was a disaster. I did not know why I was into options. I had no idea. I was clearly just in it for the money.

The big thing of the day was internet stuff. Anything with a dot-com, you could buy calls and you should be okay. I said, "Well, this can't go up forever." So I started selling calls and puts on Amazon without an exit strategy, and after a little while, I lost track of the money that was simply being deducted from my account whenever necessary. Eventually I got it into my head that it could not fail, and that's when everything kind of exploded. It took me about eight to nine months to lose a quarter of a million dollars. I did have a huge ego. I was hired by the biggest computer company at 18 years old. I was making the most money out of everyone in my family. So I definitely couldn't admit failure. There's no way I could tell anybody I was losing this much money in trading. No way at all. I had never failed at anything in my life.

Q: How did you react to that?

Jean-Francois: Well, I was hiding everything. I was running to the mailman to pick up the mail. I was running to answer the telephone first. And then one day my wife answered the phone and it was the broker saying "We need our money." That was the beginning of the end and it started the divorce proceedings and everything with it. I was introduced to trading because I wanted something new and I thought it would solve all my problems. I didn't realize how many new problems it would bring on. A lot of internal issues, problems with fear of loss. All the trading psychology stuff you're told about, it happened to me. Everybody leaves the psychology of trading for last. It got me first. I had to learn money and risk management and all that stuff. I had to overcome the losses in my head before I could actually learn to trade.

Q: Are these issues every trader faces or do you think it was only you personally?

Jean-Francois: I think everybody faces the same steppingstones to get to the profitable side. I chose the psychology of trading as the first stone to fall off of. In the beginning, I wasn't using any tools or I used all of them. I had a relative strength index, moving average convergence divergence, all that stuff trying to trade options with. All I needed was to be correct on the direction, right? But lo and behold, then options introduced time and time decay and all my money was disappearing. I couldn't figure out where and why. I was just too new for this and options were just way too complicated for a new trader. So I started removing things from the chart. I took off the indicators and all the junk. I stopped using luck, hearsay, wishes, and the television for trade ideas. Back then we were using forums. You'd log in and check what your buddies are all trading, but you have to do your own due diligence.

Q: What came after this? Did you want to get back to trading or did you want to give up?

Jean-Francois: Most of the losses came from my revenge trading. You start small, then you lose. But now you have to get that back as well. The next loss is a little bit bigger. It just snowballed and then I basically lost my house as a result. I had to sell our house to pay my broker. That initiated the divorce, so I lost the family, too. I ended up moving across the country to Jasper to start all over again about 2006. Fast-forward, it's 2016 and I'm trading prop firm money. Things changed quite a bit. Some of it came down to discipline, but the bulk of it came down to realizing that I'm responsible for everything that happened. Everything.

Q: What exactly happened between 2006 and 2016? You went from losing money to then becoming a prop trader. What kind of work did you do?

Jean-Francois: I ran into the Apiary Fund. That's where I met the mentors who helped me straighten things out. Prior to running into that group, I was trying to trade trends and it never worked for me. Once I ran into these guys, they told me, "Jean-Francois, maybe you're the type of guy who should just stop pretending to be a trend trader and instead trade the facts as you see them. Just trade sideways if the market is sideways." All the light bulbs started popping off. This is exactly what I was looking for. And from that moment forward, everything changed. And I'm now trend trading, swing trading, and doing all this stuff, but it started inside out. I had to start small and grow into big trades.

Most people try using 2 : 1 or 3 : 1 targets, right out of the gate. That never worked for me. The price always went to the stop loss before going to the target, so it was devastating to my psychology. The group of traders I ran into straightened me out. They changed my way of approaching the problem. In the beginning, I had zero money management. After a while, I became hyper-focused on money management and risk management. I was finally pointed in the right direction. And in that time period, simulated accounts, demo accounts were given away for free; they were the big thing. But I had it in my mind that I wasn't going to learn with a demo; I had to put real money in there.

Real money kind of prompted me to do it right. I had lost so much already, there's no way I could afford losing again. So now the laser focus was there. And then it just happened one trade at a time. You know, it's one trade at a time, but the key is to have a huge sample size in 20 years. In order to have a huge sample size, you reduce the actual size of each trade and now your account can take thousands of these little baby trades. So it's mathematically sound as long as you know what works for you. And that took me 10 years to figure out.

Q: It took you about 10 years to become profitable then?

Jean-Francois: Yes, 8–10 years. Prior to 2016, it was just mayhem. It was "try this, try that, a little bit of this, a little bit of that." The Apiary Fund was the first group that helped me change things. It was about 2014 when I first saw their ad. And at the time, Shawn Lucas had no beard, no hat. He was wearing a shirt and a tie. He looked like a Wall Street guy. It's very different now. About four years later, I started trading with a company from Australia called Traders4Traders. With them, I signed up for a $25 K account. I blew that up two or three times. I figured out where my issues were, tightened up my game.

And then I signed up for two $100 K accounts and got them both within days of each other. And I traded them for a couple of years until I got my diagnosis of leukemia. That's when I got a whole lot of time afforded to me. So I thought, "What am I gonna do with all this time?" I decided I'm gonna make my trading better. Fast-forward to today, I'm trading prop money and my own family office. It's all because of one strategy and never giving up on it. Once you find what works for you, don't give up.

Q: How did the leukemia diagnosis give you more time?

Jean-Francois: With leukemia, you lack an immune system, so I have to stay away from crowds, infections, certain foods, all diseases, and illnesses in general. I don't touch door-knobs. I don't touch elevator buttons. I stay away from tourists, and in Jasper National Park, we see about 2.5 million tourists per year. So I just stay home and trade for a couple hours per day. That's my own money, my own account, what I need to do for my trading business. Then for the rest of my eight or nine hours, I'll teach. I spend a lot of time educating other people.

Q: Tell me what you've achieved so far in terms of funding and in terms of a full-time trader lifestyle.

Jean-Francois: Over the years I've had multiple six-digit accounts. Once I got the leukemia diagnosis, I took a year and a half off of doing everything. My life was turned upside down there for a minute. I had to get a succession plan in place. Once I had that organized, I went back to trading. Since then, I've built an eight-figure family office, and I have a great family lifestyle. It's more of a moral, or spiritual, type of journey for me now. It's all about giving back.

Once you know how to lose, money just falls on your lap. Once you understand losing, which is the main objective, the side effect is money coming your way. Learn to lose. Don't chase the money. It's funny, once you get diagnosed with any kind of drastic eye-opening illness, you see your life in a different light and it's all about sending the elevator back down now. Somebody helped me on the way up. It's my turn to help other people. That's what it's all about.

Q: Do you consider yourself to be a full-time trader?

Jean-Francois: Yes, that's all I do. I really enjoy doing this, I bounce out of bed every morning. There's no other job on the planet I would rather do. It's not only because it's making money, it's because it's fun. It's exciting. Most people are tired when they wake up, because they have to go to work. I never feel that way.

Q: When did you move to full-time trading? Was it before the leukemia diagnosis or afterwards?

Jean-Francois: It was after the leukemia diagnosis. Once I had nothing else to do and had a track record, I decided to go full-time with trading. At first, there was the imposter's syndrome. I didn't think I was good enough so I had to prove it to myself. I had to create an environment where I understood my track record and where my problems were, so I could trust the results. It's easier to get over the fear, if you can do it and prove it to yourself. A lot of guys don't collect data on their trading. They just hope that today will be better than yesterday. You can't pay your bills like that.

You have to find consistency and that's kind of what I do now, by only trading one thing. The strategy I use now has one target, one stop loss, one take profit, one time of day, one instrument. It's only one of everything. I'm therefore the last variable. Whereas if I tried to do any other style of trading, there's a bunch of variables plus me on top. And so I guess for me to be proficient at this, I need control. The way I've structured the system I trade gives me that control. I engineer my exits instead of letting the stop loss do it for me. Managing risk is the fun part.

Q: Tell me a bit more about your style of trading these days and what you trade.

Jean-Francois: I trade only forex and some futures. I started many years ago with options and I got destroyed. I rediscovered futures a few years ago. It's an expensive game to play, but there are no tricks. Everybody gets the same price. It's one even playing field, but a very expensive playing field, so I needed to figure out something a little cheaper. Living in Canada, I can use leverage. Now with 100 : 1 leverage, I can trade micro lots. And so with micro lots, I can control my risk down to dollars and cents, instead of hundreds of dollars.

It's a very different approach to risk management using forex, because I can exploit leverage. While people are typically afraid of leverage, I use it to my advantage. Along with scaling in and out – I only trade the EUR/USD pair, but I might place thousands of trades per month, so I need to keep an eye on costs and the euro is the cheapest to trade. It's like I went down a big funnel over the years, and now I'm trading just one little thing every day for a couple of hours and that's it.

Q: What kind of patterns are you trading?

Jean-Francois: I do ranges all on the one-minute chart. It starts from the higher time frame, so I start by looking at the daily chart, but since I'm only trading for two hours, all of the work is done on the one-minute chart in the end.

Q: You have very tight targets. Tell me why that is and how you use them?

Jean-Francois: I use a long-tail stop, meaning a stop loss bigger than the average wick on a daily chart. If I'm wrong on the direction, I should still be able to survive, because a wick is a rejection. Therefore, it should be coming back. On the flipside, I ask for the smallest standard deviation that the market is willing to give me as a target. It's sort of a range, within a range, within a range. A one-minute bar at the right time of day is about three pips. If I start trading earlier in the day, it's sometimes less than three pips. And if I stay later than my two-hour window, it's also less than three pips. So I choose the right time of day to trade, which I've practiced over time.

For me, this is 8–10 a.m. in my time zone every single weekday. At that time I will experience bars that are sufficient to hit my targets easily. Because I only trade one instrument, the EUR/USD, I spent time studying it. I understand how it behaves around news, during slow times, fast times, the good and the bad. I do my best to show up on time every day. It's as if I'm driving my way to work. If something happens to my commute, I'll find a way to get to work on schedule. I can't afford to be late for work, because that's when my three-pip target is most effective.

Q: So I imagine you're not letting these trades run during trends?

Jean-Francois: Remember you've been told to not pick tops and bottoms? I do exactly the opposite, but not on purpose. I just happen to be there when the market top or bottom is forming in the range. Everything I'm doing is the opposite to a trend trader.

Q: What risk-to-reward ratio does that provide you?

Jean-Francois: My average risk-to-reward ratio can be 4 : 1 backwards on average. So I'm overall risking 4× more than what I make per trade. Once in a while, I'll take a swing trade with the same 36-pip stop loss as all my other trades and I'll set a 36-pip target on that, but only for swing trades. Everybody tries one to two times their risk as a target. Very few people will get it long term. I'm at 4 : 1 reverse.

Q: A lot of people would be scared to have that kind of risk-to-reward ratio. Why doesn't that bother you?

Jean-Francois: Because I control the environment. That 36 pip is a lot of space; I'm allowed to do whatever I need inside that space to get the job done. And therefore I'm not placing one trade and expecting one outcome. I'm placing the same amount of risk in percentage, but it's spread out within that space. In the end, it's the outcome of the averaging that pays me. Typical swing trading, when somebody is looking for a positive reward-to-risk ratio, they're usually looking in one direction. They think "It has to go from here to there." I don't really care about the direction. That's my second or third priority, because I could be wrong on the direction and still make my three pips, or come out with little to no loss.

I can reach my target many, many times before the market decides on a direction. I know where the floor and ceiling are in the market and by defining that risk, I feel free to do what I need to do. It's an averaging game. It's not one trade, one outcome. That was a huge revelation to me. The ability to open a second trade to change the outcome of the first. By adding two trades together, you're in control of the outcome. By adding a third trade, you're even more in control of the outcome. Now you've got three open, what if you remove the first one? You're still controlling the outcome by booking losses. I engineer breakeven. That's what I do all day long.

Q: So you're saying the new trade gives you a different entry price?

Jean-Francois: Yes, it changes the average price and therefore changes the exit. If the market moves 20 pips between the first and second entry, the average of the two is at 10. The market only needs to go back 10 pips for you to make money. It doesn't need to go back 20 pips. I'm giving you all the secrets here.

Q: Isn't that really close to adding risk to a losing trade?

Jean-Francois: So that's the different definition between drawdown and a loss. When you're told to not add to a loser, it's because that first trade is already closed, it's a loss. And they don't want you to repeat the same trade. My trades are still open and it's a fraction of the percentage of my risk. And I since have not gone over my maximum risk of 1% yet. I'm just putting 1/10, 2/10, or 3/10 of my risk in the market. Eventually, I've built my trade to 1% of my account and now the average move in my favor can pay me out.

Q: Do you pay any attention to news events or news releases?

Jean-Francois: If you're trying to trade the way I do, collecting three pips, three pips, three pips, then you must avoid the news. You can trade the reaction, though. You watch the news come out, wait two or three minutes, and then trade the outcome. It's a lot safer this way. I've been burned before by trying to pretend I knew what the news would do. Now I better just wait it out. I let the facts tell me what to do.

Q: Are you using any automations for your trading?

Jean-Francois: No, but I did a few years ago. I wanted to back-test a strategy and doing it automatically was quicker. But now I do all of the forward testing manually. When I was trading with the robots, I was operating the same robot across 17 or 18 different pairs. I ended up being a manager of those robots. So every day I was rebalancing 18 machines. I'm a better trade manager. I don't like managing employees or machines.

Q: How many trades do you typically have open at a given time?

Jean-Francois: Sometimes it's 40–50. Other times it's less. Today I only had 17 trades open. Ideally, I want less than 20. It all depends on the amount of money I'm trading with. And if it's a demo, just for show, I'll max it out. But if it's my money or grandma's money or somebody else's money, it's four trades per box and everything is military; it's a different set of rules. The trick is to learn how to lose. And for me, I had to blow the limits. I had to touch the stove to realize that it was hot. I happened to touch the stove with my first few trades 20 years ago.

Q: How long do you keep these trades open on average?

Jean-Francois: About three to five minutes. Some trades will be on for two hours, but that's rare. Those are the shoulders on the bell curve. The top of the bell curve is about three to four minutes per trade. So they're very short-lived trades. The target is one bar on the one-minute chart, three pips. So if I don't get the entry right or the bars are smaller than normal, I might end up waiting for a couple of bars to make my money.

Q: Can you walk me through your typical trading day?

Jean-Francois: Sure. I live in the Canadian Rocky Mountains, so I get up at 5 a.m. That's seven o'clock in New York. I go downstairs, have my breakfast, then a quick shower. By the time I get back to my computer, it's about 5:30 a.m. or so. The first thing I'll look at is what happened to the US dollar overnight. I'm typically looking at oil and bonds. The next thing I'll look at is the calendar, to see what news came out overnight and what I'm going to be faced with today. I usually look at the calendar on the weekends, so I already have an idea of what's coming up during the week. But every morning I just want to double-check. It's like looking at the traffic before crossing the street.

By six o'clock, I usually have one or two swing trades open, because I intend to be here at my computer at least until 10 a.m. I'm using that time to allow for swing trades to play out. The average session is less than two hours. In those two hours, I aim to make about a quarter to a half a percent. We're not trying to blow the barns off the door, or blow the doors off the barn. We're just trying to be consistent every single day. The idea is, slow is smooth and smooth is fast. So if I can get a quarter to a half percent per day, I'm doing great. By lunchtime New York, I'm usually done with trading and I spend the rest of my afternoon coaching people.

Q: What do you consider to be your best and worst trade so far?

Jean-Francois: Probably the IPO, the best trade where I wasn't even intending to trade. I was just there at the right time at the right place, just in time for the internet bubble. The industry that I was in was manufacturing the backbone for the internet, so I took part in an IPO that helped build the internet. That was exciting. My worst trade was probably when I blew everything up on Amazon put options.

Q: Tell me a bit more about your money management methods these days. Do you tend to scale in, scale out? Do you have floating targets?

Jean-Francois: I always use my long-tail stop. It's a standard 36-pip stop on every trade I've taken since I don't know how long. I just don't bother changing the stop because I've learned to lose within that space or the platform will eject me at the stop. So ideally I want to bring back the airplane. I don't want to be ejected from the airplane. So it's up to me to engineer a way back. And the stop loss never moves. The target never moves. I'm aiming for consistency.

It's either a three-pip target or it's a swing trade that has a three-box target. So money management, 99% flat. If I'm in trouble with that 1% trade, I'm allowing myself another 3% to fix the first 1%. And by fix, I'm talking about averaging, using drawdown to my advantage. And that's the difference between adding to a loss versus building a position that will eventually play out.

Q: Do you have any favorite tools or resources for traders?

Jean-Francois: For the newer traders, definitely an adequate calendar like Trading Economics. Even without an economics background, you can keep drilling within the calendar research and find out what's happening. Finviz is another resource. A substitute for Finviz that I've discovered recently is Koyfin. It helps me look at the bigger picture. We all need to be aware of what the bonds, yields, and the overall macro environment is doing. If you can't afford a Reuters terminal, then Koyfin is a free alternative. If you're into forex trading, http://Mataf.net is a really good website to use for a little bit of research.

Q: Tell me a bit more about why you picked the prop firms you traded with. Any reason why you picked those particular firms?

Jean-Francois: The Apiary Fund is the first one I ran into. After that, I tried multiple different ones, depending on the rules that they had and the offers that they had at the time. I'm usually focusing more on the drawdown rather than the profit split, since I want to be able to survive for months and years, not just the challenge. The firm I'm working with now has a scaling program in place to take you up to $3 million. And if you can trade up to $3 million for a couple of years, then they can open the door to more funding. And so it does depend on the track record. And to get that higher funding, you need experience. It's not going to be a 15-day challenge.

Q: What advice would you give to traders who want to get funded, and trade for a prop firm?

Jean-Francois: Focus on learning how to lose before you focus on chasing the money. Learn to manage drawdowns and your capital to avoid tremendous losses. With one trade, you can aim for one outcome. Two trades, it's an average outcome. So you control the average, and can create the environment that will allow you to exit. Don't let the stop loss do the dirty work. Learn to lose. The prop firm business serves its purpose. It has a place in the industry, but you have to learn how to lose.

Otherwise you're just paying to lose more. Like if you're renting $100,000, you're a $100,000 loser if you don't know what you're doing. And by the way, you're not trading $100,000. You're trading the drawdown limit. So they give you $100 K of imaginary money, but you're only allowed to lose $10,000, so you're actually trading $10,000. People don't see the forest for the trees.

Q: What do you think traders do wrong when trying to get funded?

Jean-Francois: I think they're chasing the money instead of managing the drawdown. A lot of the guys don't really have a goal for getting prop firm capital. If you're trying to earn a salary, you can rent $100,000 and save your own $100,000 from loss. That's an insurance policy and it's cheap. But it only works if you have the skills to churn the account and make an income. If you're missing the skills, you're out of your league. Don't even go there. Stay in your demo until you can become consistent. You have to prove to yourself that you can do it, before you start forking cash. In my case, prop firms are like an insurance policy. Instead of risking my $1 million, I take theirs and put theirs on the line.

Q: What do you think are the skills traders need to have in order to become successful?

Jean-Francois: Perseverance is probably number one. Then, the ability to learn and the willingness to change. We should never be afraid of change. Most people are stuck in a rut and they're afraid to change. Look to the future. Don't worry about the past. It's the stuff we've always been told, but kind of neglect, because society tells us it's a joke. Society tells you that if you have an $80,000 salary, then you have to make your life work with that salary. So you plan your life around this salary because society tells you to. No one is pushing you to make more or learn more. Yet that's what you need to do if you want that salary to go up. You don't need to limit yourself to what society says is right.

Q: What would you tell traders who have tried, but can't make it work profitably quite yet?

Jean-Francois: Get rid of all the garbage on the screen and look at the average true range. That should give you more than enough information, because it doesn't matter what time frame you're looking at. If price bounces off of support or resistance and you target one bar, you can probably win nearly every time. The probabilities go drastically up very, very quickly. If you bring the target as low as it can go, on any time frame, the easiest target is one bar of profit. So if I'm on the daily chart and I'm bouncing off support, there's a high probability the bounce will pay me one day. Same thing if I'm on the hourly chart and I'm bouncing off an hourly support. There's a high probability that it will bounce an hourly candle. That average true range is very significant. There's no need for anything else. Bollinger Bands are the next best thing. It's a good substitute for the little box that I use or vice versa. My little box is a good substitute for the Bollinger Bands.

Q: How would you use Bollinger Bands specifically?

Jean-Francois: The way my boxes work, it's one-half of the bands. So if I put two boxes on top of each other, it's going from band to band. It's crossing the Bollinger Bands. I'm really trying to make three pips in one half the distance between two bands. It's about understanding which half you are in. If you're in the upper half, there's a good chance it's going to keep going up. That's the probability. And a lot of people don't see it as a probability. They see it as a binary. They don't understand that you could do everything right and still not get the results you're looking for.

So yes, in the beginning with my engineering background, that was probably the biggest problem I had. I was focusing on perfection. Everything needed to be perfect. I needed the right setup, the right trigger, and everything had to be just right. Otherwise the trade would fail, but it failed anyways. So fast-forward to 20 years later, I'm okay clicking my mouse if there's a probability of 70%. It doesn't need to be perfect anymore. The tools in my toolbox don't change. I'm just better at fixing problems. Twenty years ago, I thought the stop loss was the solution. Now I engineer the solution by managing my trades.

JEAN-FRANCOIS'S TRADING TIPS

1. **A reverse reward-to-risk ratio can be very profitable.**

Contrary to most traders, Jean-Francois targets a small move with a larger stop loss. That means his win rate is extremely high and he occasionally incurs larger losses. That style of trading fits his personality.

2. **Prop firm capital is like an insurance policy for the good trader.**

You don't need to risk your own capital and can scale up more easily. But the first step should be building the skills before paying for capital.

3. **Be specific.**

Jean Francois trades one instrument in a very specific way. He always uses the same stop loss and similar targets. That consistency gives him an edge.

4. **Losing money isn't the end.**

Jean-Francois lost a lot of money trading in 2005–2007. Those kinds of experiences can hurt a trader or make them quit. Instead, Jean-Francois educated himself and found out what he was doing wrong. He turned it around and became the successful trader he is today.

5. **Use the average true range.**

It's easier to place a target when you know what the average range looks like. Jean-Francois targets the average one-minute bar on his scalping trades because it's the logical thing to do and it gets him out of trades quickly.

CHAPTER 12

Austin Silver

Austin Silver is a full-time trader and the founder of ASFX. He failed over 15 challenges before achieving success and now has over six figures in payouts across multiple prop firms. Austin's trading journey began in college, where he was known as the kid who day traded while looking at charts in class.

Austin initially entered the financial services industry by selling life and health insurance. He then transitioned to selling investments, including stocks, bonds, mutual funds, and exchange-traded funds (ETFs). It was during his preparation for the Series 7 exam that he discovered the allure of day trading and the promise of time freedom.

Austin dropped out of business school, much to his parents' disappointment. Without their support, he sought mentors online to guide his trading career. He began working for a prop firm in New York City, later traded contracts for difference (CFDs), and now focuses on futures trading using volume-weighted average price (VWAP). Austin emphasizes simplicity in his trading approach, believing that simple strategies are repeatable. By focusing on the E-mini S&P 500 (ES) futures, he gains a deep understanding of the market, making trading more intuitive and manageable.

What sets Austin apart from other traders is his entrepreneurial mindset. He views trading and the prop firm model as a business. Unafraid of failure, Austin has achieved significant payouts across multiple prop firms. He attributes his success to being adaptable, open-minded, hardworking, and relentless in his pursuit of excellence.

These qualities have enabled Austin to trade profitably and maintain a rewarding lifestyle.

Q: Austin, where did you grow up and what did you do before trading?

Austin: I grew up in New Jersey, right outside of Philadelphia. I got started in the financial services industry, selling life and health insurance initially. Then I started my transition into selling investments, stocks, bonds, mutual funds, and ETFs. As I was studying for my Series 7 exam, that's where I discovered day trading. I really liked the financial services career path I was on, mostly because it had time freedom. You had income potential and residuals that would pay you long term. I knew a lot of older guys who were not working that much in the business and still made good money. So it checked a lot of boxes, but day trading just really appealed even more to me. The upside there just seemed so much greater on top of the time freedom. And also, to be honest, I'm not the best guy when it comes to compliance with authority.

So when these big firms that I was working for, MassMutual and Northwestern Mutual, wanted me to run all of my social media posts through compliance and get them approved, it was not the way I wanted to operate. I was an entrepreneur. Before the insurance and investment stuff, I was actually working as a DJ in the private event space, doing weddings, bar/bat mitzvahs, birthday parties, quinceañeras. So I've always been an outspoken kind of guy. I can do sales and talk to people. That part of it was very natural for me, but learning all about day trading really did not start until I studied for the Series 7. They ended up making me wait four months between when I started studying for the exam and when I could actually take the test. So over those four months, all I did was look up day trading and I caught the bug. I started following Tim Sykes, Cameron Fous, and all these other people online, and that's where I got hooked.

Q: How many years have you been trading for at this point?

Austin: I took my first trade in 2015 with binary options, so not very legitimate at all. I was 20 years old at the time. I'll be in my tenth year of trading in a few months.

Q: Did you get any college education?

Austin: I dropped out of college. I was originally in a business school and at the time, I was still working as a DJ for parties on the weekend. I was making good money running a small business and had people calling me for new events constantly. But while

I was at school, I wanted to take classes like Finance 101 and all these exciting, money-related topics that interested me. But in order to take those classes, you had to take accounting and I did not pass that one. I wasn't bad at school, but I was really not good at accounting. I tried to take it several times, in person and online, because I had to pass this class in order to move on and take more classes in business school. I never cared about it enough to figure it out.

So once I realized that I couldn't pass accounting without giving it a ton of extra effort, I switched my major. I spent the last year and a half while I was still in school studying communications, which was just a waste of time. You're learning things like communication theory and all this stuff that really doesn't matter. It didn't make me a better communicator. I was already good at public speaking. I was already good at sales and talking to people. So it was kind of a joke. And that's why I dropped out of business school. The communication major wasn't worth it. I was already making money and doing this stuff with the investment industry. So I realized school's just not for me.

Q: What was your start in binary options like?

Austin: That was very short-lived because I realized it was just like gambling. Any money I made in binary options went out the window on the next trade. Then I transitioned into forex and I spent the first five years of my trading journey on forex. That's all I traded because it was a low barrier to entry. There are plenty of brokers to trade with so it was very easy to start trading.

Q: Did anyone introduce you to trading or did you start all by yourself?

Austin: All I had was me and my dad. My dad was an attorney with a large investment portfolio. He believed in investing, but not in day trading. He did not like picking individual stocks. He was never into active trading like I was. When I was in college, nobody there traded. I was the one who really led the charge. The school was called Rowan University and if you ask anybody, they all would say they knew me as the kid who was day trading. They'd see me in class looking at charts. They saw me on Snapchat. And that's how I started my brand. All I was doing was posting about it on social media. And that's what attracted people to me.

So I started with no one around, but ended up being kind of the mentor to everyone else, because nobody knew about it. Going back almost 10 years, nobody in the US was really trading forex, especially at that young of an age. Day trading did not gain popularity like it has now. I really think 2020 accelerated it. So I didn't have any mentors. I didn't have anybody to trade with other than my dad, who was sitting next to me, just kind of giving his side commentary. And other than that, it was all the online mentors: Tim Sykes, Cameron Fous, even Gary Vee. I followed Gary Vaynerchuk's content about building a personal brand. He was a huge influence on me because when I left school, nobody supported me. My dad was pissed. He didn't want to talk to me for a long time because I dropped out. So I had no mentors in person. I had to turn to the internet to find my mentors and the positive motivation I needed.

Q: What kind of techniques did you use when you first started trading forex?

Austin: The first thing I did was join iMarketsLive (IML), which was a terrible place to start. They would run a London session live trading room from Las Vegas. So he'd be up at like 1 a.m. trading the London session, chugging coffee and just calling out random trades with Gartley patterns and bat patterns and all these different patterns. I was there live, trying to follow the trades and see if I could make some money. So at first I had no strategy, no structure. What ended up happening is that I bought every video course out there about trading. I mean, literally anything I could find. I ended up buying a video course twice. The same course – I paid for it twice! Once I bought it for $250 from these guys in France who were running a free Discord or Telegram chat. I bought it because I saw their results and I didn't watch it because all these guys in the group chat were speaking French and I was like, "All right, there's $250 thrown away."

A couple of months go by and I find this other guy on YouTube who sells me the same course for $250. It was a technical analysis course, just talking about moving averages, price action, structure, things like that. So two people, two different groups that do not associate with each other, don't even know each other, are both selling me the same course that they stole from somebody else. That made me think it could be valuable.

If two different groups of people are trying this, this is where I should maybe commit. So now I finally decided to watch the videos that I had purchased twice. It taught me the basics of technical analysis beyond what I learned with Tim Sykes and Cameron Fous, which was a lot of price action. What the more recent videos that I'm mentioning talked about were EMAs [exponential moving averages]. I used to have a Traders Dynamic Index, which is an RSI [relative strength index] with some moving averages, on my chart. That taught me a lot about those indicators.

During that time, I was reading Mike Belafiore's book, *One Good Trade*. It kind of all came together. This was a pivotal moment for me. I got these two video courses. I ignored it the first time. Now I'm finally watching it and I'm reading Mike's book that talks about finding one strategy that gives you an edge. And all of that came together and I built my first strategy. I back-tested it, did hundreds of chart markups, and even ended up automating the back-testing as well.

Q: What kind of money management did you have at the beginning?

Austin: I was the worst at managing risk, because I had no guidance. The first couple of accounts I funded were with this unregulated broker who would offer 1 : 3,000 leverage if you wanted it. But I was conservative. I would only use 1 : 1,000 leverage because I thought that's what I needed. I would put in $100. I would deposit, blow it, deposit, blow it: $100, $75, $100, and so on. All my deposits would get wiped out so there was no risk management, no trade management.

And it's funny how nowadays the guys in my group compliment me because I can take a trade that someone else will lose money on, but I can still make it profitable. For example, yesterday, I took a position, ended up in drawdown. A lot of people would bail out. I stuck in and made money on the trade. So now I see how important trade management is.

At the beginning, risk management and trade management didn't exist for me. I had no guidance there. I think that's what's taken me the longest to learn. That is what traders should focus on. Entry signals should be very simple because that's just your entry into the market. There are so many different ways to make money in trading: investing, swing trading, automated trading – all these different trading strategies and indicators you can use. But nobody really teaches how to manage a trade well, because that's very hard to teach. It's something that is taught really through experience over time. As you get burned enough, you start to see what you need to do differently. You feel that pain, that's what teaches you. I had very poor risk management, very poor trade management, and it's taken years to develop it. It's very difficult.

Q: Did you ever trade in demo mode instead of risking your own capital in the beginning?

Austin: I was definitely in demo mode. I've gone back to demo many times. I got sick about two or three years into trading. I was still in college, working on the weekends as a DJ. I got really sick and I was out of commission for two weeks. That really showed me that there's periods of time where you need to go back to demo. All I did while I was sick was lose money. The money I had made that previous few months, I lost it all while I was sick. So I learned that there were periods, not only when you shouldn't trade, but when you should reconsider and go back to demo. Now I haven't traded a demo account in years, but at the beginning I did.

I do understand the people who say demo is not worth your time. It doesn't induce market emotions. It's not real; I get that. But at the same time, if you have never clicked a button before, and have never placed a trade on your platform, I would recommend taking a day to trade demo. You're going to make some beginner mistakes. You're going to put on 80 lots when you meant to put on 8 lots. You're going to buy when you meant to sell. So I think in that sense, demo can be useful, but beyond that, I didn't stay in demo very long, because you have to get skin in the game.

Q: How long did it take you to get profitable from the time you started trading?

Austin: It took me two years to have my first six months of consistent gains. Year two to year two and a half was my first six months of actually seeing and feeling the progress. Now I'm not being exactly accurate, but about two years of losing money before I got six months of consistency. And since then, I've been able to extend that into years of consistency, where I've had three green years in a row over the last three years. I think the initial drawdowns and losses are part of the game. Everybody's going to lose money. I have found very few people come in and just smash it, so you want to limit those losses in the early period. I did a pretty decent job at that. It took me two years, but I didn't go broke. I was still paying rent. I was still eating out. I still had a life. I wasn't putting every free dollar I had into trading, hoping to make it.

Q: What changed from these two years of losing money to the next six months when you got consistency?

Austin: I stopped moving my stop losses when trades worked against me. I was taking too big of losses because I didn't like to lose. So I had to learn to sit and wait. I've done a lot of self-work. You name it, I've done it. I've done my yoga teacher certification, meditation training, psychedelic mushrooms, and so on. I've done a lot for myself, trying to understand why I think the way I think. Why is my ego so big in some ways? And I've tried to humble that ego through books, exercises, and all these things. When you're moving your stop loss because you just don't want to lose, you're doing quite literally the 180° opposite of what you should do as a trader. You should be getting out of that trade as quickly as possible. So if you look at my trading when I was struggling the first two years, compared to those next six months, I just stopped taking big losses. There wasn't anything more I did to add to wins.

I was already finding wins, but by minimizing the losses, it made the wins feel bigger. It made the wins actually make me profitable. It was the losses that were chopping into my P&L [profit and loss]. I didn't need another strategy. The problem is usually the trader. When I hear traders in a similar situation today, who have been losing money for two years or more, I try to show them that if you don't do something different, nothing's gonna change. So back then I had to ask myself, "What do I know that I'm doing wrong?" Never in any of these books does it ever say, "When you're losing, move your stop loss, give it more space, take on more." No, it's the opposite. That was the big fix for me. I'm not an overly risky guy. I don't go all in on one trade. It's not my personality. My personality is that I don't like to be wrong. I don't like to lose. And once you swallow that pill, trading gets a lot easier.

Q: What have you achieved so far in terms of funding with prop firms?

Austin: I've had over six figures in payouts across a couple of prop firms just last year. That was my biggest year of trading ever. I had not made that much money previously and I think it's because of the opportunity that those prop firms give us. I'm a big believer in using other people's money when you're talking about real estate, and even now trading, using someone else's capital to scale. That is how in many industries in the past, not just real estate and trading, people became wealthy. It was one of the driving factors for me to get more funding. Because I saw my friends getting paid out six figures a year from prop firms while I was on the sideline trading my own money. Once I did get funded, it made things a lot easier for me. If you give me $500,000 to trade with, I don't need to risk 1% per trade. I can risk less now and make more money. So that all kind of clicked. And I would say that's why I had a good year last year.

Q: What do you think is required to succeed as a funded trader?

Austin: I would say the success there comes from not being afraid to fail. I failed over 15 challenges in order to get paid out. I knew I was stepping on the gas properly and that led to payouts on the ones that I passed. But if I was afraid to fail some of the evaluations I've taken, things would have been a lot tougher. Also, I am using a trade copier where I can trade on a $100 K account and copy to three $200 K accounts so I don't have to look at all of that money. That helps because I know myself. If I'm up eight grand, I'm going to close that trade and take the profit. Eight grand is good money in one trade to me. But is that really proper trading? No, not always. So I kind of keep myself within my frame of reference and copy to the other accounts.

Q: How much capital are you currently funded with?

Austin: I have multiple accounts with Topstep that I'm currently trading. Here in the United States, as of last week, we can't trade on MetaQuotes anymore. So all the CFD trading is on pause.

It seems like they're facing pressure from the CFTC [Commodity Futures Trading Commission] or the SEC [Securities and Exchange Commission], whatever regulatory agency wants to crack the whip. There's something going on behind the scenes. And that's why I've made this switch to futures because futures are regulated through the CME [Chicago Mercantile Exchange]. It's been around for a long time. And the biggest traders that I know also trade futures. So futures is probably what you'll hear more about me trading in the next couple of months to years.

Q: You went through a pretty rough phase of losing capital recently and it wasn't totally your fault. What exactly happened?

I had $300 K with MyForexFunds, which is the account that paid me the most. I was trading SPX and Bitcoin. A little bit of Nasdaq, but it just didn't interest me as much. And then as I'm funded, I have a couple of guys in our mentorship group chat who are passing challenges with MyForexFunds. That prop firm became very popular. I had one guy named Tyler in our group who had three or four resets on the account where he wouldn't hit the goal and he would hit the maximum time frame and then he had to reset. Right as he passed his challenge with MyForexFunds, they get pulled out of business. Then a couple of weeks later, now that the $300 K was gone, I had $100 K with My Funded FX. I lost that account after a payout just due to trading and taking losses with 1% risk per trade.

So two of the funded accounts I had got pulled out from me with MyForexFunds. That was not by my own doing. The other one with My Funded FX, I lost that account just from trading aggressively. So most of the time in the last couple of weeks with all this turmoil, I would say the problem has come from external, not internal. And that's why all of this is changing right now. I know guys who were in the United States, getting paid out over $10,000 every couple of weeks with FTMO [Filip, Tomáš, Marek, Otakar]. Those accounts are gone for them now. So it's a really shitty spot for some of the traders who were doing really well. And at the same time, I've talked to a guy named Mark, who is up $22 K this month on a payout trading futures. So you just have to pivot. I think that's the big thing. In trading in general, if I were not adaptable, I would not be where I am today. I wouldn't have lasted this long.

You have to adapt in the sense of strategy, the broker you use, and the prop firm you're working with. You can't be closed-minded. I'm not married to these accounts. If I lose a $100 K account, I can buy another one and pass. I've already passed enough of them that I have confidence. It's like Roger Bannister, who was the first person to run the four-minute mile. He blew everybody away. Everybody thought there's no way you can run a mile in four minutes. As soon as he did it, what happened in the next year? About 10 people did it. A bunch of other people did it. So once you pass that first challenge, then you start to see that this isn't that big of a deal. You can get over this hurdle. You've already done it once and you can do it again.

Q: How did you transition to trading full-time?

Austin: Before 2019, I worked for T3 Trading, which is a prop firm in New York City. They used to run an entire floor and then everybody went virtual. So working at T3 is when I became a full-time trader, because while working for them, I was making money for my trading, they were paying me to run a live trading room and that's when I stopped DJing. This was about 2017. I stopped all my other streams of income and I realized that now I'm gonna commit to making my money from trading, but also other streams of revenue from trading. Like now with ASFX. I make money through my own trading, through my payouts, but I also offer mentorship and some courses. So I have a bunch of different revenue streams now.

I also have four employees that we pay full time. So it's now become a bigger business where I am a full-time trader, but I am also an entrepreneur. If you look at my calendar, I am trading, but I'm also on calls for either podcasts or coaching calls or sales calls all day. I know everybody wants to be a full-time trader, but I think we should just call ourselves entrepreneurs. In reality, full-time trading can suck. I've had years where I've lost money. Why would you want to be a full-time trader and have one stream of income in a year you're gonna lose money? You have to be diversified. Some people want to try to do full-time trading and not have other streams of revenue. That's fine. I don't want to do that because I want to make sure that I'm making excess money.

I want to put more money into my long-term investment portfolio, into the US stock market, because I'm very bullish on America and I believe my family will thank me that I've been investing and making extra money, not just relying on that one income stream. So 2017 is when I really became a full-time trader because I was working for T3 running that live room from 6 to 11 a.m. five days a week. And I was doing a live stream at 3 p.m. doing a daily recap. So basically six hours a day on camera. It was a lot.

Q: Tell me more about your trading style these days.

Austin: I'm a price action trader. I have always been, but now more than ever. No fancy indicators. One of the only indicators I use is the VWAP, a volume-weighted average price. I'm a big fan of Brian Shannon. He is an amazing trader who has been very successful for almost as long as I've been alive. I use his VWAP, which is a simple break of a 21 EMA with a couple of certain parameters met. So it's a price action strategy, but I'm using the VWAP to guide my bias. And because I'm trading US markets, where do US markets typically go? Up. So if they typically go up, I'm a long bias trader for the most part, until we have extreme macro pressure to the downside, until the trend changes to the downside, specifically until we take out the previous day's low.

Because I'm a day trader, I'm looking to be in and out within a few minutes, maybe a few hours. If we're not under the previous day's low, I'm going to be a buyer on ES futures. Like yesterday, I had six trades on ES, just small little scalps long. That's all I'm looking to do. I'm not trying to catch the big move of the day. I'm looking to come in, make my nut – usually it's 5–15 points – and that's it. Because I'm usually rocking at about a 7–10 point stop loss. I'm not scouring a bunch of assets for trades either. I rock with what I like to trade, which is US markets. Since I like to follow the news, too, I know what's going on with US markets. I live here, I'm breathing it, so I feel the sentiment.

Q: Do you pay attention to news events for your trades or this is only out of interest?

Austin: I pay attention to the news for trades only in the sense of, for example, today in 30 minutes, we have the Core PCE [Personal Consumption Expenditure] price index. The Core PCE price index right now is important, because the Fed has told us they're using that and the CPI [Consumer Price Index] to see what inflation is doing. Inflation is the hot topic right now. The only other thing that's hot is interest rates. Interest rates and inflation is what is driving the market. Job numbers aren't really changing the market that much like they used to. NFP [nonfarm payroll] isn't moving the market like it used to. It's these CPI inflation-based events. So I want to know what those numbers are, but I don't make trading decisions based on them. I won't place a trade because of something happening. I will trade after the news. If it wants to pop and I can catch 5 points after it pops 15 and I can catch a little fade after it, great! That's where I'm making my money.

Q: Do you only follow one instrument or do you have more than one in your watchlist?

Austin: I follow the whole market. I know where gold is. I know what oil is doing, but I only really look at it. I'll wake up and I'll scan the market to make sure nothing crazy happened overnight. I check the news, but right now I'm a simple trader. And I think that's what some of my mentors have taught me: simple is repeatable. I don't want to overcomplicate the process. I can wake up, study the ES futures, and I know what's going on. And when you are in tune with the asset like that, it gets a lot easier to trade. That's why I'm not trading a lot of instruments.

Q: How many hours a day do you typically trade?

Austin: Two, maybe three. Usually 8–11 a.m. If I get back in the afternoon and I don't have anything going on, I will look to trade. But I found that traders have a certain mental capacity, which I can actually see when tracking my trades. Once you sit there for so long, your decision-making ability goes down. So you have to give yourself breaks. You have to step away. I don't think that when I started trading, I would have had the capacity to trade as much as I do now. I wouldn't have the discipline that I currently have. I'm always at the gym at 12 o'clock almost every single day. That's my reset to then come back in the afternoon with a new mental capacity. I think sometimes traders sit at the desk too long and they just cost themselves money.

Q: How many trades do you tend to take on a typical day?

Austin: Sometimes I'll put feeler positions in, so maybe two or three feeler positions at small size. I would call that one trade. Usually, two trades a day. Some days it's three, but usually one to two trades a day. That's all. And I have days where I'm flat, too, meaning I stay in cash. Typically those are Mondays or Fridays, because I like to take off and be with my family those days. Because I think you can make enough money in two or three days a week. I don't think anyone gets into this business to just sit at a desk all day and slug it out. I'm not trying to do that.

I'm trying to do one or two trades in those two hours when I know I can make good decisions, and then I'm out. See you at the gym. Could I keep trading? Yes, totally, of course. But that doesn't mean I should. Take the win. If I make $1 K, great. Yesterday, I made $1,700. Great. Walk off. Call it a day. Then I know in the back of my head, if I'm trading a $100 K account and copying it over to other funded accounts, my returns are multiplied. It might only look like $1,000, but if I really open up all my accounts, I'm up more than that.

Q: How long do you typically hold these trades for? You say a few minutes to a few hours, but tell me more accurately what that looks like.

Austin: I have my trade journal pulled up right here. So my average winning hold time is 58 minutes. My average losing hold time is 34 minutes. See, I have the stats.

Q: Can you walk me through a typical trading day?

Austin: I wake up, I do naked meditation, cold plunge, I'm just kidding, I'm just kidding. Just making fun of all those guys who say they have these crazy morning routines.

I wake up, I have my double espresso. I maybe have two or three of those and by 7:00 to 8:00, I'm prepping for the day. I'm looking at futures volume now. I'm answering DMs [direct messages]. I'm kind of getting caught up on things that happened in the London session before I start trading 8–11 a.m. By 11 a.m., I stop trading. Usually I'm at the gym by 12 p.m. 12–1 p.m. is the workout; 1–2 p.m. I stay home. I hang out with my kid and my wife; 2–4 p.m. is usually podcasts, coaching calls, or meetings.

Four p.m. is when I try to be done with everything. That way I have from 4 to 6 p.m. to do whatever is needed to tighten up the day. Get instructions to my graphics team, talk to my video editor, plan out my trips. And then by 6 p.m. I'm toast. I want to go have dinner. I might do my daily report card for my trading at that point and then post that and then I'm done, checked out. No DMs, no Twitter, no Instagram. I'm just trying to be with my family at that point. So that's a typical day. I'm grateful that it changes every day. I don't like having the same monotonous routine. Other people are stuck in a cubicle all day and that sucks. So I try to take advantage as much as I can. I don't wake up with an alarm clock and I'm grateful for that, too.

Q: How do you manage trading, running a business, and family at the same time?

Austin: Because I have no option. That's the answer. I want to help my wife and son and give them time and I want to grow my business. So they're all things I want or have to do and as a man, you know, you're gonna do things in life that sometimes you don't want to do and you just have to do it. So I try to find balance. Balance is that sometimes you're getting all of me, sometimes you're getting none of me. And it's up to me to try to do proper scheduling, time blocking the calendar, and thinking ahead. That is how I balance everything. But it is stressful. And anyone that acts like it's not is a liar. So you have to work out, you have to get outside. I'm grateful to live somewhere that's sunny, where I can just go sit on my balcony and soak up the sun for a few minutes every day and just reset.

You have to find those little things to make it less stressful. But life is not meant to be easy. I've had moments in my life where it has been easy to balance my business and my relationship, because I had no kid, my dad was still alive, and business was flourishing; everything was great. And I would sit in those moments two years ago, and I'd be like, things are so peaceful. Me and my wife would go to the beach, we had a boat, we were chilling, like it was just super-easy. And I knew it would get harder. Life will hand you different seasons and you just have to be forward looking to be prepared for it. We all have the same amount of hours in a day. Who's going to use it properly or not? Some people will take two hours every night to watch Netflix. Some people will take that time to be with their family and so on. You choose how to spend your hours.

Q: What has been your best trade so far?

Austin: I would say that it was in June or July of 2022. Bitcoin had been up 15% or so in three days, so I knew there was that overnight volatility. I took a Bitcoin long position with a stop at the previous day's low and I held the position overnight. That position made me almost 12%, which was enough to not just pass the challenge, it surpassed the challenge. And I didn't do anything for it, really. I just analyzed, set and forget, and when I woke up the take profit was hit.

The lesson I got from that big trade is that sometimes the best thing to do is trust the system and not micromanage the trade. But I would also add that it's being in the right instrument, knowing that it can move a lot in the Asian session. You have to know the macro climate that you're in to set yourself up for good trades like that. Otherwise you're just going to get lucky. So I was aware of the fact that Bitcoin had moved quickly in the previous two days. And when it's up 8%, it could go up even more in the next couple of days. So I know that Bitcoin expands like that. It's about knowing these things about what you're trading, not just guessing and hoping for volatility.

Q: What about your worst trade ever?

Austin: I remember it very well. So I had $80 K in a regulated broker with my own money. I took a $32,000 loss and it sucked, to put it mildly. I stopped trading for two weeks because I knew that loss should have never happened. I shouldn't even have been in the trade. It was the classic scenario of you're in a trade at a time of day that you don't need to be trading. It's in the afternoon and I didn't want to be wrong so now I'm moving the stop loss, the same mistake I had made previously years in the past. It's that mistake that always tries to haunt me, because I don't want to be wrong. And of course, it happens when I'm using my own money, so it sucks even more. It's not like I was just going to lose a funded account with a firm and have to take a new challenge. This was my own money that I had already earned and paid taxes on. And now I'm going to just blow it. That was one of my worst trades ever.

Q: Do you remember what you were trading at that time and what trade you wanted to make?

Austin: It was a forex trade either on EUR/CAD or EUR/GBP. It was just stupid, just too heavy on the lots. And then, you know, these things will slide against you very quickly and that's what happened. I moved my stop loss backward. All of a sudden you had $8 K of risk and now you're down $13 K or $16 K and it doesn't stop? Turns out $20 K was the threshold of pain. At that point that was like a fourth of the entire account and I couldn't continue. So definitely not good.

Q: How did you get back on track from that loss?

Austin: I took two weeks off. I didn't look at a chart. I didn't talk to anybody about trading. I did a complete reset. It's one thing if you lose money and you don't know what you did wrong. I knew what I did wrong. I knew it could have been an $8,000 or

$7,000 loss. And instead it was almost triple. I think knowing that I did something intentionally wrong and I did it by my own hand, I had to step away. I had to reset and give myself the space to like trading again. What I've seen other people do is they'll make a mistake and then they kind of have a bad taste in their mouth. They keep trading and it doesn't go away. Well, I've learned through time that when you make those mistakes, you have to reset until you're excited to trade again.

I don't want to trade from a place of "I have to make this money back." That is not where I do well. Some people might. I don't. So I need to completely get away until I don't even feel that loss anymore to then come back and trade well without that weighing on me. If I try to come back, I'm just going to make the same mistake again or do something more stupid, like double the position size on the next trade because I don't want to be wrong twice. That's the kind of thinking I try to avoid. Some people will lose money; they'll sit at the desk and fight it back, they won't go out with their family over the weekend, they'll just stare at the trade, stare at the charts, because they think the mistake is in the chart. The mistake was you. So you need to reset, not the chart.

Q: What's your risk management these days?

Austin: I'm always using fixed stop losses. What I'm trading is very systematic, where I'm using previous structure or a quick little fib retracement as the stop loss. That's what I've back-tested for that strategy. I'm aiming to win 60–70% of the time, which I've been able to do using a 1R target. That's it. If I risk 10 points, I want to take profit at 10 points. But where I make money, and this is controversial I think, is taking profit early. For instance, if I'm risking $1,000 and now I'm up $700, in theory at that moment I am now risking $1,700 – the initial $1,000 plus the $700 I just made – so why would I not start taking profits when I'm only looking for another $300. This isn't going to make or break me, so I start to take off that gain. I'm trying to avoid the tilt and my worst self. So if I am up $700 and then I end up down and I take a loss or if I just end up at break even, I was up $700 and now I have zero or worse, I'm red.

That's what sends me off into tilt. So all of my great trade management is rooted in not going on tilt, doing things to put money in my pocket. I'm not talking about putting all of the money in my pocket. I'm not trying to catch all of the moves. I'm just trying to get some of it. I can get in and out all day with no problem. I can get back in anytime. It means I might not get the full 1R, but I'm making money. I'm not trying to make all of the money. I'm just trying to make money and finish the day green, because that prevents the tilt. If I stack up enough green days, I look like a genius at the end of the month, even though some of my gains are 0.2–0.8%, but over the month, I could be up 3 or 4%.

Q: Do you have any favorite trading tools or resources you recommend for traders?

Austin: Not anything out of the ordinary, to be honest. I like TradingView. That's my preferred charting platform. I really like Barchart, Financial Juice, and Forex Factory. Those are three free websites that I think have helped me a lot.

TradeZella would be what I recommend as a trading journal. That's where I do my daily report cards, my weekly report cards. I can pull up those stats right away from my trading over the last year. You need to have those stats. If you don't have those stats, you're avoiding accountability. That's what most new traders do, I did it. Most new traders run away from accountability. And if you don't, you will actually grow. It's one of the many oxymorons of trading. If you run from your own actions, you don't grow. If you lean into your own mistakes, you grow faster.

Q: How did you choose the prop firms that you are now funded with? Is there a process you go through to pick which prop firm to get into?

Austin: To be honest, the main thing I look at is if they've got proof of payout. I'm just about the bottom line at the end of the year. How much do I need to invest versus how much do I take home at the end of the year? If I can invest zero and take out $100 K after all the payouts are said and done over a year, it's a good year. I'm not married to think one of these firms is better. They're all offering the same rules. They're all using the same or similar brokers. They're all probably running the same tech on the back end. So I'm not concerned with the marketing. Give me the account, pay me out. If there's any drama, I see it. I'm following the right people on social media. I see the firms who are not paying people out and I don't go with them.

Q: You have a different approach to prop firms, where you're not trying to be right and keep all the accounts forever. You're not afraid to lose an account because you can always get it back. Tell me more about that mindset of what you pay versus what you get from the prop firm.

Austin: I think a lot of guys go into it very ego-based, thinking "I have to buy one challenge and pass it." Why? If I take five challenges, 500 bucks each, so in total $2,500. Chances are if I risk 1% per trade, I'll pass one of them, especially if I start them at different points. If I don't start them all on the same day, I'll pass one of them. All I have to do on the one I pass is make 2.5%. Not only do I break even, but if I do that and I get the 2.5% payout, I may even get a refund on that account sign-up fee, which is $500. Now I'm up $500. Just the bottom line. Yes, there's four failed funding challenges along that journey, but I'm up $500 while some guys are still negative. This goes back to my point about looking at yourself like an entrepreneur. Look at the bottom line, not day over day even, but month over month, quarter over quarter, through every year.

I run my coaching business the same way. If we're gonna spend x amount of dollars in advertising and marketing, how much are we going to make in return? We have to make sure we're profitable. In the interim, I can lose money, but at the end of the year, the end of the quarter, the end of the month, I wanna make sure I'm profitable. So that's the philosophy to these challenges. No ego about "I need to pass this first one." No, you need to not waste time. Too many people are wasting time trading small in a challenge. Stop, trade bigger. Don't be afraid to fail. If you don't fail a funding challenge, I don't believe you're trying hard enough. Who cares? Stop attaching your self-worth to one challenge, one trade, one funded account. Relax. It's not your own personal money. You already lost all the money you could lose when you hit submit and paid for it on your credit card.

You can't lose any more money. So why are you acting like it's your real $100 K? Because even there, if you paid $500 for a $100 K account, your max drawdown is usually 10%. So you paid $500 for $10,000 of buying power. That's it. So it's like, you can't lose the $10,000. It's fake money. So you should be trading it more aggressively. Some guys just get roped up. They think, "I'm a professional trader trading with these prop firms." The way I see it is these prop firms could go out of business anytime. Nothing lasts forever. So you have to be looking at it as "What is the resource that I am losing?" Well, if I already spent the $500 on that challenge and I paid for it, the only other thing I can lose going forward is time. That's it. If I take too long, I'm wasting time.

Too many traders want to pass their first challenge, make it cute, make themselves feel good. No offense, but your feelings don't pay the bills. Just make sure you make more money on funded accounts than what you spend on them. That's all that matters. Even if you fail all of them except one, but you make the money back and you get paid out $5 K, you're profitable.

Q: Tell me about your risk management, specifically for funded accounts. How do you pass a challenge and then keep the account?

Austin: I find most traders will pass the challenge with roughly 1% risk per trade. Some a little less, maybe 0.7%, maybe a little bit more on some trades. I don't see a lot of traders in the funded phase trading at 1% because it's very risky and they don't want to lose that funded account. So I would just cut the risk in half. That's the conservative sweet spot for me, where I'm not overly aggressive, but I can make enough money where I won't go on tilt and keep trading. That's my sweet spot. Some people will say, "How do I know that that's enough money?" Well, you just need to scale up the capital you trade with to make that half a percent be worth enough money to you. Stop trying to squeeze $1 K per day out of a $10,000 account. That's really tough. To make $1 K a day on $400 K is very easy.

It's just like business. Wouldn't you rather risk less and make more? The answer is yes. So how do you do that? You have to scale. You're gonna have to pass a couple of funding challenges. And, of course, it depends on where you live. I'm used to living a certain lifestyle. If you're in Puerto Rico, the Dominican Republic, or Thailand, you don't need a $500 K trading account to live a decent life. You could do it with $100 K probably. It just depends on your own personal needs. So you have to think "If I want to make roughly $1,000 a month from my trading, that's 1% of 100 K." Is 1% a month attainable? Absolutely. If I want to make $10,000 a month, $100 K probably isn't going to do it unless you're trading really aggressively, which can lead to failure. So then you'd want to have more capital to scale with. You probably need about $1 million in funding to do it conservatively.

Q: What is something that you learned along the way, which you would like to share with new traders?

Austin: The beautiful thing about trading is we all can learn from each other, either what to do or what not to do. There's so much to learn because there's so many different ways to solve this puzzle. I could be in the same long trade that you're in. I could make money, you could lose money. You could learn from my trade management. Or I could make money long this morning, you can make money short two hours later trading the same asset. Both of us can make money. What makes or breaks you is your own individual trade management. Position sizing matters a little bit, entries matter a little bit. All that really matters is realizing gains. How many traders will pop trades into profit, not realize gains and then close red, thinking the strategy is the problem.

Probably not. You're the problem. And when you accept that you're the problem, like I did, and you do the self-work from the meditation stuff I've done, the yoga stuff, books, then you start to see how you need to act to become the version you want to be. "How do I act as if that guy in the future will look back on me and say, good job?" That's how I'm always thinking. When I take a trade, I think to myself, "In an hour, will I be glad I'm in this position based on how this chart looks, based on what price is right now?" If I say yes, then I know I should be in that trade. There's a really good question traders should ask themselves before taking a trade. This only works if you're trading a system. If you're just guessing every day, you're not ready for my question.

But if you have a system, you should ask yourself, "Will I be more upset if I take this trade and I lose? Or will I be more upset with myself if I don't take it and it wins?" If I'm going to be more upset that I missed this winner if it wins and I'm willing to take this loss, I'm taking that trade. If I'm going to be more upset if I take it and I lose because I know it could be a loser, but it also could win, but that win won't bother me, I'll stay out of that trade.

Q: What do you think are the most important skills traders need to have in order to be successful in trading?

Austin: I heard this from a conversation with Nick Stewart recently and I liked his answer so I'll give him the credit. It's self-regulation. You need to know how you are feeling, when you are feeling it, and why. If you can't regulate yourself, you're always gonna end up on tilt. All the wins that you have will mean nothing when you tilt. So the goal should actually not be to win more; it should be to lose less. Study your losses. Figure out what you're doing wrong. Whether you're like me, you're moving a stop loss or maybe you're trading too big. Stop doing that. You don't have to add any wins and you'll make more money over the long term. So self-regulation and limiting your downside are the two most important characteristics for a trader. If you go into it like, "I'm gonna buy two Rolexes," that's the wrong mindset.

Go at it thinking, "I'm going to find wins because I'm trading a strategy that's back-tested. I'm going to trade a system that is proven to make money. I need to limit the downside." That's the proper approach.

AUSTIN'S TRADING TIPS

1. **Mentors are important.**

   Austin didn't know anyone who was trading back when he started. He put himself out there and connected with traders online. He slowly found mentors who helped him in his journey.

2. **Look at the bottom line.**

   Austin has a specific approach when it comes to funded accounts. He looks at what he spends versus what he earns, even if that means losing some accounts.

3. **Don't be afraid to lose.**

   Traders who jump into trades with a high ego usually feel more pressure, which can lead to difficulty accepting losses. Losses are part of the process.

4. **Know yourself.**

   Austin likes to take profits on moves that go in his favor, even before reaching his take profit. That makes him more disciplined. It's all about knowing yourself and how you trade at your best or at your worst.

5. **Traders are entrepreneurs.**

   Your job as a trader isn't just to place trades. You are running a trading business. Austin treats trading like a business and has multiple streams of income in order to take pressure off when he has some bad trading months.

CHAPTER 13

Alyse Amores

Alyse Amores is a first-generation Cuban single mother from Atlanta, Georgia. She started trading in 2017 with a few hundred dollars of her own capital. In six years, she progressed from trading her own money to managing $8 million. Her success was built on the foundation of scaling capital gradually and managing risks effectively to achieve long-term success.

Alyse embodies the spirit of hard work and perseverance. While pregnant, she juggled working nights at a fine dining establishment, daytime shifts at a lunch spot, and attending classes whenever she wasn't working. Motherhood brought new challenges, particularly the high cost of childcare. Alyse found herself driving for Lyft and Uber at night while her daughter slept at her parents', striving to balance earning enough to cover expenses with spending time with her child.

Her motivation to improve her financial situation stemmed from the desire to break free from living paycheck to paycheck. Through her relentless hustle, she was able to save money for trading. She dedicated an hour each day to focus on learning and improving her trading skills. As she gained confidence and experience, she learned the importance of risk management and the potential for greater returns with calculated risks. In her own words, her approach to money management "doesn't come from a place of being smart or prepared but from a place of scarcity, holding onto my money."

Alyse's story is one of resilience, continuous learning, and a relentless pursuit of financial stability and independence. She transformed her mindset and approach to money, driven by the desire to provide a better life for her daughter and alleviate the financial pressures on her family.

Q: How did you get into trading?

Alyse: I started learning to trade in the summer of 2017, about a year after I had my daughter. By that time I was a single mother, she was very young and I felt that time was very limited. Most people are working when their child is up, but I wanted more interactions with her, to be there when she is growing up because you only get one of those.

Since I've always been a hustler, I was comfortable with being busy all of the time, stacking and saving and making sacrifices. But now, I had a reason to be at home and wanted to hustle smarter.

I knew that people don't become wealthy from a regular job. You can invest and compound for a long period of time, but it still takes a very long time. So I started researching ways to make, invest, and grow money. That's when I discovered two things – real estate and trading/investing.

I felt that one really helps the other because making money from trading or investing could provide the funds to invest in real estate. A good friend and I decided to learn and do it together. I still trade but he doesn't trade anymore. We took various courses, and while some course sellers can seem predatory, there are also those who tell you about the risks. The problem is, many people don't listen to the warnings. They want the shortcuts. They prefer listening to the person who tells them it's easy over the one who tells them it takes a long time and a lot of struggle. It might take many years to become profitable. It's not that the information isn't out there; it's that people ignore it because they don't want to invest the time without a guaranteed result. There aren't guarantees in trading or investing, so people tend to focus more on how it can fail than how to make it work.

For me, the courses were a good introduction to the basics – understanding platforms, brokers, and how to enter trades. Initially, I knew how to enter trades before I fully understood what I was doing. After going through all the basic education, I felt the need for more advanced learning, so I sought out a higher-level mentor. My advice is to find a mentor who can teach beginners and, later, one who can teach at a higher level – that's what I've done throughout.

Q: How did you balance your day job, spending time with your daughter, and learning to trade when you first started out?

Alyse: I'm a hustler, so even when I was pregnant, I was working at a fine dining place at night and a lunch spot during the day, and taking classes on the nights I wasn't working. I saved enough money before I started trading to take maternity leave since I didn't have paid leave at any of my jobs. I managed to take half a year off just from the money I saved from serving.

When I went back to work, I was at McKesson, a pharmaceutical distribution company. That was my last attempt at a corporate job. I worked in the warehouse handling shipping, receiving, and inventory. It was a good, reputable job, and I thought I would follow in my family's footsteps – get a decent career, work my way up, and go from there.

However, once you have a kid you have more expenses and childcare is very expensive. Which is probably why some families decide one parent stays home because a second job doesn't bring in enough money to cover the childcare costs or they're a single parent like me and end up doing Lyft/Ube on the side.

My main income could cover my bills and necessities, but it really wasn't enough to cover the childcare. I would leave my daughter with my parents and drive for Lyft/Uber while she slept, which was also when I was supposed to be sleeping but I wanted to spend time with her. I also didn't want my parents to have to work harder when I was trying to do all this to help everyone work less.

That's what really motivated me to do something else. You get to the point where you're still living paycheck to paycheck and something had to give. I think a lot of people find themselves in similar situations. When people ask me how I did it, I'm still not sure; it was hard but I knew that if I can have an hour a day to focus and do a lesson, eventually it'll get better.

Q: From the very beginning, even before you got into trading you had a very strong savings mentality. Can you talk about how you raised funds or in your words "stacked" your way to trading full-time?

Alyse: Honestly it doesn't come from a place of being smart or prepared but from a place of scarcity, holding onto my money. My parents were working middle class and they didn't know how to become wealthy but my mom understood that if you put everything on credit cards, you can get behind quickly. She taught me early on to be smart with credit cards; if you use them, pay them off. I respect her for teaching me the little bit that she knew even if she didn't know everything. She taught me from her experience. I also saw how hard they were working.

One thing I'll definitely talk about is my change in mindset regarding money. In the beginning I wasn't very good at putting money on the line and risking money, I think it came from scarcity, the fear of losing it all. I was trading very small numbers at first because it was my own real money. I only started with a few hundred dollars and I couldn't size up even if I wanted to. But as I practiced with demo accounts and traded larger numbers, I realized I could be making more if I risked more, so I did. Now that isn't a good long-term solution unless you have a high win rate because if you have any type of losing streak while taking high risk, the account is gone and you'll have to make a massive recovery. You learn risk management quickly if you want to be profitable.

For me, it was a phase. I was very risk averse at first and grew my account over time through trial and error. I quickly learned that sizing up too fast doesn't work. It feels like a waste of time if you make progress for two weeks and then blow it all up in one bad week. If you do that long enough, you either quit, which some people do, or you change and improve. I learned that while sizing up can work for the right opportunities, doing it all the time is not a sustainable strategy.

Q: Can you share with us your trading strategy?

Alyse: With my main strategy, I try to identify an A to B range that I'm trading, whether it's a buy-side or sell-side move. I look at whether it has had one or multiple reactions from that zone. I'm always searching for areas of interest, particularly areas of highest volume where bigger players have been before. I don't trade those zones right away; instead, I watch to see how the area reacts first. If that area continues to hold and they keep adding positions around the same price, and it breaks past and then validates as a resistance or support (depending on if it's a sell or buy), it's a continuation. If it changes direction in those zones, it indicates that the big players are closing their previous positions and moving in a different direction. When it comes to breakouts, I don't enter on the first breakout unless it has a very strong reaction. The first breakout is often a fake-out or manipulation. I usually wait for that initial breakout and then look for the true move.

I also try to narrow it down to price as much as possible. Early on, I would get into trades too early and wasn't patient enough. I had to learn to wait for the setup and be comfortable with sometimes missing the move. If you want good confirmations and high-probability setups, you'll occasionally miss moves and have to accept that. Or you can take more trades and risk losing more when you're wrong because you get trigger-happy. For me, I feel better letting the trade set up and taking what I consider a valid reaction in those areas versus trying to guess before I have enough information.

Q: What time frame do you trade?

Alyse: Seventy-five percent of my trades are scalp trades on the minute charts, and the rest are intraday trades from the four-hour or higher time frames. I typically trade the same areas consistently but my intraday trades usually occur on days when the market continues in the same direction as the initial play. However, if the price ranges around that price, it can't be an intraday trade for me because it hasn't continued and will either hit the full stop or the stop profit. These are the days better suited for scalping.

   Intraday trades for my strategy only happen a few days a week. I take them when they set up and I let them run when it happens. I also take some swing trades during the year, but these are mainly for my personal accounts. I don't swing trade much on the larger accounts, and when I do, it's usually with oil and commodities.

Q: What's your trade management for your scalp trades?

Alyse: I always have targets for my scalps. I used to do a lot of partial exits, but over time I started trading more positions and set one as the scalp target, meaning it's out regardless, and everything above that is extra, a bonus. So my scalps became what I call my *bag trades*. I assess a certain amount of risk for these calculated trades. Either my risk is hit and I'm out, or I make my bag, and anything beyond that is a bonus.

Q: So your scalp trades don't transition into intraday trades. You scalp within the ranges and then wait for a breakout to take a new intraday trade, right?

Alyse: Yes, that's correct. Some of my scalps do end up turning into higher time frame plays because I have multiple positions, allowing me to let one run. For higher time frame zones, I set deeper targets because my targets are based on where I'm entering. If it's a higher time frame zone, I want a higher time frame target because that type of volume will match the magnitude of the move. So typically, if I'm entering at one of those higher time frame prices, those are the ones I'll try to let run longer because they have a higher probability of achieving that.

For example, let's say I have a daily time frame entry and I'm expecting it to reach a specific level, which may take two to three days within that week. It might pull back along the way, so my scalps could be trades that capture the moves in between. I will take some profits off the initial entry, but I always leave some positions running for the higher time frame targets.

Q: Your approach sounds very practical: you have a view, either positive or negative, and you scalp in that direction while waiting for a breakout move.

Alyse: Right. I have my initial bias, but I don't ever get attached to it. I take the entry where I get confirmations and it continues to confirm the trade for me. This was one of the biggest lessons for me – I used to hold onto losing trades for too long. Part of that was because I was trading with too big of a size and it was hard to take the loss when I was wrong. Then I started trading with the right size and I was able to let go of my attachment to the trade and the need to be right.

Q: Do you make more money scalping the range or taking the intraday breakouts trades?

Alyse: The intraday trades are great when I get them, but for consistency, I'm stacking my accounts with scalping and those small gains every day compound over time. Some people only take high risk-reward trades, but you have to understand that those trades happen less often than a simple scalp with a 1 : 1 or 1 : 2 risk-to-reward ratio. So, you either trade those higher risk-reward plays less often or trade more frequently and gradually stack your account. I've found a strategy that allows me to do both but when I broke it down and analyzed it, I was surprised at how clean my equity curve stays because I'm consistently adding little by little.

Q: What instruments do you trade?

Alyse: I started with forex and still trade some forex today, but I don't trade all the pairs. In the beginning, you want to trade everything every minute of the day, thinking you'll make more that way. I realized early on that I didn't like the slowness of the majors. I enjoyed the exotic currencies like the Singapore dollar and South African rand for a while because their volatility was great during moves. However, they were less predictable and always paired with a major currency like the US dollar or euro. It was fun for a period, but the spreads were huge. I eventually stopped trading them because I experienced significant slippage on price a few times because there wasn't enough trade volume.

I got interested in oil and gold mainly through other traders, but I was already studying them for correlations with currencies. With commodities, there are large amounts of money moving around in those markets for large purchases and investments, they're going to have pretty smooth bullish and bearish trends and they have really good movement throughout the year. So I thought, I could swing trade these. That's what got me into it.

Now, I find gold better for intraday trading than oil, which I only keep oil for swings. Gold has enough volatility and, even though I trade gold, it's paired with either the US dollar or euro, so it's still currency-related. I look at correlations a lot and use them as an indicator for divergence. I usually have Gold-USD and Gold-EUR charts pulled up and look for divergences between them.

Q: Do you back-test?

Alyse: I like to test the structure and rules of my strategy to see if they really hold up. It's similar to a scientific hypothesis, when you're trying to test to see if things are valid. I do this a lot in the market as well. Whenever I'm learning something new, I incorporate it into my strategy by working on one thing at a time. I test that one thing to see its limits – what it can and can't do, when it will work, and when it won't. Building a new strategy involves a lot of learning, understanding the basics of the rules, and then testing those parameters to see how I can evolve it.

Longevity in trading is very important. One of the main things I stress to people is that when you learn a lot, you tend to complicate things. Sometimes you need to come back and resimplify. When you're a beginner, you're trading out of ignorance, and it's easy to overcomplicate things before realizing the need to return to simpler, more effective strategies.

After trading for several years and experiencing different markets – whether it's during elections, economic events like wars, or periods of economic growth or inflation changes – you learn the discretionary part of trading. You understand that certain strategies work well in specific market conditions but not in others. This flexibility allows me to trade in more market conditions, rather than adhering to a one-size-fits-all approach. It helps me recognize when not to trade and wait for the right conditions, ensuring better performance and adaptability.

Q: Can you talk about your transition from part-time to full-time trader? At what point did you feel ready to leave your full-time job?

Alyse: I was getting paid biweekly, so my first goal was to make from trading what I made daily at my day job – I think it was like $160–$200. Once I hit that, I aimed to make my biweekly paycheck weekly, which was about $1,600–$2,000. When I realized I was making that amount each week from trading while still working my day job, I was effectively earning three months of pay in one month. I continued to compound that, putting a few hundred dollars from each biweekly paycheck into my trading account, building it up. Some of it was savings that I used to trade larger sizes. I stacked money for a whole year before I left my full-time job. The only reason why I was able to leave after that period of time was because I did not take any withdrawals during that time.

Q: That's a really good way to think about it: to focus on first making your daily pay, then your biweekly in one week instead of two.

Alyse: The hardest part was staying consistent with the risk, because that's where most people mess up. They do well, get too confident, and they kill it. Many people have a larger loss that wipes out a day or week, but when it's months of gains, that's completely reckless. That's when people often mess up and end up quitting. I knew someone who built up $50 K and lost it all in one day.

Q: How do you avoid that?

Alyse: I tend to take 1% or less risk per trade. Depending on how many positions I have, I might risk 0.25–0.5% per position. If I feel very confident about a position, I'll risk the full 1%, but I understand that if that trade loses, I have to stop trading for the day. On days when I feel more confident and the market conditions are favorable, I might risk up to 2%, but that's definitely my maximum.

Q: How did you transition into managing money?

Alyse: One member of the group worked at a venture capitalist firm and knew a firm looking for female traders. There was only one female trader in the entire fund, and she wanted to bring more in to show that we can do it too because the market doesn't care if you are male or female. It wasn't just about female traders, though; she wanted to prove that a decent pool of retail traders could be brought into the fund. Despite having a track record, I still had to audition. The track record is just the starting point for them to consider you for managing money. I always tell people that while a track record is important, it's not a guarantee. You still need to audition to ensure your trading matches up with the track record and is consistent. The process can take a long time, from a few quarters to half a year, or sometimes even a year. Consistency is key, and many people don't last through the process because it requires maintaining performance over an extended period.

The audition was a multiple-phase process. The first month was to see if you were consistent – it was straight fire, people were in and out. Either your stats matched your previous performance, or they didn't, and you were out. Both females and males auditioned together, and groups of people would fall off in each round.

Q: Was it different trading your own account compared to managing a seven-figure portfolio?

Alyse: The one big change when trading with a fund is that they care about risk management more than a retail trader. Protecting capital is number one over everything. I got really good with risk management because I had to in order to make the cut, and it evolved my view on trading.

When I was trading PAMM [percentage allocation money management] and prop accounts, they were only six-figure accounts. I didn't really get to a million plus until I started trading with the fund. I got to the smallest risk when I traded seven figures. The allowed risk was 1.5%, meaning that once you hit that number, you're out. As a trader, you make a percentage of the profit, so if I'm trading that account and compounding, it just takes time. I later traded for another fund based in Florida that scaled up to seven figures. I started with $1 million, did well, and then moved to $3 million, $5 million, and eventually $8 million but bear in mind this scaling happened over a period of about a year and a half.

Q: What type of return were you looking for on a seven-figure account?

Alyse: The fund was fine with 1–2% returns a month, which a lot of people don't like because when they are trading their own accounts, they are used to doing that in a day. However, it's important to realize that with the fund, you're using smaller risk, so those returns are still good if you're only risking 0.25%. The profits are small because the main focus is on protecting capital. On a personal account, you might take more risk, but with a fund, I tend to focus more on better opportunities because, with that capital size, you can't trade recklessly. When trading with a fund and generating 1–2% a month, they considered that satisfactory enough to scale up the size. Typically, my goals are to achieve somewhere between 6 and 10% a month, but if you make 3% a month, you'd be hired at the fund forever.

Q: How quickly did they scale up the account for you?

Alyse: The first account scaled up fairly quickly because I performed well and stayed disciplined with my risk, which made them happy. Within a month, they increased my account from $1 million to $3 million. However, I want to be very clear that this is not the standard norm. Keep in mind, I had already auditioned for a few months and had been consistently matching those results, so I have my track record. That's the biggest thing. Their goals are in the lower realm of what I aim to achieve, so even if I have a bad month, I've typically made the numbers they want.

Q: Why did you decide to trade for a fund and not prop?

Alyse: There is a pro to prop trading because you're not trading with your own money. You're leveraging other people's capital, even if it's a synthetic trading environment, as long as you're getting paid out. That's the online model, whereas with in-person prop trading desks, you are trading their real capital. Regardless, the same truth remains: you're not risking your own funds, so that option is always there if I decide to go that route. I have the same capital size to trade as what props offer, but trading my own money gives me the freedom to follow my own trading strategy.

For example, many prop firms have rules against hedging and stacking positions. They consider this Martingale, but unless you're increasing your position size in a drawdown, it's technically not Martingale. Many intraday or swing traders add positions in a drawdown if it's in their entry zone, and I feel that as long as risk is being followed, it should be allowed. Still some prop firms limit you to only two positions, and I don't want to worry about getting flagged or breached. I just want to trade the way I trade without having to think about all those restrictions. My main rules are about risk management rather than the technicalities of how I execute trades. Firms say they welcome all types of traders, but not all the rules welcome all strategies.

Q: What are your favorite trading tools or resources?

Alyse: Most people don't like reading books but once you start learning online and do the research you realize you could have just learned it all in this book. I mainly use TradingView for my charting and MetaTrader is my go-to platform but I also use Sierra Charts and NinjaTrader for futures. When it comes to fundamentals I'm using MyFxBook or ForexFactory. I also know someone who has access to a Bloomberg Terminal and sometimes we'll analyze fundamentals together. Although I'm not in many groups, I do have one or two traders who stay aligned with fundamentals, and we share tools and resources.

Q: What advice do you have for traders who want to become funded or trade full-time?

Alyse: Focus more on progress than the results. People focus on results first; it doesn't matter how they got there and they ignore the important details. This is why I emphasize the mistakes people make – they see the end result but overlook how they achieved it. For example, once you have your strategy in place, a good trading day should be based on adhering to your strategy, regardless of whether you win or lose. People often view it purely in terms of making or losing money. However, if you took bad moves against your strategy and got lucky, it's not a great trading day because you're building bad habits that go against what you've worked hard to establish. Evaluating your progress and staying disciplined with your strategy is crucial.

Another tip is to work on one thing at a time. When I was learning, I focused on one aspect at a time. People get overwhelmed because they want to do everything at once. When I was focusing on risk, I worked on that individually. When I looked at pinning orders or liquidity parameters, I tackled them one at a time. This approach makes it less overwhelming and more manageable.

Q: In the beginning you talked about having some nonnegotiables for trading and some that allow for more creativity. What are some of those nonnegotiables?

Alyse: My nonnegotiables are typically
- When I'm trading
- What I'm trading
- My entry parameters

I'm really big on not chasing price. The areas I mark are where I'm looking for entries, period. When I chase price, that's when things get rough. My variables may be my sizing, which is why I mention a range of risk – it depends on what I feel is more probable or less probable. I'm okay with getting into a trade that's less probable with smaller size rather than not taking it at all. At the same time, if I have a trade that I don't feel good about and I miss it, I'm okay with that, too.

Q: What happens when the trade goes against you? Will you stick to the stop or try to repair the position?

Alyse: It depends on how much it is going against the position. Since I tend to enter in high-liquidity areas, if my trade is invalidated, it usually happens quickly. For swing trades, where I'm allowing more breathing room, I'll add positions once I see confirmation again. However, if the trade is completely going against me, I won't stack positions. In that case, I let the stop loss do its job.

Q: Do you add to positions on retraces or new breakouts?

Alyse: Retraces, but I'm looking for that breakout reaction. For retracements, I need to see a high volume impulse in that area and then it continuing again, respecting those previous highs if it's a high, or a low if it's a low.

Q: What do you think is the number-one skill that it takes to be a successful trader?

Alyse: It feels like an easy answer, but it's not. I would say resilience is the most common trait that I've seen in all traders. Our styles, from swing trading to scalping, have different edges, but regardless of the style, all the traders I know are very resilient. We've all experienced major losses or losing streaks. After these events, will they quit? You've got to be able to see the bigger picture and not be overwhelmed by the small setbacks. You'll definitely have times in your trading that are just tough, no way around it. Either you have a purpose bigger than yourself, see past those tough times, apply the lessons, and remain resilient, or you let them overcome you and end up doing something else.

Q: Speaking about overcoming bad trades, what was your worst trade ever?

Alyse: My worst trade and my best trades were both on gold, and they both happened within my first year or two of trading.

The worst trade was in my small account. I don't always measure my biggest loss by the actual amount but rather by the percentage of the account size. I made the mistake of not letting the trade invalidate and held onto my bias. This experience created one of my trading rules.

When people see an all-time high or low, and it breaks, they often think it's going to reverse and get in on the opposite side of a strong pushing market. They hold onto that bias, thinking any candle in their direction is a good sign. They might hold, hope, or even add more positions, but is the trade really ready? In my case, I had one bearish candle and kept holding, which resulted in my largest loss because I didn't let the trade invalidate. I just let it run until it took out a major part of the account. It was a small account, but it took a long time to build and I let it blow away months of hard work which was really frustrating.

So the trading rule that came from that: the market makes new highs and lows every day; enter trades based on other confirmations. I still trade areas of high volume, points of supply and demand, and previous highs and lows, but not the same way. Before it was off one expectation. Now I use an if-then scenario. If the market does this, then I do that. Many of my trading rules are based on this if-then logic.

My best day was also on a gold swing during one of those bullish movements. I held the position for months, and it paid off extremely well.

Q: How did you have the patience to hold onto it for months if your personality is to day trade? Did you trail your stop?

Alyse: I identified that high time frame target and I really wanted to see it hit. Along the way, I took partial profits but also added new positions because I was using the zones. Once those zones were cleared and the momentum continued, I put on new positions. The significant profit came from all these positions combined, not just the initial one. It ended up being my longest-held trade and one of my most profitable.

Q: Do you think that being a woman makes you a better trader?

Alyse: I definitely think it helps me. I believe in my intuition a lot, and I think people can build trader intuition regardless of gender. I think I trust my intuition more because I often make decisions based on it. My intuition helps me have really good reaction time on a lot of my trades because I've seen the patterns so many times, every day for seven years. This has made me trust myself on my trades much more than I used to.

ALYSE'S TRADING TIPS

1. **Budget for the leap from part-time to full-time trader.**

   If you are looking to make the leap from part-time to full-time trader, set trading goals based on your current earnings. Start by aiming to match your daily earnings through trading. Once achieved, strive to consistently earn two weeks of earnings in a week. As you continue to trade, compound your gains by adding a portion of your regular income to your trading account and reinvest your trading profits. Avoid taking withdrawals to allow your account to grow. By following this disciplined approach, you can build the skills and the financial cushion to enable you to transition to full-time trading.

2. **Keep your equity curve clean with 1 : 1 risk–reward trades while waiting for big ones.**

   High risk–reward trades can be lucrative, but they occur less frequently than simpler, more frequent trades like scalps with a 1 : 1 or 1 : 2 risk-to-reward ratio. Alyse's methodology involves stacking her account with small, regular gains that compound over time, helping to keep her equity curve steady. Additionally, she uses higher time frame breakout trades based on volume that she lets run further, and during these periods, she may also scalp the moves in between. This balanced approach ensures her equity curve remains smooth and consistently growing.

3. **Refine one part of your trading strategy at a time.**

   Avoid getting overwhelmed by trying to learn everything at once. Focus on working on one part of your trading strategy at a time. Concentrate on a single element, such as risk management, before moving on to other factors like pinning orders or liquidity parameters. This approach makes the learning process more manageable.

   Emphasize progress over immediate results. Many traders fixate on outcomes without understanding the process that led to them. A successful trading day isn't just about making money; it's about adhering to your strategy. Even if you win by taking moves outside your strategy, it's not a good day because it fosters bad habits. Consistently evaluate your progress and stay disciplined with your strategy to build long-term success.

CHAPTER 14

Matthew Miller

Matthew Miller, widely known as "Trades by Matt," is one of the most popular funded prop traders. He started trading penny stocks when he was 18, switched to crypto a few years later, and has been trading futures prop since 2019, withdrawing more than $309,000 over a period of 85 trading days.

Matt's trading philosophy is based on mastering a single instrument, Nasdaq futures, to the point where his trades become almost instinctual. Matt's approach is all about precision and expertise. He quickly grasped the importance of sticking to prop firm rules, building a rock-solid, disciplined strategy.

A scalper at heart, Matt zeros in on 10-point trades. His favorite setup is an initial balance (both IBH [high] and IBL [low]), which relies on confluence. For Matt, an A+ setup occurs when the initial balance breaks out, retests, forms a hammer on the one-minute chart, and shows Delta sky-rocketing – an indicator showing the change of market buying and market selling.

Matt's philosophy is simple but powerful: take the base hits, pocket the points, and wait for the next play. He likens his strategy to filling up on bread-crumbs, understanding that the market always offers new opportunities. This disciplined method has been key to his sustained success and popularity in the trading community.

Q: Were you always fascinated by finance in school?

Matt: I went to school for supply chain management. I thought I wanted to study finance, so I took an intro to finance class, but

I hated it. I thought finance was all about stocks but quickly realized it encompasses many other areas. Then we had this intro to business class, where industry speakers would come and talk about their jobs to help us figure out what we'd want to do.

One of the speakers was the leader of Boeing's supply chain for the International Space Station, and it blew my mind. I've always been interested in planes, not space but planes and this job sounded fascinating. I learned that supply chain covers finance, logistics, warehousing – basically, every tangible part of a business falls under the supply chain umbrella. So that was a cool area for me to be involved because I'd learn everything. Then the more important side of it was that at Baylor, this was the number-one salary coming out of school with a 99% after-college job placement rate. I wanted a job and to make good money, so I chose supply chain.

Q: Not all college students are wise enough to choose their future careers based on the highest pay and best job placement opportunities. Do you think this approach carried over to your trading, where you seek a certain level of certainty in your setups?

Matt: I think it does, and it's funny you mention that. Just yesterday, my wife and I went to In-N-Out for a milkshake. It reminded me of when I applied to work there in high school. I've always had a job, starting in middle school. At the time, I was working at Best Buy for about $8 an hour, while In-N-Out was offering $15 an hour. I thought, why not switch to make more money? My wife said it was crazy I was thinking about earnings even as a high school kid, but I told her, well, I was broke.

Q: Did your parents inspire your strong work ethic?

Matt: More or less. I had a great upbringing, and my parents definitely taught me the value of money. My dad's a pastor, so we were comfortable, but I wasn't going to summer camps or things like that. If I wanted something, I had to spend my own money on it. From a young age, I understood the value of a dollar, both in saving and spending.

I started working very young, passing out door flyers for my godfather's roofing company in middle school. I sweated in the hot sun all summer for a couple of hundred dollars, so I wasn't going to waste it.

Q: Do you think your understanding of the value of money and how hard you worked for it has influenced how you manage your trades and the level of risk you're willing to take?

Matt: I think so. When I first started trading, I was into crypto. I traded penny stocks for a long time. It would be a stretch to even call it trading. I had no idea what I was doing and I wasn't fully focused. I got serious with crypto trading because making money seemed easy. Honestly, at that time, it was very easy to make money with hardly any investment. I started thinking, "$500 a day is more than what I make at my current job, and I did it in 15 minutes. I prefer this over that. How can I make it happen, and what's the best approach?"

Of course, the journey is a cycle: you start with smaller numbers, then grow into bigger numbers. Then you get cocky, assuming big numbers will always happen, then you get humbled and hammered, and eventually, you reestablish what the numbers actually mean.

Q: How did you get into trading?

Matt: When I turned 18, my buddy and I downloaded the Robinhood app because I knew I wanted my money to work for me. I'd heard the stock market could do that, so I bought GoPro at its peak, around $90, and it immediately dropped by $20 in a few days. I bought one share, got hammered, and sold it. But it sparked my interest – I realized I could buy and sell stocks. So I started researching and learned about day trading. Google often leads to penny stocks, which seemed perfect for someone broke like me. However, I quickly discovered the dark side of penny stocks with pump-and-dumps and all that.

Q: Were you in college at the time?

Matt: Yeah. I'd put in a couple of $100 and try to trade it up. Sometimes I was a bit successful but then it would get evaporated. I'd get slapped by the PDT [pattern day trader] rule constantly. That was my first few years of college. Then I was ready to jump back into the stock world. I started trading Nvidia with a coworker, and then a buddy hit me up about crypto. That's when I migrated over, but *trading* is an aggressive word – it was more like figuring out what I was doing. I had a friend making $5,000–$10,000 a month trading, and I didn't understand how. I thought I could turn $100 into $5,000, but that's just not accurate.

Q: What type of research were you doing at the time?

Matt: At the time I was just starting to get into watching YouTube as an educational space for trading. It was still mostly random Reddit forums or reading about something that's pumping and I would get in, and then it dumps. I didn't discover StockTwits until after I graduated college, which really helped propel my research for stocks.

Q: How did you find time to trade after graduating college and working in supply chain management?

Matt: I was a software analyst at the time, and the company I worked for built all their software in-house. I acted as a liaison with the business side, the operations side, and our developers. My role involved understanding the business needs, then working with our developers to figure out how we were going to solve their problems and build the necessary software.

In terms of time, crypto trading was a bit easier back then because we didn't have as many crazy coins – it was mainly Bitcoin, Ethereum, and Litecoin. I would trade on exchanges like Bitmex, which isn't allowed in the United States anymore, and a bit on Binance. I traded with a couple hundred dollars, but the nice thing about crypto is you can trade in incredibly small increments. I didn't know about paper trading back then, and I'm not even sure if crypto had paper trading options. So, everything I learned was with my own money, but I was trading in such small fractions that the risk was minimal. I would wake up and trade.

My now-wife and I were long-distance, and I didn't have any friends in San Antonio. So I would literally wake up early to trade or learn new trading principles on YouTube, like support and resistance. I'd map out charts, come home for lunch to trade some more, and then trade all night after work. You can even find old videos on my YouTube channel from seven to eight years ago, where I'm in my suit and tie on my lunch break, filming videos about technical analysis before heading back to work.

Q: Were you a trading junkie at the time?

Matt: Yeah, I was obsessed with it. I loved it. That's when I truly found my passion because I was living, breathing, and sleeping it – it was all I wanted to do. At the time, many people were making crazy money with crypto, and I joined a Discord group to understand it better. I saw people doing crazy numbers, crushing it, and I realized that while the money was enticing, the constant problem-solving aspect was what really drew me in. My brain loves solving problems, and the combo of trying to figure it out and make money was great.

I ended up turning a couple of hundred dollars into $10 K, which I used to buy my wife's first engagement ring (we've since upgraded it). At the time, it was all crypto money, which is a fun story to share now.

Q: So you started off with a couple hundred dollars and rolled it into $10 K. Did you add money in between?

Matt: No, I never did, and I attribute a lot of that to luck. I was involved right before the big runup so it didn't take much. It took leverage, getting long, and riding with the wave to make a ton of money. I was very long-biased and heavily into the crypto scene. Back then, it didn't take a whole lot of skill – unlike trading futures nowadays. It was basically just "up only."

Q: Did you buy and hold, or were you frequently trading in and out?

Matt: I was in and out all of the time. I think I could have made so much more money if I just held it but leverage can prevent that. I learned the concept of scalping in that time frame.

Q: When you were scalping, did you have an exit strategy or target in mind?

Matt: It's hard to remember; this was seven years ago. I do know that I was trading a lot off the DOM [depth of market] back then. Bitmex was notorious for heavy spoofing – when someone would put up a massive order on the ask, making everyone think the price would drop, then pull the order, causing the price to explode. I wasn't spoofing myself but rather riding those spoofing waves. I traded using basic support and resistance strategies, buying dips into support, and waiting to see if there would be a spoof. I'd take a couple hundred dollars' profit and kill the trade. It was definitely P&L [profit-and-loss] trading at the time.

Q: Why did you move away from crypto, and was it directly into Nasdaq?

Matt: About 2018, I had a job change and went into consulting. I was on the bench, meaning I wasn't assigned to a project, so I had a lot of free time, especially since my boss was in Virginia. While I got all my work done, I wasn't the best worker. I was actively trading at this point, spending eight hours a day trading during work and then trading in the mornings and evenings. It became a full-blown obsession.

When Bitmex became illegal in the United States, it was a red flag for me. I didn't want to do anything illegal. Without access through a VPN, I started looking for alternatives that offered similar movement and leverage. I didn't want to deal with the PDT rule for stocks and I didn't like using screeners. That's why I liked crypto – I could trade the same thing every day, focusing on Bitcoin and knowing exactly the setups I wanted to see without running a bunch of scanners.

In late December 2018, I learned about futures and immediately opened a personal account. I didn't know about paper trading at the time and made $1,000 on my first day, which I have recorded on YouTube. It was exactly what I wanted – regulated, centralized, and allowing me to trade the same thing every day. Futures are always moving because they're index-based and incredibly leveraged.

Q: How much did you start your futures trading account with?

Matt: Honestly, I don't remember exactly, but probably about $2,000–$5,000 if I had to guess. I didn't know I needed more money in the account. When I saw margin requirements on a broker's site, I thought I could stick close to the bare minimum. I didn't have anyone advising me that I needed more wiggle room in my accounts, and not to mention I was still broke. Not *broke* broke, but I didn't want to put $20,000 into something when $20,000 was a significant part of what I had, and I was still learning. I knew it would be silly to throw a lot of money into something I had just picked up.

Q: It appears you're cautious about how much you invest but very aggressive with the portion you choose to trade?

Matt: Yeah, and a big part of that comes from my crypto days. I've seen so many projects get rug-pulled and had money on exchanges that got taken away. I'm only going to put money in that I'm okay with losing, whether through my mistakes or external factors. I don't want my whole life savings in there. I've seen people lose everything, and I never wanted to be in that position.

As for trading aggressively, yes. Things are different now but my mindset at the time was that I could trade aggressively because I knew the stakes. If I put myself in a position where I really needed a trade to work out – not to pay rent, but to avoid a nasty hit on the account – I'd wait for something I really liked and then be very aggressive in executing it. This approach kept me from being overly exposed to the market, allowing me to be more aggressive because my brain was at a heightened level of focus. I wasn't just clicking "buy" and walking away; if I was in, I was fully engaged.

Q: It sounds like you are a day trader from the very beginning focused on short-term moves?

Matt: It's been like that for forever. For the most part, I've gone through my fair share of trying to have more swing-style trades and it has never worked out for me. I just know I'm a scalper at heart.

Q: Can you share what type of strategy you were using to trade Nasdaq and how you learned it?

Matt: When I got into futures, I met a bunch of awesome people through Discord. We would be on video calls for eight hours a day, talking through what we were learning and the different strategies we were trying. We were always searching for additional alpha and constantly experimenting with new approaches.

This is crazy because you can see the history of it on my channel. I tried Renko charts, moving averages, pivot points, MACD [moving average convergence divergence], naked charts, just trading price action, and just trading the DOM [depth of market]. I've gone through all of these different cycles.

The strategies I use now have been part of my approach for a long time, but I still add new elements occasionally. Each cycle of my trading life lasted a few months, and I usually found at least one useful aspect from each cycle that I still use today. I ended up keeping the valuable pieces and discarding the rest.

Q: So you basically had a squawk box system with your trading buddies to get feedback on your trades?

Matt: More or less. It wasn't a professional setup, but we trusted each other for the most part. We all had the same goal: to pull a ton of money out of the market. We understood that we thought about things differently, so we'd run ideas off each other and back-test together. Obviously, three minds are better than one, and at that time, 10 minds were even better. We provided feedback and inspiration to each other and did outside research as well. I was introduced to Delta through those guys. One of them discovered it, and we all started trading with it, and I found out I really liked it. We were all grinding it out together every day during market hours.

I definitely remember voice calls at the market open, with everyone saying, "I'm in a trade," "I'm out of my trade," and so on. We'd post screenshots and discuss them afterward. I have streams from that time frame with all those guys in the voice chat while I was at work. Again, I wasn't the best worker. I didn't realize it at the time but if you can distract yourself a little, your trading usually improves. Being hyper-focused on every single tick of movement isn't a good spot to be in.

Q: Why did you start streaming your trading?

Matt: I started my YouTube channel right at the very beginning. Initially, it was meant to be a journal of what I was learning. I had gained value from other people's journal-style channels, even though I can't remember any of their names now. I thought, why not pay it forward? If I could offer value to anyone, that would be awesome.

Using the channel as a journal, it eventually morphed into a way to meet like-minded people. It's very hard to meet traders in real life, at least from my perspective. I've rarely met anyone in person, so I used the online community and videos to connect with new people and generate new ideas.

The goal, then and now, is to make more money from trading. That's why I still do it. You might encounter 1,000 duds, but finding that one person who can change your life a little bit makes it all worthwhile.

Q: Let's dive into your trading strategy. Since you only trade Nasdaq, which time frame chart do you primarily use?

Matt: If the Nasdaq is really struggling, I'll occasionally trade crude oil. I don't really trade the S&P; I always think I want to because that's what all the old guys do, but when I try it once every year or two, I quickly realize it's not for me. I would say I'm a 99% Nasdaq trader, maybe even a bit higher – about 99.5% by trade volume.

When you focus on one thing every single day, you understand how it moves, you understand the typical increments, how news affects it, when not to trade it, your position sizing, and your P&L movements. All of that becomes second nature. This is much easier than trying to refigure out the value of a tick for different instruments. With the Nasdaq, I just know it's $5 per tick, and that's it. This approach significantly reduces stress and emotional strain. I don't need a screener or multiple charts with different indexes; I simply trade the Nasdaq.

As for time frames, I trade using the 5-minute chart, 1-minute chart, and 22-range chart. I also keep a 30-minute chart up for some perspective, but it's mostly a space filler – I don't actively trade off of it.

Q: When does your trading day begin?

Matt: I don't trade the overnight sessions. I log on at 8:30 a.m. central time but I don't trade the first 15 minutes. I've been burned too many times over the years. Trading the open puts me in a weird mental state because it can either make or break my day because the movements are so volatile at the open. There have been many times where I was thrilled to be up $1,000 in 15 minutes, but just as many times where I was frustrated and down x amount of money. I would think, why did I do that? I still have 7.5 hours left in the trading session, and now I can't trade because I've tapped out by being super-aggressive in the first 5 minutes.

So I implemented a rule for myself. I'm going to sit here at the open and watch the volatility so I can get an idea for the pace for the day. So I can understand, how are we actually moving? If we're super-trending, if we're going sideways, or if we're going to V bottom, and so on. I'm religious about sitting there for the first 15 minutes and disciplined enough to not take any trades.

Q: How long did it take you to establish that rule?

Matt: Too long, probably a couple of years. I was really into journaling in 2019 and 2020. At that time, I was consistently making a lot of money before lunch – around $1,000 or $950 – but then I'd go to lunch, come back, and piss it all away.

That's when I turned to my data. Being a big-data guy, it's easy for me to make decisions based on clear-cut information. If the data tells me not to do something, I follow it. When I looked at my P&L by time of day, it was clear: green, green, green in the morning, followed by massive red in the afternoon. This made it obvious that I needed to stop trading after lunch.

At that time, I was making a lot of trades – probably 20 or 30 round trips a day. Nowadays, I trade significantly less, which allows me to sit and observe the market longer without feeling pressured.

Currently I take a more corporate approach to my trading. I've gone through extremes: avoiding afternoon trading entirely because I was getting killed after lunch and then switching to aggressively trying to make all my money before lunch. Both approaches were equally bad.

Now I've found a happy medium where I treat trading like a job. At the beginning of this conversation, we talked about understanding the value of money – $500 a day adds up over a year. I'd rather sit in front of my charts for eight hours day, make $500, than work for someone else and do the same amount of money or less. Understanding the value of both money and time has allowed me to sit at my desk without feeling the need to crank buttons and constantly trade.

So now there are days where I feel very comfortable walking away at 11 a.m. There are days where I'm trading until 3 p.m. I traded until 3 p.m. yesterday and the day before, but last week I was pretty much done by noon every day. It's really open ended for me, and I like to keep it that way so that I'm not forcing myself into a mental battle. The hardest parts of trading for me are all mental at this point but it is not a mental battle of feeling like I need to be done at a certain amount of time, because then I start making stupid decisions.

Q: Can you describe the strategy that you are using now? Are you looking for a breakout followed by a retrace test at a certain time of day?

Matt: Yes, I do. This involves the initial balance, which is the first hour high and low. After 9:30 a.m. central, if we break out of the initial balance, I'll look for a retest to get long and ride the trend. If we reject the breakout, I look for a mean reversion play back into the range. On clear range days, if we reject the initial balance high for example, I'd look for a short back into the mean.

I use the volume profile heavily for range trades and look at Delta to help determine if we're going long. I hate buying breakouts and will never use a buy stop to let momentum carry me. I prefer to buy on dips because it feels like I'm getting a discount, even if I'm not.

Q: For your two setups, do you find that one tends to work better at specific times of the day compared to the other?

Matt: It really depends on the given volatility of the day. There's plenty of days that we range out. There's plenty of days that we don't. Take Monday, for example. We had an amazing initial balance retest. The Nasdaq went super-high up, then came all the way back down into the initial balance. It was about a 60-point sell-off, and then we had an 80-point rebound about 12:30 p.m. or 1:00 p.m. These moves can happen at different times: sometimes at 10 a.m., sometimes later. It's not time-based from my perspective.

Some of my favorite setups are wick tests, which are pullback continuation trades. These happen all day long. I really dislike thinking in terms of specific times, like expecting something to happen only at 11 a.m. or between 10:30 and 11:30 a.m. If it doesn't happen during that window, it could lead to frustration or missed opportunities. It's not good for my head, so I just don't think about it that way.

Q: Do you enter trades with a full position right away and exit completely, or do you adjust your position as the trade develops?

Matt: Yeah, I'm all in, all out. Emotional capital aside, this is super-important for me, and this approach makes it so much easier. I've tried scaling out, I don't like it. I've tried to trail stops up and let things run exponentially and I hate that. For me, if I feel like I should be getting into a trade, then I should be getting into a trade so I will put on what I'm comfortable putting on.

I don't enter a trade thinking I'll put on more later if it comes back down. If I think the price will drop, I'd rather wait and buy lower. I have no desire to be in a trade that I might need to add to. I'm full size right away and prefer to have a set take profit target rather than trailing a stop loss.

For example, if I have a 20-point trade target on the Nasdaq, which nets $400, I'd rather the trade hit that target directly and keep going than watch it go up 40 points, trail my stop, and then come back down to 20 points. Both scenarios result in a 20-point trade and $400 in your pocket, but it's harder for me to see a trade go up significantly and then drop back down. I prefer ending on a positive note, with the trade hitting my desired target.

Q: Do you have a fixed stop and target for every trade or do you vary it based on market conditions?

Matt: I'm very consistent about 10 points on the Nasdaq. Sometimes I'll move it up a bit, but never for the first few trades of the day. I want to build a cushion before considering any adjustments. My stop loss is set at 25 points as an "act of God" stop, meaning if there's a sudden sell-off, I want to be out immediately. I don't want to be a part of that, get me out.

However, I base my actual stops on market structure. I look for points where the market would indicate that a trade is no longer valid. The market doesn't care about my risk-to-reward ratio, so I focus on where it makes sense to place my stops based on market behavior. This approach naturally leads to a good risk-to-reward ratio because I'm looking for cheap trades where I can enter close to the point of invalidation.

Q: What do you look at for market structure? Is it classic support and resistance?

Matt: More or less. Volume, the pace of play on the DOM, and how fast are buyers moving around or sellers moving around with Delta. Then classic support resistance structurally based on a one-minute chart.

Q: Let's say the trade moves against you, you're moving your act of God stop. At what point is the trade wrong?

Matt: Yes, I would have moved that act of God stop up to wherever that market structure point is. So plenty of times I'm getting into a trade, I'll have my 10-point target and I'll have my 25-point initial stop. As soon as the trade fills I'll drag that stop loss up to 5 points or 10 points, wherever that invalidation point is. If it takes me out, it takes me out and it is fine at that point.

Q: Now when you are in profit, do you trail the stop to lock in partial profits like +5?

Matt: I'll go breakeven but I'll never go +5. Again I'm looking for 10 points so going +5, that's semantics for the Nasdaq. It is just a two-second wiggle, which is nothing. If the trade goes up 6 or 7 points and kind of stalls there and doesn't fill me out, I'll usually pull it up to breakeven, but a lot of times I've already decided where I think the trade is invalid so I'll just leave it there.

If the trade is invalid at a certain point, why should I place a stop at my entry? I don't think the market really cares about where I entered or exited, so I let the trade play out. In my mind, I believe the market cares about its structure and where the volume is being conducted, so I let the trade work with the initial stop because that's where the trade is truly invalidated. If the price comes back to my entry, hangs around there, and then goes up, I would have been stopped out if I had set a breakeven stop. Placing a stop at breakeven is usually driven by fear and a lack of trust in yourself. There's no reason to do that if you trust your analysis and the trade setup.

Q: How many trades do you take per day?

Matt: It really depends. Ideally, I'm taking 2–4 trades on my prop firm accounts. After that I switch to my personal account for the rest of the day where I'll typically take 2–5 trades depending on volatility and how much movement we have.

Q: Do you have a daily profit target?

Matt: I don't have a fixed target every single day. On my prop firm accounts, I have set targets because I'm rewarded for consistency. It's a bit of a game – I'm not rewarded for having a big standout day, so I focus on being consistent rather than having big swings. I've experienced the emotional and mental toll of those big swings, and it's not worth it. Consistency is key for me. Ideally, I aim for around $400 per account. I'm currently trading $20 K of the $50 K Apex accounts and have withdrawn $240,000 from them. I've been funded by other companies in the past, too.

Even on my performance accounts [PAs], I don't enjoy having a fixed target. There are days when I make $200, and that's fine. There'll be times when I make 100 bucks and I'm not going to continue to grind that out for the sake of some money. If the market isn't clear, I don't force trades. I've tried that before and know it doesn't end well. There are days I make more than $400, but on average, $400 is my goal based on Apex's rules. That's just two 10-point trades on the Nasdaq, which is very doable. For the personal accounts I don't have targets because I just want to trade what the market's giving me.

Q: Do you trade your PA and personal accounts at the same time or do you switch between them?

Matt: I don't trade them both at the same time. I'm either only trading the PA accounts or I'm only trading my personal. For my PA accounts, just based on how much money you can withdraw and things like that, $400 is a comfortable target that allows me to meet my goals and maintain a smooth equity curve. For example, today I had two trades on my PA accounts, each up about $410. With those accounts done for the day, I now focus on my personal account and will continue trading on it for the rest of the day.

Q: Do you trade your personal and PA accounts differently?

Matt: No, I trade my personal and PA accounts the same. There are times where if I get two good 10-point trades on my personal account, I'll let the trade run a bit using more structure to structure instead of a set 10-point take profit. This is because I have more wiggle room on the day. I trade both accounts the same way, especially the first couple of trades on my personal account, which are always 10-point scalps. The main difference is the mental aspect and some fill issues, as the PA accounts are simulations. Currently I'm trading 20s, which means one contract per each of my 20 PA accounts, which is a 20-net contract trade. On my personal account, I'm trading 20 contracts at once so there are times where I will get half-filled because the market didn't want to fill all 20 contracts.

Q: Is that your rule? Trade one contract per PA account?

Matt: Yeah, it comes back to a principle I wish I had learned earlier: being overfunded and under-leveraged. The goal is to stay in the game as long as possible, and the best way to do that is by being overfunded and under-leveraged. On my PA accounts, I trade one contract even though I'm allowed to trade up to 10. Most people blow up their accounts by trading larger sizes with less wiggle room. It's not a good combination, so I stick to trading single contracts on my PAs.

Q: How and when did you discover that solution?

Matt: I don't know exactly when, but I can tell you how: through pain. I understood the idea was right, but I didn't have the equity to hold onto the trades. That was a pretty glaring issue. To fix it, I got under-leveraged and overfunded. I need to have money in the account in order to live to fight another day. If I have three bad trades and that completely wipes out my account, that's a massive problem and a red flag.

Q: Speaking of bad days, at what point do you know it's time to stop trading that day?

Matt: I follow the "three strikes, I'm out" rule. Sometimes, I stop at two strikes if it's blatantly obvious that neither trade was even a tick in the money, so I'm just going to call it because I'm clearly not seeing the market right. But generally, if I have three strikes or losing trades in a row, I'm done for the day.

Q: How long have you traded prop for and has your trading style changed during this time?

Matt: I've learned to be more patient. The last eight months have been particularly defining for me. There was a lightbulb moment when I realized I had strategies that work, so I asked myself what the next step was to make more money. Naturally, sizing up was an option, but I also wanted to avoid natural drawdowns. It took sometimes a second of self-reflection to understand that I needed to be more patient with setups that I think are A+. I need to be able to take those and if I am already at my loss limit on the day, I can't take those setups.

It goes back to what we were talking about earlier: being patient and focusing on base hits. I know I'm a scalper at heart, and every time I go for a big hit, it might work the first couple of times. If I get a 50-point trade on the Nasdaq, I'll be tempted to look for another 50-point trade because the dopamine hit feels great. But for me, a 50-point shot on the Nasdaq is an outlier. I don't need to be doing that regularly, nor do I want to. So, I focus on base hits, which you'll hear me talk about a lot. Base hits are number one, and patience is number two. The combination of the two is lethal for me.

Q: What would you consider an A+ setup?

Matt: It would be one of my favorite setups. So an IB [initial balance] trade retest – it's basically based off confluence. So if we break out of initial balance, we come back down to retest it, and we hammer on the one minute, and Delta is skyrocketing showing like a ton of market buyers and volume never flipped up – that would be like an A+ setup that I want to take.

One-minute structure wise – there is a nice hammer after a nice little comeback that typically shows some buyers coming in, Delta showing a buying trend going in, and it's at initial balance, which is a level that I love. That's a lot of things coming together to say, BUY THIS and get your 10 points. That's the other thing: just because it's an A+ setup doesn't mean I need to be looking for more than 10 points.

If it is an A+ setup for me, take the base hit. Take the money that's given to me, and the market's always going to be doing something else. It will always continue to go up, or it will always go back down, so I take my 10 points, and I'll play it later. I'm fine with breadcrumbs. I'll get filled up off breadcrumbs.

Q: What's your trading setup like? What do you have on your screens?

Matt: I use Sierra charts. I have the five-minute chart with volume profile. I have a one-minute chart with initial balance, which is just a high and low marked out. I have a DOM, the depth of market, which shows liquidity and you can see based on how it's flowing, the aggression of the buyers and sellers. Then I have a 22-range chart that has Delta on it. That's the whole setup that I use.

Q: Your 22-range, is it on one-minute chart or five-minute chart?

Matt: It is a range chart and a range chart is not time-based, which is why I love it, especially when used with Delta. It is price-based. The number in front of it represents the number of ticks it has to move to print a new candle. For me, that's 22 ticks of price movement, equivalent to 5.5 points on the Nasdaq.

You'll notice that the candles don't print as frequently during the overnight session because the market is less volatile. However, when prices are highly volatile, moving 20 points every second, the chart prints a lot of candles. This really gives you an idea of the speed of the moves, and you can see how much buying or selling is happening within that 5.5-point range. It shows you how significant a particular price area is based on the volume of buyers and sellers, helping to indicate the importance and speed of what's going on. The fact that it's not time-based is why I love using it.

Q: Have you ever done paper trading or back-testing, or have you always jumped straight into live trading?

Matt: Yeah, I did with prop firms. That was the closest I ever got to true paper trading – paying a small fee, going through an evaluation, and having a lot of upside potential. I also did some back-testing in 2019 with a group of traders. That's how I discovered my 22-range chart; it worked best with what I was doing then, and I've stuck with it because I'm used to it now.

I've also learned that back-testing isn't very effective unless you have tick-based data, which is hard to get. So, when I'm practicing new strategies, I prefer to do it in a live environment. I might not execute trades, but I watch live price action to see how things react to whatever I'm testing.

Q: When did you realize that you were ready to be a full-time trader?

Matt: It made the most sense about four years ago. My wife was the one who encouraged me to make the switch. I think I've always had some money baggage in my life. I always wanted to work, and I was doing both – working and trading – thinking I could handle it.

The job I had was very demanding, requiring about 80 hours a week. Despite that, I would still wake up at 4 a.m. to trade. My wife pointed out that I was making much more money trading than from my job and questioned why I was still juggling both. She suggested that I focus 100% of my effort on trading and also explore other business opportunities outside the trading world. She really pushed me to make that change, and I thank her for it all the time.

Q: How many prop evaluation accounts did you blow up before you got funded?

Matt: The very first time I got funded was in 2019 with TopStep and I passed on my very first try. Then I blew up 100 evals on Apex and 21 PA accounts.

Q: What kept you going? Why didn't you give up?

Matt: I was doing all 20 at once, which meant five different tries basically. It wasn't a long period. I've had bad months, but I've also tasted the goodness. You have a little bit of the sweet honey of trading and you understand the upside and it's worth fighting for. Yes, I've blown up evaluations just like everybody else by wanting to get through them too fast. That's probably my number-one thing because I knew how to trade and I knew that I need to be on the PA or a funded account so I rushed through the eval and then you blew up.

Q: What do you think are some of the biggest mistakes that people make in trading?

Matt: People blow their savings without having any idea of what's going on. Many traders lack patience. As soon as the market opens, they start clicking buttons and firing off trades without a strategy. They get too locked in and over-leveraged because they get a taste of the money and aren't positioned for long-term success. They don't have the patience or the proper risk management to sustain their trading.

Q: What advice would you give to a new prop trader?

Matt: I recommend starting with a simulated account. You need a lot of screen time as a trader just watching the market and experimenting with different strategies. This helps you understand what's going on and figure out what works for you and what doesn't. There are many profitable strategies out there, but the challenge is keeping your money, which involves psychological discipline and risk management.

There's a lot of ways to make money. You either buy or sell – there are only two options. Once you start making money consistently in the simulated account, move to a prop account. The risk is low, and you don't have to invest much to have significant upside and get funded. Take withdrawals from your prop account and put that money into a live account, where you can keep all your profits and have no restrictions. By then, you should have established your rules and strategies.

In a live account, your money can be gone in a day if you do something dumb, so having the right foundation for all of that is crucial. Understand leverage, contract sizing, trade execution, and the importance of patience.

Q: Speaking of rules, what are your thoughts on the need to play by the rules for prop firms?

Matt: I think it's their house, their game. I absolutely stand by it. If you don't want to trade a live account, there's plenty of options. If you don't like the rules, open up a live account and trade your own money. If you need their money, then follow their rules. If you see the upside, follow their rules.

Q: Do you feel that it's hard to follow the rules?

Matt: Not for my strategy. For some people, sure, but for me not really. I'm not trading max size and I'm not averaging into a bunch of trades.

Q: What advice can you give to prop traders on adhering to prop firm rules and avoiding violations?

Matt: It depends on the prop firm. There are tons of different props, tons of different rules, tons of ones that don't have as many rules. You need to establish what those rules are – read the website and understand them. Then think about whether you even need to change your strategy. Don't look at outlier days. You need to be looking at your whole sample size. A lot of people have one bad day, and they assume they need to rewrite their entire strategy and the way they approach the market. No, you had one bad day. Everybody has had a bad day. Even if you have a 70% win rate, you're losing 30% of your trades. I think a lot of people try and rewrite what they need to be doing to follow the rules. I don't think you need to be doing that. Just establish what the rules are and move forward. Most of the rules are not very complicated.

For example, at the prop firm I'm with now, one rule is not to add to losers more than once. If you add to losers twice, you've broken the rule. So, if you want to add to a trade, close your current trade and open a new position. That's the workaround. Another rule is you can't make more than 30% of your total withdrawal in a single day. So how do you go about that? Be consistent. Make $400 a day. Don't push the limit of trying to make $750 a day, because then you're not going to get a payout. Learning to walk away probably is one of the biggest things people need to figure out.

Q: What one skill would it take to be a successful trader?

Matt: Patience and understanding your brain. That second part is a loaded answer but if you don't understand your own emotions, you'll never make it in trading. It's so emotionally heavy. You can do your best to try and be emotionless, which is arguably just as bad as being heavily emotional.

Patience is the easy answer. If you cannot sit in front of your screen and not take a trade, you're never going to make it as a trader. You have to be able to not take trades and watch the screen.

Q: How do you think being part of a trading community contributed to your success?

Matt: Community is so important! Everyone needs accountability in their life in some capacity, and accountability and vulnerability are key to getting better. How can you improve if you can't acknowledge your flaws? How can you improve if no one else acknowledges your flaws? Vulnerability and accountability in trading communities are powerful because most people don't understand trading. When you share your mistakes and wins with someone who truly understands and can provide feedback, it makes a huge difference.

For example, if I had a really bad day and didn't follow any of my rules, I can share that with my accountability buddies. The next day, they can encourage me: "Hey, Matt, I know yesterday was tough. Be patient. You got this, keep your head up, you know what you need to do. Execute it right." This support helps me stay motivated and bounce back.

On my YouTube live streams, I do a vibe check every day as an accountability measure. I ask, "Are you red or green on the day? What are you doing that you like? What are you doing that you don't like?" There's always something to improve and something to pat yourself on the back for, whether you're losing or making money. You could be red on the day but had a good entry and just managed it poorly, so you need to work on management. Or you could be green with a bad entry but got lucky and exited well. The goal is to think about how you can be better every single day.

MATT'S TRADING TIPS

1. **Master one instrument, one setup.**

If you want to make trading more effective and less stressful, focus on one setup, one instrument. Ninety-nine percent of Matt's trade are in the Nasdaq. By trading the same instrument every day he intimately knows its typical movements, the impact of news, when to avoid trading, what each tick is worth, how to manage his position sizing and P&L like the back of his hand. The more you trade the same instrument and the same setup, the more confident you will become. This familiarity not only makes trading more intuitive but also boosts your confidence, allowing you to trade with greater certainty and reduced stress.

2. **Focus on base hits.**

For prop firm accounts, setting targets and focusing on consistency is key. Instead of aiming for big standout days, prioritize steady performance to stay within the rules. Matt's ideal target is about $400 per account, achieved through small, consistent trades across 20 accounts. One effective approach is to focus on base hits. While aiming for large, infrequent gains can be tempting, those big wins are outliers and will probably breach the rules of some prop firms. Instead, aim for small, consistent gains: base hits. Aiming for two 10-point trades on the Nasdaq may seem small like breadcrumbs, but you can fill up easily doing it multiple times a day.

3. **Be overfunded and under-leveraged.**

One of the best strategies for long-term trading success is to be over-funded and under-leveraged. This approach helps you stay in the game longer and manage risk more effectively. Having more funds in your account than needed creates a financial cushion, absorbing losses and reducing pressure to recover quickly. This stability allows for more strategic and less emotional decision-making. Trading with less leverage means each trade affects a smaller percentage of your total capital. This reduces the impact of losses and helps avoid large drawdowns, preserving your capital. Overfunding is also beneficial because trading with too much leverage can be stressful and lead to quick losses. By staying under-leveraged, you maintain a clearer mind and stick to your plan, even during market volatility. For prop traders, this can be achieved by trading with fewer contracts across multiple accounts.

CHAPTER 15

Nick Syiek

Nick Syiek, known as "Trader Nick" on YouTube, made over $3 million by the age of 23 trading forex and indices. Unlike many traders, Nick focuses on fundamentals, skillfully combining economic growth, interest rate trends, and news with technical levels to identify swing trades.

Nick's entrepreneurial spirit ignited early. At 15, he started a landscaping business, and by 17, he was flipping yard equipment like pressure washers, lawnmowers, and tractors. By 19, he used the capital from these ventures to dive into stock investing, eventually making the leap to active forex trading.

"I think I was the only kid at my high school with a pickup truck because I needed it for work, not because it was cool. My truck wasn't cool at all, but it was my first investment. I bought my dad's old truck for half the price. That truck kickstarted my business ventures."

Nick studied computer science at Auburn University, where he honed his tech skills to develop software for scanning, studying, and analyzing financial markets. A proud Atlanta native, Nick balances a strong work ethic with a love for trading.

He believes in trading small with tight stops and aiming for open-ended profits on his winners. Combining his computer science background with his passion for trading, Nick Syiek embodies the entrepreneurial grit, tech-savvy, and discipline that makes him a widely followed figure in the trading community.

Q: How did you get into trading?

Nick: I became fascinated with trading through my experience in land-scaping. I noticed how you could buy big-ticket items like a four-wheeler on Craigslist or Facebook Marketplace and sell them for a higher price. This gave me the idea to buy an iPhone from someone for $200 and sell it to another person for $300, making the spread. I essentially created a market for both sellers and buyers, acting as a middleman.

My dad, who has always been my biggest supporter in my entrepreneurial endeavors, pointed out that I was essentially engaging in stock trading. I was buying low and selling high, a fundamental concept in trading. This realization made me wonder what it would be like to do the same with companies and stocks. So, I opened a Robinhood account and started trading stocks, but I was initially terrible at it.

Q: What were you doing in the beginning that made your trading so terrible?

Nick: When I opened up the Robinhood account, I received some free shares. I think I put less than $1,000 into my first trading account. I remember my first strategy was the dumbest strategy. I started by buying well-known companies like Ford because I thought they made cool cars and were good investments. Whenever the stock went up by 25 cents per share, I would immediately sell it, thinking I was making easy money.

Then I tried trading Snapchat. I bought it at $24, watched it rise to $27, and thought I was doing great. But suddenly, it dropped below $20. My strategy was to hold on to losing stocks until they recovered and to sell winners as soon as I saw a profit. As anyone experienced in trading will tell you, this approach doesn't work well. Fortunately, I was only trading with a small amount of money. Now, I focus a lot more on fundamental analysis and macroeconomics to guide my trading decisions. It's far less dumb than it used to be.

Q: How much of your money did you invest?

Nick: I think it was no more than 2% of what I had. It was not a lot. I wasn't dead broke when I first started trading, I had a reserve, but money meant so much to me because I worked so hard to get it. When I found trading, I fortunately knew how hard it was to get that money, so I didn't burn through all my savings right away. I traded with a really small amount, and instantly found out in a good way that this stuff is really difficult. I lost money first, and I think that's made all the difference. Often people will have a good start in their trading and then make big mistakes. I was humbled right away and realized how difficult it is.

Q: What happened next? Did you put more money into the account and continue to trade?

Nick: After this, I went to school for computer science. I had programming experience and I wanted to combine that with trading. This led me to the technical side of trading when I discovered MetaTrader, which ultimately got me into currency trading. Initially, I was fascinated by stocks, but then I wanted to create scripts and back-test strategies. My computer science itch was tingling, which drove me to write code to test some trading ideas. MetaTrader has one of the most approachable coding environments. I spent a lot of time on YouTube and Google, learning how to program trading robots and back-test strategies.

I feel my approach was honestly not terrible. I made dumb mistakes like everyone else but pretty quickly, I wanted to test the ideas. I was too scared with my money to start out, which I think served me really well because I still didn't become profitable for some time and I still lost money, for years after that. The idea that I want to back-test and combine this with software simply because that was my interest, ended up being a real advantage for me. I realized pretty quick, once I started getting into programming trading strategies, which were purely technical for starters, that there is no magical simple edge that can be derived from a moving average crossover or anything like that.

I would encourage anyone who has programming skills to get into MetaTrader and start programming trading systems, robots to trade, and you'll find very quickly that it is very difficult to find huge amounts of alpha from just purely technical strategies. Are there ways to make money from technicals? Absolutely. I still use them in my trading but it didn't take long before I started realizing that creating 20% gains in the market every year is really, really hard. It's really hard to find a system that can do that reliably without taking a tremendous amount of risk.

So back-testing really served me well. I got obsessed with it. I stopped putting my money at risk, and just kept staying in a back-tester. I didn't even demo trade. I was just really interested in writing robots on MetaTrader that would trade the market and back-testing strategies out. I really didn't want to put any money in until I felt like I had a reasonable strategy and a large sample size of back-tested data to go off of. I did kind of slowly find that. For a while, I was just in the tinkering phase until I started to get a little bit more confident.

With some time, I started realizing that you can also back-test fundamentals. Sometimes people wonder how do you back-test fundamentals? I started wanting to understand what's really driving the currencies that I'm looking at or the stock indices. I've always been all encompassing. I've never really niched down to one specific market. I've always been rotating to different markets and I think that fundamentals allow you to do that. So I was fascinated by what drives the market, what really pushes the market around.

That slowly landed me to CNBC and listening to places where people were debating what's driving the markets right now. The more I listened, the more I realized they're not talking about moving average crossovers as why the entire stock market is performing poorly or well this year. So I started testing and employing those concepts, trying to see how does that typically perform in a pre-election year, for example. I just had so much fun with that and I still do to this day. I love testing and understanding forces on the market, going back and looking at it historically.

Q: Were you in college at this time, when you were coding and back-testing?

Nick: Yes, I would back-test all the time throughout college. I left individual stocks behind because I really got into currencies. I feel that currencies, indices, and gold, those three can coexist within the same macro forces like the Fed and economic figures. I was digging deep into those, trading the big picture, the macro not the micro side.

Q: At what point did you put real money on the line again?

Nick: I constantly continued to back-test but I also started trading. I think about two to three years in I actually started to be breakeven to slightly profitable. What I think a lot of people get wrong is, they think that from there the next step is you become ultra-profitable. That's where I think a lot of people get mixed up. I realized the more and more I back-tested that slightly profitable is great. Slightly profitable is all you need. You don't need to be this ultra-profitable guru. The players whom you're going up against in the markets have a floor full of PhDs trying to figure out where the market's going next. It's going to be really hard to beat that. If you can get to a point where your strategies and systems are producing profits slowly and steadily over time, these small positions can equate to big gains. That was the breakthrough for me. You can make good money with a lot of different strategies, a lot of different approaches if you also accept that you're not going to make a lot of money very quickly. If more people accepted that, there'd be a lot more profitable traders.

One of the things that I learned the most from back-testing was that the actual position sizing and risk management part of your strategy matters more than the technical entries and exits. And it makes a lot of sense. When you think about, why do people struggle to make money in markets? If you just reverse all the things that they spend all their time on, it's actually a really good place to start. Most people obsess over the entry, psychology, and risk management. Reversing all of that was a really important starting point for me.

Q: Were you more confident to trade larger size after back-testing?

Nick: From the beginning up until now, I haven't been a huge risk taker, which might sound counterintuitive that I've started businesses and currently run my own software company. However, I don't like to take huge risks, which is one of the reasons why trading has not come natural to me. It has taken time. I also have a systematic approach with my position sizing, which I have programmed. So if you visualize a bunch of checks and balances that I do for positioning, if I have a lot of things that agree with my strategy, I'm not just talking about technical confluences, but rather fundamental confluences, I may risk slightly more, but it's still very small overall. Most people get very frustrated with the idea of risking really small. The idea of risking small gives me a lot of room to bounce back from drawdowns and manage positions. I stay away from leverage. I always try to risk less than 1% because I'm all about that slight, slow, and steady performance, rather than huge ups and huge downs in my trading.

One of the things that I've really landed on is when a good story is there, when something is very fundamentally bullish or fundamentally bearish for me, I try and take out as much of the technical timing as I can. So, I might enter a market and let's say

I'm long and prices come down to a level I like, the story overall looks real good, the checks that I'm looking for are all checked, I may take a position size that's still less than 1% but close to it. In that case I have a stop loss. I always use a stop loss for my trading but I don't use a take profit. So if market just tanks goes through my stop, I'm out of the trade if it rips from there, and I was right about entering into the market at that level, I will try and let it run as much as I can.

One thing that I really liked about indices is that from a lot of my back-testing they go up over time, and they have very strong rallies. This sort of strategy favors my style of trend following where I can buy and stairstep to the upside on the indices. That's why indices are my favorite, but I also trade currencies and commodities, because sometimes the fundamental trends can be very, very clear. For example, one central bank wants to cut rates and the other does not. I love those sorts of stories in the currency world.

Q: If you don't have a target, at what point do you exit a trade?

Nick: On the record, for me entries are more difficult. Everybody wants that perfect entry where there's no drawdown and it's instantly in profit. Entries are hard and a lot of times I'll mark up two to three levels and it might not be until my third entry that the market actually does well. I might try more than once with a relatively tight stop but even though I'm entering multiple times, let's say I finally catch the runner and I'm in a trade and now it's working well.

So for exits, I use trailing stops. I like market structure, the simple stuff. Let's say we put in a higher low, and we're in an uptrend and that higher low breaks through the highs, I'm trailing a stop behind that higher low. That's my risk management. I'm going to lock in portions of the trade. I know a lot of traders take partial profits. I don't think there's anything wrong with them, but for me my exit style is trailing a stop and letting the market tell me when market structure has changed paths and it's time to get out. Most of my trading is on the four-hour and daily chart.

Q: Does that mean you that you have a single entry with a tight initial stop and single exit with a trailing stop for profits?

Nick: Yes, with a willingness to try a couple of times if I am stopped out quickly. I'm all in and I'm all out. I have one position on, I won't ever get to two or three added positions. Now, in rare cases, however, I will add to a winner if I really like this story and if

I really like the fundamentals and the technicals. If they all look really good, I may add to a winner, but I don't add to losers in my primary momentum trading. I usually don't add to winners, either, but in rare situations where my indicators are screaming all of the right things, I may add more but I usually won't do that until my initial risk is completely off the table and my profits are locked in. So I'm not adding risk to the trade; I'm only reintroducing risk to the position if I like all the checks and balances.

Q: What are those checks and balances that you look for?

Nick: There are three pillars that I really look at when it comes to positions. I have the technical side, the sentiment side, and the fundamental side. So for example, I like to look at the commitment of traders' report, I like to look at put–call ratios, I like to look at investment or investor surveys.

When it comes to sentiment, I'm looking at both the retail side and how institutional traders are positioned. When it comes to institutional positions, I'm usually agreeing with what they're doing for the most part. Whereas with retail side I'm generally looking at it as more of a contrarian indicator.

In my checks and balances, in the system that we've written I have a couple of people on my team. We've built a tool that will fetch this data, then look at it, and automatically assign a numerical plus or minus 1, 2, 3 scoring system that will look at the commitment of traders' data and retail positioning as displayed by forex brokers, for example. So, looking at positioning from a retail and institutional level. That's one area that I look at.

Then on the fundamental side I have the four main categories. Economic growth, which is going to include metrics like PMIs [purchasing managers' index], retail sales, and all the standard indicators. Then, on the inflation side you have numbers like the CPI and PPI [Consumer Price Index and Producer Price Index]. All of these are getting numerical scoring within the systems.

A lot of the actual scoring falls under a systematic approach because we're talking ones, zeros, and minus ones. So there's a lot of stuff there and then, of course, the final being interest rates and labor stats. All of these things are factoring into the checks and balances. There's some discretion involved but what converted me into a systematic trader is my background in software and realizing that I can't do all these things off the top of my head. I can't anecdotally consider everything from PMIs to NFPs [nonfarm payrolls] in my head all the time for every different asset that I trade. I just can't do that. So I have to have software that helps me and that's what built the foundation of our Edge Finder tool. There is some discretion involved on the technicals side using market structure, which is not predefined hard rule sets, it's more support and resistance trend lines. Those things can be a bit more subjective.

Q: You trade on four-hour and daily charts but sentiment and fundamentals do not change often. Does that mean on a day-to-day basis, you have a fundamental bias and then you're looking at your indicators for the entry?

Nick: If I only looked at sentiment, you're right, it would be mostly weekly or monthly signals, but there's constantly news coming out, and those components of the scoring system that I use will always be changing. For example, last week, when we had NFP come out, all the columns that score the US dollar–related currency pairs, gold, and indices got a stronger read in favor of the dollar because we had a blockbuster jobs report. Everything was in line for a stronger dollar so that component changed, which means the overall total scoring of all of these independent metrics changed.

With the sentiment indicators and fundamental indicators, when you combine the total score of all of them, that score is changing pretty frequently but it's not every day that you're getting a totally different read. For example, during 2022 the US dollar was bullish the whole year because the inflation numbers were high and that was ratcheting up the score very consistently in favor of the dollar. So there are forces that can remain bullish or bearish for a very long time but then there're other areas that are changing throughout the week and day-to-day. It doesn't change constantly; it changes slowly.

Q: Does this mean you are looking at your trading tool and waiting for a change in the scoring, then going to the charts? Or looking at the charts and then checking to see if the scores changed?

Nick: That's a great question. I start on Edge Finder. For example, if USD/JPY is getting a bullish reading right now, I don't take the trade just because of that. I have to do my markups on the charts and look for proper entry points. This sort of discretionary side comes next, so the charts are the final decision point for me.

Everything else is what will get me to look at that chart. If something is getting a strong read but I don't like the technical signal, I may not take a trade.

Q: Do you use this information for day trading or swing trading?

Nick: I'm not a day trader. I'm a swing trader. The Edge Finder scoring takes into account new data as it comes in but I always weigh the data against the week before. I take it as a full picture and when the new data comes in others are lagging, but when you listen to Powell speak, the data might have been several days before but he'll still referencing it, so it is still important to them just because it is not today's data. My tool is probably built more for swing traders since it's not generating a signal every day. It's more of a week-to-week signal system that helps to spot lots of different metrics.

Q: How often do you trade?

Nick: I take about two or three trades a week and my average trade duration is anywhere from one to seven days but my really big winners could last a long time. The losers are really quick and I get smacked in the face right away, sometimes more than once in a single day. When I'm trying to enter on a pullback, and that pullback becomes a bigger pullback, I might get stopped out a few times in a single day, but psychologically, a little rule for myself is I don't like to take two losers in a day so I usually will stop trading after that. It's just easier to make mistakes, so after two losses I have to step away. Not that it really bothers me, because my position size is small, but I know I'm not going to be as sharp as a fresh day.

Q: Your strategy is a trend-following strategy, correct?

Nick: I am a trend follower, but not only technical. I think anyone who's a fundamental trader will say the same thing here. You're always a trend follower if you're fundamentalist because you're constantly waiting for data and reacting after the data. At the end of the day, as a true trend follower, which is the cheesy nickname for my trading strategy, because true trend following means you don't know when a trend is going to end. That's why I don't have strict take-profit levels on my trade and I don't think there's anything wrong with that. I know many traders who do well taking partial profits, but as a fundamental and technical true trend follower, I recognize and accept that I'm following the data. I don't know what the jobs number is, I'm not sure where the price is going to go perfectly but true trend following, if you think of a simple moving average, is waiting for the price to become a bearish trend before you cut the trade.

Q: What's your best trade ever?

Nick: I love talking about my best trade, and I hope you don't ask me about my worst trades after, but I know you will. My best trade was in 2023. I was pretty bullish on the Nasdaq all year going into 2023. Everyone hated the stock market and again to be clear I was also bullish in 2022, which did not work so well for the Nasdaq. However, my best trade actually was toward the end of the year, when everybody saw the market just absolutely rally and the dollar sell off at the same time. I had some dollar shorts on and at the same time S&P longs. This is a perfect testament to my entry style, because as price was pulling back on the Nasdaq and S&P 500 in October of last year, I took two losses before my third trade, which was an absolute rock star. I held onto the trade for a month and a half until late December. I did get trailed out for a profit that ended up being one of my best trades ever. So while it took me a couple of entries to get into it the result was a really nice move. Toward the end of the year I just kept trailing the stop and it just kept going and going and going. One of my favorite things about it is that I remember all of my big winners, whereas a lot of counter-trend traders remember all their losers because they become big problems. What I will remember, though, are the really long losing streaks but they're small losses that pile up.

Q: Your best trade ever was S&P, Nasdaq, and the dollar. How many markets are you watching at the same time?

Nick: The main ones that I trade are the major currencies, and within that, I really watch the euro, pound, and the Japanese yen against the dollar. Those are the primary currencies that I trade.

       Then on the commodity side I really just trade gold, then the S&P 500, Nasdaq, and the Dow I rotate based on the outlook for the markets. That's pretty much it, there's like 10 things that I seriously watch and trade.

Q: How do you consider correlation risk, because you've got a few of these positions all in the same direction? How do you manage that?

Nick: That's a great question because correlation risk is a thing that I don't think a lot of traders consider. Somebody will tell me I'm long EUR/USD, and I'm short GBP/USD. I'm like what's going on, you're taking two different trades on the same thing. For me, it goes across all markets. If you're trading gold and the dollar, it really starts by just saying is this current environment more risk on or, is it more risk off? If it is risk on right now, I don't want to be long the dollar and long the Nasdaq at the same time because there's some inverse relations. Also I don't want to take too many of the same trades so usually I'll just total it up. So remember I said 1% or less on a trade. Sure, I might have two trades on currency pairs at the same time but I don't want to take on the US dollar specifically more than 1% risk because even though I might trade GBP/USD and EUR/USD, if the dollar flies or drops, those two trades become the same thing. It's like, if you ever look at correlation in a stock market drop, every stock just becomes super-correlated and the same thing can happen in currencies when one currency just becomes super-dominant all of a sudden on a big news drop, or something like that.

Q: How long did it take for you to become consistently profitable?

Nick: About 2.5 years to get to a point where I wasn't losing money. Three years was about the time that I started making some money and when I say *some* it was very modest amounts of money. I did have a good starting capital basis and I slowly deployed more of that to make it a little bit more meaningful. At the end of the day, the game of money in general is you have to have it to make more of it and I know that that's not a popular way of thinking but it's what I believe.

I think with trading you can totally find ways to take your talents and ratchet them up. Many people go the prop firm space route or many people find an investor; there are many ways to scale yourself up. I got into trading in 2015/2016 so prop wasn't that big. So I kind of did it the old-fashioned way. I saved money and saved everything I could. I never wanted to buy myself stuff. I just wanted to put it in my trading account. I feel like I was interested in the markets for the right reason. Most people won't make it two to three years in if their only interest is to make money. Obviously everybody wants to make money, there's no question there, and there's nothing wrong with that but that interest won't carry you as far as if you had a passionate interest in the markets, and I think that took me a long way.

Q: When did you become a full-time trader?

Nick: When I left school, I got a contracting job on site at Delta Airlines but I spent the night studying the markets, making videos, and trading. I had a membership group that I was running, although it was very small at the time but that was the basis. I got to a point when, between YouTube and my own trading, I was making not as much as my job, but enough to say okay, if I had every waking hour to put into this, maybe I can make it. But it ended up working out really well because when COVID happened first thing Delta Airlines did was cut out a lot of their contractors, which was no fault to them. If you have nobody going on planes, you need to cut costs. So while it was almost like I took a risk, my entire job was at risk and I didn't know it. While it may seem that I took a risk to leave my steady paycheck, that paycheck was not steady; it got cut right away after that.

Q: Not everyone has the time or motivation to work after their day job. Would you say that it was your passion for trading or your passion for being an entrepreneur that pushed you to commit to trading?

Nick: No, and it's not healthy, either. At that time my commute was horrible because the Atlanta Airport is on the south side of the city and I was living with my parents for a bit and that was on the north side. My commute was awful to get through the city every day. I was driving all the time and working long hours there. There was a period when I felt that I couldn't do two of these things at the same time; trading is so hard and creating content is a lot of work, too.

If you're going to be an entrepreneur, you've got to work some crazy hours. I did that for a while but I realized I couldn't do that forever. What drove me to stick around with trading is a combination of the two. I really love markets and I just love that the challenge to entrepreneurship is never-ending. There's always more to learn. There's always more challenges ahead.

Q: Now, getting back to your worst trade. What was your worse trade ever?

Nick: I'm going to pull up MyFXBook quickly because I remember the pain of trying to put out a public track record. It is so painful because when you're losing and everyone's just telling you your strategy sucks and comments on your YouTube, it is hard. It's very hard to trade, period, but trading in front of others is something that is ridiculously hard. My worst drawdown on record, I have two different ones. In 2021 I had a pretty steep drawdown. I can't remember exactly all the trades, because remember there are a lot of small losers. A lot of it was just being on the wrong side of the currency market. During this time, I took several losses along the way. I think I was wrong about gold in 2021, so there was a string of losses in some specific assets. The other one was in 2022 and because my trading style tends to be small losses, it's like death by a thousand cuts. The market just kept selling and selling and selling and I was wrong about the Nasdaq and gold that year.

I wouldn't say it was a mistake because I still stuck to my rules but I took a lot of losses trying to catch a breakout. If you look at the Nasdaq on a chart during 2022 obviously with hindsight, it's just a straight downtrend but there were times where things might be breaking out. Breakout-retest kinds of setups and they just would fall apart so my loss streaks were pretty substantial. I think my peak drawdown during 2022 was 30% on my account, which was a lot.

I actually think my position sizing saved me. My trading style worked phenomenally well in 2020, 2021, and 2023. In 2022 I had a horrible drawdown even though I thought my position sizing was small. So it just goes to show you can prep all you want for trading, do all your back-testing, but at the end of the day position sizing has saved me many times from steep drawdowns. The year 2022 was pretty much the worst I've seen for my trading style and strategy to date. So those were tough times.

Q: When people have these drawdowns, especially when it is prolonged, they start to question their strategy. How do you mentally recover and return to trading?

Nick: It's so hard. Here's something that drives me crazy. In the markets, a lot of people will say, "You just need to turn off your emotions and trade like a robot," and I know we're in the revolution of AI [artificial intelligence] right now but I'm not an AI, I'm not a robot, and I still have feelings. So when I go through a losing streak and it wasn't a year straight of losses, I had wins, I had losses, but the net equity on my account trended lower for an entire year, there's no getting around the fact that it's hard to show up to work. It was incredibly painful. For me personally to get in front of a camera and talk markets, it's hard when you're going through a drawdown. It's not fun. So that's the human side. The constructive approach is that fortunately I had years before where I had drawdowns, they never quite got to 30% but I stuck to a system.

Also, it's not as if I'm trading this money and if I don't make a profit my lights get shut off. I'm not trading with that kind of pressure and I don't think anybody should because trading is really hard. You should have other sources of income or other diversified investments. I don't trade solely for a living. Maybe I will someday but if I do, it's going to be selling puts way in the money and super-low risk and I'll probably underperform the S&P 500. That's probably when I will trade solely for a living.

The markets are very hard to look at when you're experiencing drawdown and I have other things that I'm doing with my day to keep me preoccupied. So I think that that's been a healthy way to approach that. I got married in 2022, so that was a good kind of healthy distraction.

I almost got into a stage where it doesn't hurt, you almost get numb where you're sticking to the plan. It's like when things get really hard for Jeff Bezos at Amazon, he doesn't walk out and never come back, he continues chugging on. You've got to have that vision that is more than pure hope and dreams. I back-tested it a lot beforehand so I felt some comfort there.

Q: What are your favorite trading indicators?

Nick: I love the fed watch tool and I love the analytical tools that WeBull gives me. There're so many stats to look at my trading performance versus traditional brokerages. In terms of indicators I like simple momentum indicators on Tradingview. I have this indicator that I use that's basically two moving averages and it shades between the two. I love that stuff like that gives me a visual of momentum or no momentum in the market. So simple moving average cross-over indicators just help me to get an idea, but they are not the lead driver to why I'm entering a trade or not. Just helpful resources to spot momentum.

Q: Can we sum up your strategy as being a trend follower that who looks for pullback in the direction of your fundamental bias with entries on four-hour or daily charts?

Nick: Yes, without any indicators on the chart, I'm just looking for higher highs, higher lows with a moving average crossover to help visualize it. You can see it really quick when you're flipping through charts. You can say, oh, that one just flipped from bullish or bearish, the other way. So it's just a visual helper but, yes, I'm looking for a pullback into a market structure area.

I like break and retests. I know it is the most standard technical analysis that you could possibly pull out of a technical book but that's what I use. It is simple and that's why it kind of works for me because it's coupling with the fundamentals that really makes the difference. I had a conversation with somebody just the other day; they're asking, how do you know if a breakout is false or not? And I said, wouldn't we all love to know that? But I feel that with a good fundamental catalyst, a breakout can be understood a little bit better. Like when the dollar broke out last week on NFP: this is a breakout on the technicals aligned with a really strong report that could have lasting effects and that's why I'm long the dollar.

Q: Do you make all your trading decisions yourself or do you have a team that you confer with?

Nick: I have lots of trading friends and I do a show on Monday through Friday where usually a guest joins me and one of the most regular guests is Frank, a guy who works for me. He'll join me on the show, we'll talk markets and oftentimes we challenge or confirm each other's thought processes. I love that, and I think it's a really healthy thing to have a trading partner, somebody to bounce ideas off of and to push back on, but final decisions are just me.

Q: If you had to give one tip to a new trader, what would it be?

Nick: The one tip? Easy. It's one that I would be forwarding from somebody. I learned a lot of things from Rob Booker, whom I used to watch back in college every day. He would have this live stream and it was my happy place. He would come on in his office. I thought it was the coolest thing in the world; he would say, "Hello!" Everybody was just so happy, and he also was always coding bots on MetaTrader. So that was a big influencer for me. His thing was there would be a lot more profitable traders if they learned to shrink their position size. He had a tip on there that he would always say, which was if you want to make $1,000 a day, you've got to learn how to make $1 a day and keep it first. I love that way of thinking. Most people just come in with big position sizes.

My one tip would be: reduce your position size, and see what happens in your trading. It will make you trade with a more level head. It will allow you to handle drawdowns a lot better. You still need to incorporate an edge and do all your back-testing, but assuming that you've done a lot of that, reducing your position sizes is the biggest tip I can give anybody.

Q: Do you think there's a specific skill that it takes to become a successful full-time trader?

Nick: I think it's less of a skill and more of a genuine interest in markets. I don't think I've ever met anyone who is very successful in markets who isn't absolutely in love with learning about them. It's like anybody who's top of their class. It's something they like, it's not agonizing for them to do. It's the same thing for starting a business.

Q: Any tips on the transition from the comfort of a paycheck to a full-time trader?

Nick: If you're thinking about transitioning, you should be profitable before you do it. You should probably see several months of profitability before you do it or try and get funded. By the way, a lot of people make that mistake. They try and get funded to try to leave their job and they get too excited. Like when the crypto crazy stuff happened a couple of years back. A lot of people said I'm going to quit my job and do this because I'm making a bunch of money, and it was because the chart only went up.

You should not quit your job until you feel like you've had some really tough times, you've learned a lot, and you've had several months of overall consistent profitability in different market environments. If you've only been trading in Superbowl market and you've been bullish the whole time, that's not a true experience. You haven't seen it all. So make sure you've seen a good diversity of markets in your trading, and you don't have to jump two feet into the river when you go full time. You could switch to part-time; I think that's healthier.

What many people might be surprised by when you have all the time in the world to trade, your trading might take serious dips because you might force too many trades, you might be too obsessed with the profits, you may break your rules because you're staring at it too long. I think there is a path to becoming a full-time trader that does not incorporate just binary all in, all out. Having some other source of income to supplement your time and income is a much healthier way to approach trading.

NICK'S TRADING TIPS

1. **Let your winners run.**

The key to Nick's trading success is taking small losses and letting his winners run. He always uses a stop loss but rarely sets a take profit.

If the market moves against him, Nick's stop loss protects him; if it moves in his favor, he lets his winners run. This strategy aligns perfectly with his trend-following approach, especially with indices, which tend to rise over time and have strong rallies.

Nick also trades currencies and commodities, where fundamental trends can be very clear, such as one central bank cutting rates while another holds steady. Nick maintains a disciplined approach with one position at a time. In rare cases, if the fundamentals and technicals are exceptionally strong, he might add to a winning position but never to a losing one. Even then, he only adds to winners when his initial risk is fully covered and his profits are secured. This way, he doesn't increase his risk but reintroduces it only when all indicators align positively.

2. **Trading smaller keeps you in control.**

Trading with a smaller size keeps your head cool and helps you handle drawdowns like a pro. While risking small might seem boring, it gives you the flexibility to bounce back from drawdowns and manage positions like a boss. As an experienced trader, Nick believes that the position sizing and risk management part of your strategy matters more than the technical entries and exits. Most people obsess over the entry and they care less about the exit, psychology, and risk management. As Nick's mentor Rob Booker wisely said, if you want to make $1,000 a day, you've got to learn how to make a $1 a day and keep it first.

3. **Experience different markets before committing full time.**

Don't quit your job until you've had losses, learned from them, and achieved several months of consistent profitability in various market environments. If you've only traded during a strong bull market, your skills haven't truly been tested. Also, there's no need to dive in headfirst. Transitioning to part-time trading can be a healthier approach. Surprisingly, having all the time in the world to trade can lead to serious setbacks. You might force trades, obsess over profits, or break your rules from over-monitoring the market. The path to becoming a full-time trader doesn't have to be all or nothing. Maintaining another source of income to supplement your trading can provide financial stability and reduce the pressure to perform, leading to better trading decisions.

CHAPTER 16

Vince Koehn

Born and raised in southwest Kansas, Vince Koehn has built a remarkable journey crisscrossing the globe to manage his businesses in China, Southeast Asia, and the US. Vince began prop trading in 2017 but only got serious about it during the COVID-19 pandemic when he was often stuck in Asia due to travel restrictions.

Vince's trading journey is nothing short of extraordinary. After blowing up hundreds of evaluations, he eventually turned a $1 million profit on his prop accounts. He specializes in trading Nasdaq futures, particularly during the New York open. Vince's strong work ethic is evident from his early career, starting at a sheet metal business in southwest Kansas at the age of 19. Despite having no college degree or formal training, his relentless desire to learn and excel led him to work many 20-hour days. He eventually took over the business from his father-in-law, growing it from a $700,000-a-year operation to a $6 million-a-year enterprise in just five years.

Vince carried his strong work ethic into learning about trading, dedicating countless hours to mastering the intricacies of the market. His commitment to understanding and applying trading strategies with the same intensity he brought to his business ventures was key to his eventual success. His trading strategy focuses on looking for confluence of Fibonacci retracements and price levels. Vince's journey from a self-taught business owner to a successful prop trader exemplifies his dedication, resilience, and ability to adapt and thrive in competitive environments.

Q: How did you get into trading?

Vince: I was about 25 years old when I really got into stocks. When you're on a shoestring budget, you start off with pink sheets and penny stocks, thinking that's going to work. Then you find out that doesn't work very well or you get stuck in positions, but I learned a lot. From the stock side, I got introduced to options and their potential, which intrigued me. At the same time, the one thing I learned very quickly with the stock side is that it takes a lot of research. You really have to understand and research the companies. I tended to do better with companies that I understood. I think that's pretty popular across the board. So I tended to focus on companies that were involved in aviation because I'm a pilot. I also started looking at companies that were in the tech side because I'm fascinated with that.

Q: When did you become a pilot?

Vince: I was 20 when I got my license. In the aviation world they call it *experimental*. You can buy a kit and build it in your garage. These are very fast, very modern, and very capable airplanes. Inspectors come out before you fly the first time to go through it, and then you get a certificate to fly. I built my first one when I was 22 and flew it for the business. I flew it all over the US, everywhere I needed to go. I flew it back and forth from Vegas four or five times a year for trade shows. That's how I got around. It was a two-seat airplane, but I was primarily by myself. I've built one airplane and owned four.

Q: How did you find the time to build an airplane while working crazy hours?

Vince: I worked on it every morning from about 4 a.m. till noon and it took six months. I had another guy helping me most of that time. Then at lunch I would go back to my office and typically work there until about midnight, sleep for four hours and then went back to building the airplane.

Q: Fascinating. So back to the markets. You started by analyzing companies mostly from a fundamental basis, position trading stocks, holding them for a couple of weeks or months. Why did you make the switch to day trading?

Vince: I think I got bored with stocks. That's when I started looking at the leverage that options provided and thought, "Wow, I can make exponentially more by doing this." I was never really that successful on the stock side and was only marginally successful with options because I always tried earnings plays that never worked for me.

About 2017, I noticed some prop firms popping up online and wondered what they were doing and what type of financial vehicle it was. I didn't know anything about it, so I started to study. That's when I got exposed to futures. Once I got into futures, I quickly left stocks behind because the opportunities with futures, especially at prop firms, are unbelievable. I looked at oil, the Russell, the Dow, and Nasdaq (NQ), but I predominantly trade NQ.

Q: How did you settle on NQ as your favorite market to trade?

Vince: Even when I was looking at stocks, I hadn't been introduced to charting, Fibonacci, or any technical analysis. I had no training of any kind. When I discovered the prop firms, I started looking into how to start charting.

When I discovered the future side, I immediately jumped in with both feet, bought the accounts, blew them up, bought more, blew them up, and it was just this vicious cycle. That's when I started to research – how do I learn more, how to trade this? I discovered stock chart pros, took their six-month Fibonacci class. That course really taught me the fundamentals of what I still use today – Fibonacci, support and resistance, trend. A lot of those things are sometimes overlooked by traders. They traded multiple things such as oil and gold but predominantly ES [E-mini S&P 500 futures] and NQ, that's what drove my interest.

What they taught was something I still do today, and that is you start looking for Fibs on a higher time frame, like a daily or a weekly chart in some cases and you start marking off support and resistance. Then you start drilling it down into the lower time frames all the way down to a five-minute chart. The one thing that I took away from that course and still do today is you just can't ignore high time frames.

You've got to look at the big picture and understand, where are we at in the big picture? That's really what helps. Even today, I'll mark off support resistance on higher time frame charts, and color-code them according to the time frame. So if it's a daily or weekly level, or even a monthly level, in some cases, I'll color that one color so that when I drill down to my five-minute charts I can identify key levels. For example, if I see a red support line,

I know it's a significant monthly support or resistance level. This method is something I still use today.

Q: Do you do chart Fibonacci levels manually or do you have a program that helps you do that?

Vince: I chart Fibonacci levels manually in thinkorswim, now Charles Schwab. Then I use Trade Devils, a company that I've bought quite a few indicators from that has a support and resistance indicator that you can use in NinjaTrader and that works quite well. It's taken a lot of refining because there are a lot of settings that you can do but I've actually tailored it to where it's working very, very well because you can have it plot, support, and show resistance off higher time frames on a five-minute chart, for example. It'll auto-plot, support, and show resistance off of a daily chart on my five-minute chart.

Q: Drawing precise Fib levels can be a challenge for many traders. How would you recommend they start?

Vince: Start by looking at the previous day's levels. If you dive straight into Fibonacci, it can become overwhelming very quickly. Focus on the previous day's levels first. The market reacts to these levels, which can include Fibonacci levels, as well as the previous day's open, high, low, close, the opening range, and initial balance. These are simple yet very effective strategies for trading.

Q: How do you use the previous day levels?

Vince: My recommendation is to first understand the previous day's movement and the big-picture levels. Then you just need to see what price does around those levels. Does it accept it? Does it reject it? How does it respond around those levels?

I'm fascinated with market profile. My market profile charts separate the regular trading hours from the overnight session. I'm not that concerned about the overnight session, but I like to see it separate from the regular trading hours. When you set up a market profile chart correctly you can very quickly identify those levels easily.

Then I mark those levels off on 30-minute charts so none of it happens quickly. A lot of times I'll set alerts at the previous day's level so I don't have to be watching it. If an alert goes off, then I'll usually wait to see on a five-minute chart if price establishes or rejects the level. I want to see it enter value and the next candle on a five-minute chart open inside of there either above the level or below the level. If I'm looking to go short, I want to see that next candle open in the direction before I take the trade. I don't enter on the first touch.

The great thing with Fibonacci is that it gives you targets. When NQ and ES are trading at all-time highs, you can use Fibonacci extensions to put potential price targets. It's interesting to me when you start putting those Fibonacci levels on a chart where price never traded before and then you start looking at software like Bookmap where you can see liquidity levels, you can start to see liquidity build out around those Fibonacci levels.

I'm always looking for confluence, and anytime I can have three forms of confluence at a level, I feel pretty confident in that trade. I generally would never take a trade based on Fibonacci alone. I need a support or resistance level, a previous day's level, or some sort of level there for me to feel confident in taking that trade.

Q: Would you consider yourself a trend trader or a reversal trader?

Vince: It depends on whether I'm trading a prop firm account or my own brokerage account. In my own brokerage account, I would rather wait for really high time frame confluence and then trend trade, meaning, I would try to get in and hold a position.

Many futures prop firms have trailing drawdowns so that's a little more difficult to do, plus you usually need to get flat by 4:59 p.m. eastern time [EST]. So with prop accounts, you need to scalp. You need to get in and out for few ticks and take the profit. There's nothing wrong with that. That teaches traders to bank the green and build those accounts over time. There's nothing wrong with that approach. It also depends on what time frame of chart I'm looking at – whether I'm going to scalp it, or get in and try to look for a runner.

Q: What type of scalp trades do you look for?

Vince: When people hear the word *scalp*, they start thinking that it means simply entering and exiting quickly and hoping that it works out. But that's not what scalping the markets is about. You still need to have some sort of confluence, or some reason why you took that trade. You still need to have a strategy behind it and if you lack a strategy, you're probably going to fail. You have to understand that there are a lot of people who are susceptible to trying to call tops and bottoms. Even throughout my entire trading career, I've been susceptible to this, and it simply doesn't work.

When you see a strong trending up day, a lot of traders will try to call the top. If it's trending down, they will try to call the bottom, and that doesn't work. I always look for pullbacks. On a day that has an established trend, I let it trend and if I miss that entry, I look for the pullback. I like to see some sort of confluence on a pullback, to enter and scalp in the direction of the trend. I only ever scalp in the direction of a trend, and if there isn't a trend on the day, that's probably a day I'm going to sit out.

Q: Would it be accurate to say that you use higher-time-frame Fibonacci levels to identify longer-term support and resistance, and then use Fibonacci on intraday highs and lows for short-term levels? You look for retracements to intraday support in the direction of the uptrend and exit when it reaches longer-term Fibonacci levels?

Vince: That's it in a nutshell. I'm also always watching the previous day's value area, which is very important to me. If you open inside the previous day's value area, it can often lead to a choppy open. However, if the price action driven by Asia and London opens outside the previous day's value – which encompasses 70% of the previous day's activity – and then trades back into that value area and gets accepted, there's an 80% chance it will fill that value area. I think the value area plays are often overlooked by many traders. It's a very simple concept to understand and a great play for new traders. When the price accepts into the value area, there is an 80% chance it will fill to the top or bottom of that area. Even if it doesn't completely fill, it usually offers a great scalp opportunity as it moves up or down within the value area.

Q: How do you incorporate Bookmap and liquidity levels?

Vince: I used to trade levels to the tick, placing my exits or entries precisely at those levels. But not everyone will use Fibonacci the same way, and not everyone will have the exact same support and resistance levels marked. We may be close, but on NQ, for example, we could be 8–10 points apart. While that may not seem like much, it can be more than most people are comfortable with during a drawdown.

Bookmap helps by showing where liquidity is building. When I draw my levels, I look at Bookmap to see if there's liquidity slightly off from one of my levels. One could argue that market makers are trying to front-run certain levels, and you can see where that liquidity is parked. So, I might adjust my levels based on this information. I might get out my target or enter a bit after my target. That's where Bookmap is really helpful from a liquidity perspective.

Q: How do traders get access to Bookmap?

Vince: Bookmap is a completely stand-alone platform. You need to purchase a separate Rhythmic connection to see certain features within Bookmap. I have a dedicated connection just for Bookmap, which has its own platform that I run. So, I usually have three platforms open at all times: Bookmap, thinkorswim, and NinjaTrader. I execute all trades in NinjaTrader, while Bookmap is a visual reference to see where liquidity is and set alerts for big orders.

Q: It sounds like you trade manually?

Vince: One hundred percent. I have several bots that I've purchased over the years and I still tweak and back-test some but I've never got them to be consistent enough to put my own money on the line. I've run them in evaluations to see how they perform, but I enter all my trades manually.

Q: Were you successful in prop right away or was there a learning curve?

Vince: Since I first started in 2017, I've blown up hundreds of prop accounts.

Q: Why didn't you give up?

Vince: The potential was there, but every morning as I brushed my teeth and looked in the mirror, I realized I was my own worst enemy. I knew the problem was staring back at me. I was comfortable with the technical analysis and confident in the levels I identified, but I kept front-running entries. During the Trump presidency, for example, news breaks and tweets would cause the market to spike, and I would impulsively jump in, only for it not to work out. At the end of the day, I would reflect back and see that my levels were correct, but I had jumped in too early or tried to catch a spike, which didn't work. When I finally decided to sit back and wait for the price to reach my levels before entering, things started to change. It was a difficult journey, but that shift in discipline made a significant difference.

Q: It took four years for you to be profitable. What are some of the rules that you've created along the way?

Vince: I don't trade the news. I don't trade the open and I don't trade the close. I know not everybody is going to agree with that because there are a lot of really good traders who specifically trade the open and the close. I don't have any luck with that. I never did and I think that's important for traders to understand – what works for one person isn't necessarily going to work for the next.

Early on, I started logging my trades in an Excel spreadsheet to identify patterns in my success. I found that my best trades typically happened between 10 a.m. and 11 a.m. EST. Outside of that window, I didn't have much luck. I realized that I tend to do well within that time frame and often give back my gains if I continue trading beyond it. It's also crucial not to just jump into the charts. You need to understand the overall market sentiment, upcoming earnings reports, and any breaking news. Even though I don't trade the news, being aware of it is essential.

Q: Why do you think this time frame is so effective for your pullback strategy?

Vince: I think the market gets its jitters out in the morning, then there's a little intraday trend that you can capitalize on. Sometimes it goes both directions, then you're kind of pushing into the Eastern time frame zone's lunch period where things kind of stagnate, go sideways. Overall that's the time frame that works best for me.

Q: What do you think is happening in the first 30 minutes of trade that makes it challenging for your strategy?

Vince: I think a lot of retail traders try to capitalize on the quick movements in the morning, but that doesn't work for me. The market opens with very rapid moves, and if you're wrong, you can burn through a 15-point stop in a heartbeat and that sets the tone for the rest of the day. I don't like starting my day with a loss that I then have to recover from, as that usually doesn't end well for me. Instead, I prefer waiting for the first trade at a great level or confluence to ensure it works. I start to build that little cushion for the day, even if it's just a couple of hundred dollars, to set a positive tone.

Q: How many trades would you take between 10 a.m. and 11 a.m. EST?

Vince: When I was actively trading prop, it might have been 15–20 scalps during that time frame. Now, it's nothing like that. I'm looking for just a few. I have a whole different expectation now. A part of me doesn't want the anxiety and stress so I look for the higher time frame or the better confluence, and try to take fewer trades.

Q: In that one-hour period that you were trading, what was your entry and exit strategy? Did you enter the entire trade at once or scale in or scale out?

Vince: I typically enter and exit with one to three contracts. If the price quickly moves in my favor and I build a good cushion, I pull my stop into profit to protect against the downside. If the price continues in my favor, I might scale in much bigger but typically it is one to three contracts in and out.

Q: How are your targets determined?

Vince: Everyone talks about risk/reward. That's just not my style. I enter one to three contracts based on the confluence that I see. If I have only one or two pieces of confluence, it's going to be a one contract entry. If I have multiple pieces of confluence and its higher time frame confluence, I'll enter much more aggressively and those targets are based on that entry. That's what I like to tell traders, that I trail my stops when I can. If I'm in a trade that's moving in my favor, I like to trail based on confluence. I enter on confluence, and place my profit targets on confluence.

I never anticipate. For example, if I enter a value area play at the low of the value area and the price moves up to the top, I will definitely set my profit target a few ticks or a point or two below the top. As the price moves up, I tighten my stop really close within three points to see how the market reacts. If the price doesn't pull back, I start moving my target up.

Q: When you hit your $1,000-a-day target, do you protect it at all costs?

Vince: That really came from trading evaluations. When you're on evals with a trailing drawdown, you might have a trade that goes $4,000 or $5,000 in your favor, but if it pulls back by $3,000, you've lost that $3,000 from your trailing drawdown because it's calculated from your peak balance, whether realized or unrealized. For example, if you are running more than three or multiple contracts, you have to use tighter stops because you cannot afford that drawdown.

I always look at an eval based on my profit target. For example, if my profit target is $9,000 on a $150,000 evaluation and I had to trade for five days, I would set an average daily target of $1,500. I knew I had to trade for five days anyway, so why push it? As soon as I averaged $1,500 a day, I would protect those gains, knowing I still had to trade for four more days. That's why I would pull the stop up, protect the downside. If you're trading an evaluation for a prop firm, you need a slightly different strategy than when trading your own brokerage account.

Q: The five-day rule is for passing the Apex evaluation but once you were funded did your strategy change?

Vince: What I tell traders is that the strategy that allowed you to successfully pass the evaluation, you should carry that over into your funded account. Don't change the strategy. Even after I got my PAs [performance accounts], I built them well past the point where the trailing drawdown stopped. I continued to scalp because that worked. I figured I would keep building the accounts that way, so I never changed my strategy.

Q: You lost $350,000 before you started to make money – can you tell us about that?

Vince: That was when I was in Taiwan. I had 20 $300,000 PA accounts with Apex, and across those 20 accounts, I had made $350,000. However, one technical glitch after another – and the biggest glitch being my own mistakes from pushing trades when I shouldn't have – I lost that $350,000. I returned to the US, bought 20 more evaluations, and traded those through to funded accounts. This time, I took those funded accounts to a total of $1 million.

Q: What challenges did you face in making money previously, and what adjustments did you make to succeed?

Vince: I knew what I was doing was wrong. I was sitting in an apartment in Taiwan, using a notebook computer on Wi-Fi – not even a hardwired connection. Aside from running speed tests, I had no idea who was providing the internet service. I was trying to take advantage of news spikes, which doesn't work. The failure was due to pushing trades when I knew I shouldn't have. I knew very well that it was a bad idea and that I shouldn't be doing that. Even though there was some lag, I can't blame it on the lag. The responsibility lies with me. I should have known pushing 20 accounts with trade copier over Wi-Fi on a notebook without a graphics card is a recipe for disaster.

Q: Did it make any difference that it wasn't $350,000 of your own money, it was a prop account?

Vince: Everyone says that, but you have to treat it like it was real money because it was money that I could have withdrawn. I hear a lot of people argue that technically it wasn't, but it felt like it was because starting over meant going back to evaluations, getting through the eval stage, and then back to funded accounts. To me, it felt no different than if someone had taken $350,000 out of my bank account.

I hadn't withdrawn anything from those accounts because I didn't feel comfortable doing so until I felt like I had enough cushion. I wanted to get the accounts to $320,000 before I withdrew. I was getting those accounts to that point, with the trailing drawdown fixed at $300,100. Then I hit the threshold, all the accounts were liquidated and they were done. I was left with nothing. It takes time to build $350,000 – you don't do it in a week. We're talking 15, 20, 30, or even 45 days of trading. Starting over meant getting back into the regimen of slowly building those accounts and working them away from the trailing drawdown, all while coping with the loss of $350,000. It was a very tough pill to swallow.

Q: Did you stop trading for a bit after that?

Vince: I was in quarantine when that happened. I had just entered Taiwan and was spending two weeks in my apartment. After quarantine, I was going to spend three months working in a factory office. During those three months in Taiwan, I purchased more accounts and started trading them, but I hadn't fully recovered. Mentally, I wasn't in a state to be trading and started pushing those accounts again. From the time I blew those funded accounts until I returned home, I fell back into my old habits of recklessly blowing up accounts. When I got back to the US, I had to sit down and have a period of self-reflection. I realized I needed to change my approach.

Q: Between August and December of 2022, you were trading 20 accounts, $50,000 each. This was when you made $1 million dollars in profit but it wasn't a straight line to those profits, right?

Vince: Yes, when I got back to the US, I was back to blowing up accounts like a fireworks show. That's when Darrell, the owner of Apex Trader Funding, called me, and it was such a turnaround for me.

In the trading world, you have to look out for yourself. I always encourage people to become part of a community because communities help. You can see other people's successes and failures and you can learn to judge your own performance based on that. It might not all be good, but I think community is very important.

I remember Darrell telling me, "You're not a bad trader. You do quite well in the mornings, but then you give it all back in the afternoons and blow the accounts. Then you reset and start over the next day. Just take that morning profit – whether it's a couple hundred, $500, whatever it is – bank it, and stop. Bank it, and stop. Do it again the next day."

That phone call lasted only a minute or two, but it really resonated with me. First of all, it was Darrell Martin, the CEO of Apex, which was significant. I hung up the phone thinking, "I've got to listen to him." I had followed Darrell on the Apex investing side with the sniper course, so I was familiar with his expertise. It also spoke volumes about Apex's qualities and built a lot of confidence in me. If the CEO of a company is willing to reach out personally and offer advice, it's meaningful. He didn't change the way I traded; he just said, stop trading, just stop, make a couple hundred dollars and stop. I took his advice to heart, and it was a profound moment in my trading career.

Q: What was the lightbulb moment that changed your trading performance?

Vince: As soon as I realized that you could scale with accounts, not with contracts, that was the key. I stuck to the same rules that I was using for just one account and things started to work. Previously, I would over-leverage a single account with lots of contracts. Instead, I began trading 20 accounts with fewer contracts. I might make only $500 per account, but that adds up to $10,000 a day across all accounts. By stacking $10,000 every day, it adds up very quickly. However, you have to be careful of the trailing drawdown when you've got multiple contracts. The more contracts you have with a trailing drawdown, the tighter you need to run your stop to protect against downside risk.

Now, I don't advise trading 20 evals at the same time – that was just my approach. I was willing to accept the risk and pay the price of failure, which I did. Instead, I tell traders to trade them in groups of three to five accounts at a time. Get those to a mini target for the day, then select another group. You can trade

20 accounts, but it's very difficult to trade 20 in fast-moving markets. Look at the big picture over 30, 60, or 90 days. Even with just a couple of accounts making $250 a day, over 90 days, you're looking at substantial earnings. So, scale with accounts, not with contracts. These strategies were very effective for me and allowed me to succeed.

Q: What is one major mistake you see new prop traders make?

Vince: They'll trade 35 contracts on a news event during their evalua-tions. What they don't realize is that market orders aren't always filled at the expected price and there could be a lot of slippage, resulting in their trailing drawdown getting taken out. Then they think, "I had a stop there; why didn't it get filled?"

To avoid this, you need to trade prop evaluations with just a few contracts and avoid over-leveraging. When you move into a funded account, trade it the same way. Don't over-leverage. Focus on the big picture over 30, 60, or 90 days. If you have a few accounts making $250 a day, spread that out over 90 days and look at what you actually put into the bank. You could be making a lot of money so scale with accounts, not contracts. Those were all things that I did that were very effective for me and allowed me to pass.

Q: When do you think is a good time to start withdrawing your profits?

Vince: My suggestion is to never withdraw part of that trailing draw-down. Keep at least that much in the account to protect against the downside because you're going to have losses. That trailing drawdown is what you were comfortable with, it's what you worked with, and it's what got you there. At Apex, once you hit your threshold in a funded account, your drawdown gets fixed. For example, in a $300,000 account, once you reach $307,600, your threshold gets fixed at $300,100, giving you a $7,500 draw-down. Technically, if you met the minimum number of trading days, you can make withdrawals, but people often dip too much into that. I would never take a withdrawal if I only had $7,500 profit in the account. I would aim for $10,500 before withdrawing $3,500, so I keep my full trail intact. Personally, I wanted to reach $20,000 before making a withdrawal to have a big cushion.

I see traders who always withdraw down to the minimum balance, and it seems to work for them. However, I prefer keep-ing the balance as far from the minimum as possible. I wasn't comfortable trading close to that minimum even during evaluations. When you get a little bit past that, you feel very excited, thinking, "I'm past the dark zone." I just don't ever want to trade close to that level again.

Q: Has your trading or approach changed after such a big withdrawal?

Vince: Trading has taught me a lot of lessons in humility that I didn't otherwise know. My approach hasn't changed much. I had a lot of risk exposure in my businesses, and trading was just one part of that from a risk perspective. Now, I try to be content with less. I don't need to hit home runs every day; base hits are perfectly fine.

Q: What's your top advice for traders looking to trade full-time?

Vince: I see traders who have been successful for a few months and start wondering if they can go full-time. Everyone's situation is different, but I typically advise them to test the waters first. Try living off your trading income while continuing your current job. Put your employment income in the bank and don't touch it; live solely off your trading income for a few months. If you can manage that, then you might be ready to go full-time. If you can't, then you're not ready yet.

This approach keeps your bills paid, your mortgage up-to-date, and keeps the kids in college before taking on the full-time trading challenge. Once you commit to full-time trading and leave a stable job, there's no turning back.

If you're working a full-time job and feel ready to trade full-time, this test shouldn't be a problem. By banking your job income and living off your trading income, you can see if you're truly ready without risking anything.

VINCE'S TRADING TIPS

1. **Maximize success with daily profit goals.**

If you need to achieve a $9,000 profit target on a $150,000 account over five trading days, break down the target into manageable daily goals. Aim to make $1500 each day, for instance. Setting a daily target of $1,500 ensures steady progress toward the overall $9,000 goal, while also protecting your profits and minimizing the risk of large draw-downs. If you hit your daily target, protect your gains or stop trading; if the market offers more opportunities, you can take advantage, but always make protecting your downside your number-one priority. Remember, trading a prop firm evaluation requires a different strategy than trading your own brokerage account. Focus on steady, consistent gains, and disciplined risk management.

2. **Scale with accounts, not contracts.**

To succeed with prop accounts, focus on scaling with multiple accounts rather than increasing the number of contracts in a single account. Stick to disciplined rules for each account and avoid over-leveraging. For instance, achieving $500 per account might seem modest, but if you trade five accounts, it amounts to $2,500 in total daily profits. This approach can quickly add up to substantial gains, such as $12,500 over a week. By breaking down your targets, you can trick yourself psychologically into maintaining discipline and consistency. However, be cautious of the trailing drawdown; managing multiple contracts requires tighter stop losses to protect against downside risks. Maintaining strict discipline and protecting your downside are key to sustainable success.

3. **Try living off your trading income first.**

Before making the leap to full-time trading, test your readiness by living off your trading income while keeping your current job. Continue working and save your employment income, using only your trading profits for daily expenses. Try this for a few months to see if you can sustain your lifestyle solely on trading income. If you can, it's a good sign that you might be ready to go full-time. This approach ensures that your bills are paid, your mortgage is up-to-date, and your family's needs are met before you commit to trading full-time. It provides a safety net, allowing you to evaluate your ability to live off trading income without risking your current job or financial stability.

CHAPTER 17

Ultimate 10-Step Checklist to Jumpstart Your Prop Trading

1. **What is your trading experience?**

   If you are completely new to trading, it's time to start learning. Begin by deciding which market you want to trade – whether it's contracts for difference (CFDs), futures, or forex – and determine your trading style. Once you've made these decisions, dive deep into understanding the specifics of your chosen instrument. Learn what a tick or point is worth, the margin requirements, and the leverage available. Familiarize yourself with the spreads, as they can significantly affect your trading costs. It's also important to identify the most active market times, as these periods often have the highest volume and best trading opportunities. This foundational knowledge is your ticket to building a successful trading career.

2. **What do you want to trade – CFDs, futures, or forex?**

   The next step is to decide what you want to trade – futures, CFDs, or forex. CFDs are popular because they offer higher leverage and no fixed expiration dates, giving you plenty of flexibility. Futures contracts, however, are loved for their transparency and are traded on centralized exchanges with fixed expiration dates and larger contract sizes. Futures prices come straight from the exchange, while CFD prices are set by the broker. The key difference between CFD and

257

forex trading is the variety of markets: CFDs let you trade a wide range of assets like indices, energy, and metals, whereas forex focuses purely on currency pairs. Each trading instrument has its own unique flavor, and as we've seen from our interviews with seasoned traders, many prefer to specialize in one instrument. Your choice should depend on your risk tolerance, trading style, and market knowledge. Dive in and find what suits you best!

3. **Choose your trading style – day trading versus swing trading.**

Next, it's time to decide how you want to trade by choosing a trading style that suits you best. Consider your schedule and lifestyle: Do you have the time to day trade, or is swing trading a better fit? Are you patient with your trades, or do you find yourself checking quotes every few minutes? Answering these questions will help you determine the trading style that works best for you.

The traders we interviewed for this book have diverse methodologies, but most find day trading more compatible with prop firm rules. This is especially true for futures prop firm challenges, which may have consistency rules or require closing trades before the weekend. Many traders favor day trading for its cash flow and consistency. If you prefer the flexibility of swing trading, look for a prop firm with rules that support that style.

4. **Understand the difference between picking tops or bottoms and trend trading.**

After that, think carefully about the type of trading setup you're looking for. To help you decide, ask yourself if you're often skeptical of extended moves and tempted to pick tops and bottoms. Or do you thrive on the excitement of riding big trends? This will help you determine whether you're more suited to trend following or counter-trend trading. Many seasoned traders prefer trading breakouts but always wait for a pullback before entering continuation trades. While this approach is popular and effective, it doesn't have to be your style. Consider it as a starting point and find what works best for you.

5. **Learn an effective strategy.**

Use resources like YouTube, live streams, and online classes to learn new trading strategies. Don't rely on just one or two gurus; instead, watch a variety of experts to identify common patterns and key takeaways. Immerse yourself in how these strategies work in real-life environments. Understand the trading rules, observe how different traders execute their strategies, test various approaches, and refine your methods based on what you learn.

6. **Determine your trade management.**

Determine what type of trade management strategy you will use. Consider whether you prefer to use a one-in-one-out method, where you close the entire position at once, or scale out of positions gradually to secure partial profits as the trade progresses. Alternatively, you might prefer to let winners run, allowing profitable trades to continue until they hit a higher target.

Decide on your risk/reward ratios – whether you aim for small, consistent targets or larger, occasional wins. Many day traders prefer conservative profit targets, opting to build their accounts slowly but steadily through frequent, smaller gains. This approach minimizes risk and helps in maintaining a steady growth curve. However, some traders might aim for bigger wins, accepting that this strategy may result in fewer but larger profits.

Think about how you will handle losing trades as well. Will you set tight stop-loss orders to minimize losses, or give your trades more room to move? Your risk management strategy should align with your overall trading goals and risk tolerance, ensuring that you can trade confidently and sustainably.

7. **Practice your strategy in a demo environment.**

You've probably heard that even successful prop traders blow up hundreds of prop accounts before turning profitable. You don't want to become part of that statistic. Before committing real money, make sure you can turn a profit in a demo environment. Most major CFD and forex brokers offer demo accounts, and an increasing number of prop firms provide this practice option as well. While prop firms allow you to trade with limited risk – meaning you only lose the amount you paid for the challenge – that's still hard-earned money you don't want to waste. Make sure you can be consistently profitable trading your strategy on a demo account before committing your time and money to a paid prop trading challenge. Use these demo accounts to practice trading the instrument, refine your strategy, and hone your risk management skills.

8. **Set daily and weekly profit goals.**

Many traders trade aimlessly with no goal except to make money. If you want to become a full-time trader, setting clear trading goals is absolutely essential. Establish realistic profit targets and strive to meet them consistently over a few weeks. Aim to achieve your daily or weekly salary through trading.

Some traders use trade copiers to amplify their earnings. For example, they might set a daily profit target of $400, with 2, 3, or even 20 trade copy accounts mirroring their trades. That $400 target can then become $800, $1,200, or even more. If you can achieve your goals regularly, you'll know that you are ready to transition to full-time trading.

9. **Choose the right prop firm.**

There are hundreds of prop firms to choose from, but only a few are truly reliable. Make sure to thoroughly research the prop firms you're considering. There have been instances where prop firms shut down, resulting in lost challenge fees, floating profits, and pending payouts. Here are some key factors to consider when doing your due diligence:

- **Longevity:** How long has the prop firm been in business?
- **Technology:** Do they have in-house tech, or are they relying on third-party solutions?
- **Liquidity providers:** Who are their liquidity providers?
- **Professionalism:** Do they have a professional website and online presence?
- **Reputation:** Check their YouTube channel or Instagram account. Are they flashy without substance, or do they have real trading and life experience?
- **Broker backing:** Are they backed by a reputable broker?
- **Reviews:** Look at customer reviews on sites like Trustpilot and Propfirmmatch.
- **Customer service:** Do they have a dedicated team providing real-time, quality customer service, or is it just one or two people responding slowly?

- **Trading rules:** Do their rules align with your trading style, such as allowing expert advisors (EAs), news trading, or swing trading?

By considering these factors, you can find a prop firm that is stable, trustworthy, and suited to your trading needs.

10. **Review all terms and conditions.**

You'd be surprised how many people don't thoroughly review all the rules and prop firms have a lot of them. Carefully examine their website to understand ALL the prohibited trading rules and ensure your strategy complies with them. Do they require you to close positions before the weekend? What are their payout terms? Is there a minimum number of trading days required before you can make a withdrawal?

Additionally, explore any restrictions on the types of trades you can execute, like news trading or using automated systems (EAs). Check out their policies on scaling your account and any associated fees. Knowing these details in advance will help you avoid any unwelcome surprises. There's no worse feeling than having your account terminated because you missed a crucial rule. Stay informed and trade confidently within their guidelines!

Last but certainly not least, make it a habit to take payouts; your profits only become real when they hit your bank account. We wish you luck in scaling your account to success!

Index